DANGEROUS WORLDS

DANGEROUS

LIVING AND DYING IN BIBLICAL TEXTS

WORLDS

MARK McENTIRE

SMYTH&HELWYS
PUBLISHING, INCORPORATED • MACON, GEORGIA

Smyth & Helwys Publishing, Inc.
6316 Peake Road
Macon, Georgia 31210-3960
1-800-747-3016
©2004 by Smyth & Helwys Publishing
All rights reserved.
Printed in the United States of America.

The paper used in this publication meets the minimum requirements of
American National Standard for Information Sciences—
Permanence of Paper for Printed Library Materials.
ANSI Z39.48–1984. (alk. paper)

Library of Congress Cataloging-in-Publication Data

McEntire, Mark Harold, 1960-
Dangerous worlds : living and dying in biblical texts / by Mark McEntire.
p. cm.
Includes bibliographical references.
ISBN 1-57312-433-8 (pbk. : alk. paper)
1. Death in the Bible.
2. Violence in the Bible.
3. Bible–Criticism, Narrative.
I. Title.
BS680.L5M34 2004
220.6–dc22

2004003515

Contents

Reading
in Dangerous Places

We are the roses in the garden,
beauty with thorns among our leaves.
To pick a rose you ask your hands to bleed.
What is the reason for having roses,
when your blood is shed carelessly?
It must be for something more than vanity.

—10,000 Maniacs[1]

INTRODUCTION

For a previous book, I read a selection of biblical texts in order to discover what they communicate about violence.[2] Following that detailed analysis of limited texts, I now wish to step back and take a more panoramic view of issues of danger and death in the Bible. In this study, I intend to read whole biblical books and ask questions about death and the threat of death in these books. The approach to the biblical text will necessarily be different. Concise discussions of whole books cannot rely on close readings. Instead, I wish to use the concept of "narrative worlds"[3] to explore whole books. The past three or four decades have witnessed an explosion of attention to biblical narrative. With varying success, numerous critics and theoreticians have attempted to describe how biblical narrative, and narrative in general, operates. This exertion of effort is in part a backlash against the historical tendencies of the previous two centuries, which tended to devalue the stories found in the biblical text in favor of analysis of the events and transmission processes that lay behind them.

This book begins with a discussion of the nature of biblical narrative, but I hope it will not be one that ultimately removes, or even obscures, a sense of mystery about how stories operate. The narrative books of the Bible create worlds of their own. I invite the reader to enter these worlds with me to observe how violence operates within them.

How and why do we read the Bible differently than we read other books? Gabriel Josipovici made an enlightening attempt to answer this question.[4] Many may be uncomfortable with his analysis because he demonstrated the inadequacy of the most common kinds of answers, those emphasizing the sacred content of the Bible. Josipovici came closest to the heart of the matter in his assertion that only in reading the Bible is "our childhood way with books…prolonged into adulthood."[5] Indeed, many people begin "reading" the Bible long before they learn to read by listening to Bible stories in their church, synagogue, or home. Some continue reading the Bible fervently until the end of their lives. No other book is treated this way by a significant number of people. Only certain parts of the Bible receive this kind of usage, however. Nobody reads Leviticus or the Epistle to the Hebrews to four-year-olds. The parts that are read in this way for a lifetime are stories.

Such use of the Bible, however, presents special problems in regard to the subjects of violence and death. The Bible stories we read to children, like those we listened to as children ourselves, are edited.[6] Two favorite stories illustrate this practice most clearly. In 1 Kings 18:16-40, the Hebrew prophet Elijah engages in a contest against hundreds of prophets of Baal on Mount Carmel. The humble Elijah wins the contest by praying successfully for YHWH to send fire from heaven to consume a sacrificial offering that he soaked with water. For children, the story almost always ends with v. 39, when all the people in the audience fall down and worship YHWH. It can be a shock for adolescents or adults who come to this story later in life and, reading all the way through v. 40, discover that the people, under the leadership of Elijah, brutally murder the 450 prophets of Baal.[7] Something similar takes place in the popular usage of the story of Daniel in the lions' den from Daniel 6:1-24. In the story, royal officials observe Daniel as he prays in violation of a specific decree. He is sentenced to death in the den of lions but is protected by God. The king and his officials find Daniel alive and well in the lions' den the morning after they throw him in, and here the story often ends. In many situations where the story is read, v. 24 is omitted. In this verse, Daniel's accusers and their wives and children are fed to the lions. Daniel does not participate explicitly in this act, but neither does he raise any objection. In the case of both of these stories, the narrative world created by the text is radically altered, from violent to peaceful, by the reader's choice to omit a single verse. It is understandable that we want to omit these portions of the story. The Bible is not supposed to be like that. At some point, however, a childish reading must give way to a mature one. Omissions like the two illustrated above are among the tendencies I hope to overcome by reading whole books of the Bible and exploring the narrative worlds they create, without editing disquieting passages.

Josipovici carried his understanding of reading further when he expressed the ability of literature to "draw me out of myself." This ability of a text is destroyed "if I only accept as belonging to it what I have already decreed should be there."[8] What the text draws the reader into may be called a "narrative world." This concept is difficult to define, particularly in its relationship to the reader's own world. Nevertheless, my use of this approach demands a preliminary discussion of theoretical and methodological issues.

UNDERSTANDING BIBLICAL NARRATIVE WORLDS

Modern attention to biblical narrative and how it operates can be traced to the foundational work of three individuals: Erich Auerbach, Hans Frei, and Paul Ricoeur. In 1953, Auerbach published his highly influential work titled *Mimesis: The Representation of Reality in Western Literature.* Though not a biblical scholar, Auerbach opened his study of general narrative theory with a comparison of biblical narrative to other ancient narratives. His primary illustrations are the story of Odysseus's return home in book 19 of the *Odyssey* and the *Akedah* story in Genesis 22.[9] One intriguing feature of Auerbach's work is that it seems to provide fuel for all sides in modern debates about the function of narrative.

The most prominent feature of the current debate over biblical narrative focuses on the problematic use of the term "realistic" to describe it. The term has been brought to the center of the debate by the influential work of a second writer, Hans Frei. Frei defined "realistic narrative" as "that kind in which subject and social setting belong together, and characters and external circumstances fitly render each other."[10] Frei argued further that because of these qualities, realistic narrative is much like history. Therefore, he also labeled biblical narrative "history-like." Frei's conclusions, despite the problems I will discuss below, have provided a great service for the field of biblical interpretation. He has been at the forefront of bringing narrative, or stories, back to the center of attention. Most importantly, he has reminded us that a story and its meaning are inseparable. Biblical stories do not illustrate meanings that can be extracted and stated as principles.[11] The way to their meanings is to enter the stories and hope to emerge transformed. Frei cited Auerbach in support of his argument that the biblical world is not just *a* real world but *the* real world.[12] Frei went on to argue that the neglect of realism, as the Enlightenment moved on to modernity, led to a separation between biblical stories and the real world of history. Thus, in Frei's words, the narrative was "eclipsed." Rather than fitting their life experiences into the real world of biblical narrative, readers began to try to fit the Bible into their perceived reality.[13] Frei's position has received support from George Lindbeck, who argued that "no world is more real than the one [the biblical stories] create."[14] Consequently the task of theology is to "redescribe reality within the scriptural framework rather than translate scripture into extrascriptural categories."[15]

The shortcomings of Frei's understanding of narrative are best illustrated by examining the narrative theory of Paul Ricoeur. Extensive attempts to compare and contrast Frei and Ricoeur have been made by others,[16] so only a brief summary is called for here. Among other differences, Ricoeur's theory of narrative places greater emphasis on the role of the reader. While Frei's insistence on the realistic nature of biblical narrative led him to stress the autonomy of the text,[17] Ricoeur has argued for the importance of the reader's contribution to the determination of the meaning of biblical language.[18] Mark Ellingsen, a strong critic of Ricoeur, has correctly understood that "correlation" is vital to the hermeneutics of Ricoeur and others who take a similar view.[19] Correlation may be understood most simply as the need for some experience of correspondence between the world of the reader and the narrative world of the text in order for a narrative to have significant meaning. Ricoeur illustrates this mode of reading in his recent collaborative effort with André Lacocque. Ricoeur even goes so far as to suggest that the narrator of Genesis 2–3 assumed a correlation of experience between the reader's world and the world of the text. Readers of the Edenic creation story, following the narrator, seek "to return to an origin starting from experiences belonging to their own sphere of observation."

Ellingsen has insisted, more strongly than most others, that Ricoeur's approach is inappropriate because it requires correlation between the experience of the reader and the biblical story. Drawing on Auerbach, Ellingsen has defined the task of narrative preaching as one of helping the hearer into the realistic world of biblical narrative.[20] Ellingsen was incorrect, however, in supposing that meaningful reading of narrative can take place without correlation.[21] Somehow, the world of the text must fit together with the world of the reader. The text cannot remain completely autonomous and self-referential once the act of reading has begun. Lewis Mudge observed the problem in his statement that "It is hard for us to see scriptural language, full as it is of figure, metaphor, vision, and myth, as having to do with reality."[22] Mudge has aptly labeled Ricoeur's approach "anti-Cartesian."[23] Our pure, objective, and unaccompanied minds do not enter biblical narrative worlds.[24] Simplistic notions about readers inhabiting biblical narrative worlds and experiencing them as the real world do not stand up to close scrutiny. Amos N. Wilder stated that "the ancient rehearsals may be recognized in some sort as the archetypal molds of our own histories and fabulations."[25] In plain terms, when modern readers travel through biblical narrative worlds, they carry a great deal of baggage.

The world of metaphor and symbol has been the focus of Ricoeur's hermeneutics. Through metaphor and symbol, narrative opens up a pathway to understanding. It is one thing to say that this newly opened world is "real" and quite another to say that it is "realistic." The former description may be used of a narrative's ability to draw people in so that they may experience something of the story. The narrative world is real at that moment, in the sense that the reader is capable of entering the story.[26] But, as Walter Brueggemann has observed, the biblical texts' ability to generate a world is at least partly dependent upon a lack of the "checks and restraints" of reality.[27] Reading is an interaction between the text and the reader's experience and choices.

There are important issues at stake in this debate. Perhaps the most important is the Bible's ability to transform readers and the world in which they live. For those who follow Frei, it is vital that the Bible be able to stand apart from human culture, in critique and judgment.[28] The supposed autonomous nature of biblical narrative, which means that the text does not rely on the reader or the reader's culture and experience to determine its meaning, would seem to guarantee the Bible's supra-critical position. This notion of how narrative operates, however, relies on a highly idealistic understanding of the reader and the reading process. Many critics of Frei have noted this problem. Francis Watson, for example, has contended that "it is one thing to identify the role these texts outline for their implied reader, quite another to show how a real reader might be able to fill that role."[29] This gives rise to the key question of whether complete textual autonomy is the only situation that allows for reader transformation. Might readers' experiences of their worlds interact with the world of the text within the reading process in a way that transforms both the text and the reader?[30]

The preceding question, offered from a narrative perspective, blends into developments from the fairly recent application of reading theory to the study of the Bible. Wolgang Iser and Umberto Eco have most successfully analyzed the role of the reader. Iser identified the problem of a supposed "ideal reader." Such a reader would have to have what he calls an "identical code" as the author of a text.[31] In Gadamer's terms, the author and reader would have to share the same horizon from the beginning. Of course, this is impossible for modern readers of the biblical text. Iser placed limits on the reader's role, however, by asserting that "competent" reading narrows the possible meanings of a text.[32] If the text is not autonomous, then neither is the reader. Eco labeled opposing views of textuality as "opened" and "closed." The latter roughly corresponds to the notion of autonomy. Eco rigorously questioned this understanding of texts, at the same time emphasizing the role of the text in defining a "competent" reader. In the end, the need for the reader to perform a large set of tasks that Eco has outlined causes all texts to remain open.[33]

A profound illustration of the effect readers' choices have on their experiences of biblical narratives can be observed in the African debate about the meaning of the Cain and Abel story in Genesis 4. The character with whom the reader chooses to identify, Abel (murdered herdsman) or Cain (dispossessed farmer who responds with violence), determines how the narrative world is experienced.[34] Allen Boesak's reading represents the traditional understanding of Cain as the powerful villain and Abel as the innocent victim.[35] In opposition to Boesak and the traditional reading, Itumaleng Mosala took the side of Cain, who represents the dispossessed farmer. Stories such as Genesis 4 that characterize the dispossessed as murderous savages function as propaganda to justify the taking of their land by an elitist group that poses as morally superior.[36] To illustrate the problem in a different context, we might pose the question, how can the story of the battle of Jericho in Joshua 6 operate autonomously when read by a modern Palestinian Christian, for whom this text is supposed to be the inspired word of God?

VIOLENCE AND DEATH IN THE BIBLE

Mention of the Cain and Abel story brings us to the issue of violence and death in the Bible. My earlier work focused specifically on violence. Though I wish to expand that horizon to examine death and danger in the Bible, violence cannot be separated from the biblical understanding of death. This subject of violence has received rapidly growing attention over the past two decades. The impetus can probably be attributed to the work of literary critic René Girard, who has often applied his general literary and anthropological theories to biblical texts.[37] Studies of violence in the Bible have continued and multiplied in the work of Walter Wink, Robert Hamerton-Kelley, James G. Williams, Mieke Bal, Regina M. Schwartz, and many others. What explains the sudden prominence of this issue? The texts have been there all along. Something has changed in the collective manner of reading. Surely this has something to do with the increasing awareness of violence and changing attitudes toward violent death in our world. Late-twentieth-century culture has produced readers who approach the Bible with a new set of questions, who find a stunning correspondence between their dangerous world and the dangerous worlds of the Bible. Those who enter the

Bible with an awakened sensitivity find that it is filled with violence and death from beginning to end. The book of Genesis establishes a pattern of violence, death, and the threat of death that continues straight through to the book of Revelation.

My earlier work, *The Blood of Abel*, concluded that violence is a central issue about which the Bible is concerned, and it pointed to three key conclusions about biblical violence. The ideas themselves may not be as surprising as the indications that the biblical narrators are so keenly and consistently aware of them. First, violence alters human identity. Both victim and perpetrator are changed by acts of violence. The Bible's protagonist, Israel,[38] experiences a series of changes in identity through the course of the biblical story. These changes in identity are brought about by acts of violence committed against, by, and for Israel. Second, violence is an inevitable and ultimately uncontrollable element of human existence. Any attempt to harness violence for carefully controlled use eventually fails. Even visions of peace and order, so common in the visions of Israel's prophets, are consistently predicated by violent preparation. Third, God's involvement in violent events is typically indirect and ambiguous. Biblical narrators go to great lengths to keep God's hands from getting bloody. The destroyer in Exodus 12:23, the ark of the covenant in Joshua 6, and the confusing syntax of 2 Chronicles 36 all serve to keep God at a distance from bloodshed.[39]

At least the first two of these conclusions fit well with Girard's theory of violence, and the third is not inconsistent with it. Girard's theory, therefore, will continue to play a role in this study of danger and death in the Bible.[40] He began with the observation that both in the real world and in the worlds of literature, human relations are thoroughly infected with mimetic desire. This desire to have what the other has and to be like the other brings about rivalry and conflict. Left unchecked, such conflict threatens to disrupt or even destroy the entire human community. Therefore, some mechanism to control this process is necessary if human civilization is to be ordered. Individuals and groups resolve their conflicts by choosing a surrogate victim. By joining together against this victim, they temporarily overcome the threat of uncontrolled violence. This mechanism of victimization becomes institutionalized because the effect is temporary and must continuously be renewed. What Girard has described is a rather delicate mechanism, so it is not surprising that it frequently breaks down. The result of these failures is the overflowing of violence, perhaps in intensified form, after being pent up for a time. This is illustrated in 1 Kings 12:18 where Israel and Judah avert war for a moment by tacitly agreeing on Adoram as a unanimous victim, sealing their peaceful division. The ensuing relationship between the two nations, however, is characterized by warfare (1 Kings 15:6). The surrogate victim mechanism ultimately fails.

Regina M. Schwartz raised the discussion of biblical violence to a higher pitch with her work, *The Curse of Cain: The Violent Legacy of Monotheism*. The foundation of her poignant analysis is the Bible's preoccupation with the "myth of scarcity."[41] Life is a zero-sum game, according to the majority voice in the Bible. Therefore, violence is typically the result of struggles for identity and status. Such a conclusion sounds like the precise converse of my assertion above that violence alters human identity, but this is probably a chicken-and-egg argument. More important is the question of how the Bible functions in relation to human violence. Does the Bible promote violence by asserting the myth of scarcity? Schwartz has called for a reforming of the canon that replaces the biblical focus on scarcity with an emphasis on plenitude and generosity. Apart from the problem that the relevant canons (Hebrew, Catholic, Protestant, etc.) are far too entrenched to be changed, I have to ask whether Schwartz's new canon would do anybody any good. She arrived at her conclusions, with which I largely agree, by an astute reading of the Bible as it is, combined with careful observation of the world. That other people have read the Bible and used it to condone and promote violence is undeniable, but were they reading the wrong Bible or reading the Bible wrongly? I believe the latter is truer than the former and that if the same people were handed this new Bible, they would read it wrongly too. Hamerton-Kelly addresses this question with great insight in his debate with Pieter Tijmes concerning Girard's reading of the New Testament. In Hamerton-Kelly's words, "It does not seem important to settle the question whether Girard discovered the sacrificial [or surrogate victim] mechanism in the Bible or whether he merely found it disclosed there with exceptional clarity. We all come to the text with preunderstanding."[42]

The discussion of narrative hermeneutics with which this chapter began and this discussion of the implications of canon may both come down to a fairly simple question of the Bible's purpose. Is the Bible's primary purpose to give us the right answers to all of life's questions? If so, then we are discovering that it does a rather poor job. Instead, might we accept that the Bible's primary purpose is to lead us to ask the right questions and to live in this world with those questions burning in our hearts? Increasing sensitivity to issues of violence in the Bible is an indication that Bible reading changes in response to the changing world of the reader. For centuries, the Bible was typically used to justify the practice of slavery and promote the cause of war. The latter use has not entirely disappeared, but the past two centuries have witnessed a significant shift in the way the Bible is read in relation to issues like war and slavery. The same Bible is being read, so this change must come from readers' changing perceptions of their world and how they bring their world into contact with the world of the Bible. In addition, such shifts may be attributed to the increasing access to the Bible enjoyed by people living on the margins of society. Perhaps the most important new directions in biblical hermeneutics today are the result of the increasing influence of interpretive voices from Latin America, Asia, and Africa.[43] The lives of real readers apparently have a tremendous impact on how they read the Bible.

My earlier book, *The Blood of Abel*, presented a picture of violence in the Bible as it emerges when selected texts are read closely, giving careful attention to details of language and structure. The question posed in this study is what picture emerges when the reader backs away and experiences the world created by an entire biblical book, without focusing too closely on how such narrative worlds are created. How do stories of death and the threat of death in the Bible affect modern readers? How do readers' experiences of violence, danger, and death in their own "real" worlds interact with their perceptions of the world in the text?

ORGANIZATION OF THE BOOK

The remaining issue is the choosing of biblical texts on which to focus. These choices will be somewhat arbitrary and will be questioned by some readers, but they must be made. The biblical books selected should consist primarily of narrative. Beginning with the book of Genesis is an obvious necessity. It sets the tone for the rest of the Bible, both in terms of establishing a narrative pattern and portraying human violence. The next selection is more difficult. I will move on to the book of Judges, primarily because it portrays a significantly different world from Genesis. This is a world in which Israel is settled into the land but beset by dangerous neighbors. Israel is also a danger to its neighbors and to itself in the chaotic world of Judges. The books of Samuel portray another different world, one in which Israel is busy establishing itself as a nation working out its monarchical institutions and its ways of relating to other nations. The grand, sweeping story of the Israelite monarchy stands in contrast to the colloquial world of Ezra-Nehemiah. Death and danger in Ezra-Nehemiah are less overt, and the narrative is of a different character, particularly because of the halting pattern caused by the narrator's insertion of written documents. In the New Testament, the Gospels and Acts clearly fit the narrative pattern established in the Hebrew Bible. Acts is an obvious choice because it tells the story of the church in the Mediterranean world. The remaining question is which of the Gospels to choose. I have chosen the Gospel of Matthew because it establishes patterns at the beginning of the

New Testament, much as Genesis does at the beginning of the Hebrew Bible. Matthew invites the reader into the world inhabited by Jesus. In addition, its position and a number of literary elements provide the clearest sense of continuity with the story of Israel.

Each chapter will begin with a discussion of the narrative shape of a particular biblical book. We are not the first travelers in these narrative worlds, and much work has been done to find a way through them and to produce useful maps. I will attempt to trace the path of past attempts to describe an overall narrative structure for each book, and move toward my personal perception of the narrative shape that will provide the map for my reading to follow. Each chapter will then provide a trip through the book, which follows the contours observed in the discussion of narrative shape, paying careful attention to issues of life and death. The end of each chapter will present observations and conclusions about how human experience in the modern world might connect with experiences of life and death in the given biblical world.

Thus, we will examine the worlds created by six different biblical books that form part of a continuous story beginning with the misty portrait of the creation and ending with Paul's arrival in Rome. Hopefully, the observations about danger and death in these worlds will apply in many ways to the Bible as a whole.

NOTES

[1] From the song "Eden" on the 10,000 Maniacs album *Our Time in Eden* (Electra/Asylum, 1992).

[2] Mark McEntire, *The Blood of Abel: The Violent Plot of the Hebrew Bible* (Macon GA: Mercer University Press, 1999).

[3] It is not easy to establish who first used this term. It certainly represents an ancient idea. The modern understanding owes much to the work of Erich Auerbach, Paul Ricoeur, and Amos N. Wilder. I will discuss the work of each of these critics in more detail below.

[4] Gabriel Josipovici, *The Book of God: A Response to the Bible* (New Haven: Yale University Press, 1988), 1-28.

[5] Ibid., 8.

[6] Jonathan Kirsch, an American journalist, tells the story of deciding to read the bible to his five-year-old son. Upon reaching the story of the drunken and naked Noah in Genesis 9, he discovered that he needed to do careful editing and paraphrasing to make many of the stories suitable for his young audience. See *The Harlot by the Side of the Road: Forbidden Tales of the Bible* (New York: Ballantine, 1997), 2-4.

[7] Some adults who do not read freely on their own continue to avoid the full ending because lectionaries and devotional reading guides sometimes leave off the final verse of the story.

[8] Josipovici, *The Book of God*, 15.

[9] *Mimesis: The Representation of Reality in Western Literature* (Princeton: Princeton University Press, 1953), 7-23.

[10] Hans Frei, *The Eclipse of Biblical Narrative: A Study in Eighteenth and Nineteenth Century Hermeneutics* (New Haven: Yale University Press, 1974), 13. Frei acknowledged the influence of the work of Erich Auerbach on his own understanding of narrative. Most significant is Auerbach's discussion of the *Akedah* story of Genesis 22 in *Mimesis*.

[11] *The Eclipse of Biblical Narrative*, 280.

[12] Ibid, 3.

[13] Ibid., 3-8.

[14] George Lindbeck, *The Nature of Doctrine: Religion and Theology in a Postliberal Age* (Philadelphia: Westminster, 1984), 117.

[15] Ibid., 118.

[16] The most balanced and informative of such analyses has come in a pair of related articles by Gary Comstock. See "Truth or Meaning: Ricoeur versus Frei on Biblical Narrative," *Journal of Religion* 66 (1986): 117-40 and "Two Types of Narrative Theology," *Journal of the American Academy of Religion* 55 (1987): 687-717. In the end, Comstock gives much credit to Frei but positions himself closer to Ricoeur. A somewhat polemical attempt to analyze Frei and Ricoeur has been made by Mark Ellingsen, who follows Frei closely and rejects Ricoeur's views entirely. See *The Integrity of Biblical Narrative: Story in Theology and Proclamation* (Minneapolis: Fortress, 1990).

[17] Frei, *The Identity of Jesus Christ: The Hermeneutical Bases of Dogmatic Theology* (Philadelphia: Fortress, 1975), xiii-xvii.

[18] Paul Ricoeur, *Time and Narrative*, vol. 1 (Chicago: University of Chicago Press, 1984), 77-82.

[19] Ellingsen, *The Integrity of Biblical Narrative*, 13.

[20] Ibid., 43-52

[21] Ibid., 43-52. Here, in a sample of Ellingsen's own narrative interpretation, he relies on correlation. Comstock has also noted a "tacit" need for correlation in the interpretations of Frei. See "Truth or Meaning," 124-27.

[22] Lewis Mudge, "Paul Ricoeur on Biblical Interpretation," in *Essays on Biblical Interpretation*, ed. Lewis Mudge (Philadelphia: Fortress, 1980), 4.

[23] Ibid., 8-10.

[24] Note that this idea is close to Hans George Gadamer's influential description of a "fusion of horizons" as a model for the hermeneutical process. See Gadamer, *Truth and Method* (London: Sheed and Ward, 1975), 269-78. Dan R. Stiver has provided an excellent illustration of the advantages of Gadamer's "fusion" model over Frei's concept of "absorption" in *Theology after Ricoeur: New Directions in Hermeneutical Theology* (Louisville: Westminster John Knox Press, 2001), 50-55.

[25] Wilder, "The World Story: Biblical Version," in *Jesus' Parables and the War of Myths: Essays on Imagination in the Scriptures* (Philadelphia: Fortress, 1982), 52. Note also that Wilder's description of biblical narrative raises problems with notions of realism: "The human actions [in the Bible] burst the wonted course of affairs and explode, as it were, into the hyperbolic. They go over the limits of human scale, in heroism or immolation, in ecstasy or horror" (58).

[26] On this capacity of biblical narrative, see Robert Paul Roth, *The Theater of God: Story in Christian Doctrine* (Minneapolis: Fortress, 1985), 10; Thiselton, *New Horizons in Hermeneutics: The Theory and Practice of Transforming Bible Reading* (Grand Rapids: Zondervan, 1992), 351; and Bernard Brandon Scott, *Jesus, Symbol-Maker for the Kingdom* (Minneapolis: Fortress, 1981), 14.

[27] Walter Brueggemann, *Theology of the Old Testament: Testimony, Advocacy, Dispute* (Minneapolis: Fortress, 1997), 57-58. Here Brueggemann draws on Ricoeur's understanding of a "world in the text."

[28] See, for example, Ellingsen, *The Integrity of Biblical Narrative*, 27; or George Lindbeck, *The Nature of Doctrine: Religion and Theology in a Postliberal Age*, 117-18.

[29] Francis Watson, *Text and Truth: Redefining Biblical Theology* (Grand Rapids: Eerdmans, 1997), 36-37. In addition, the self-referential view relies on an unclear notion of how narratives are related to history. This problem has been described by a number of critics. See Watson, *Text and Truth*, 39, and Stephen Prickett, *Words and the Word: Language Poetics and Biblical Interpretation* (Cambridge: Cambridge University Press, 1986), 194-95. According to David Lee, Frei may have been moving late in his life toward a second stage that emphasizes a consensus reading of the Christian community through history as the "literal sense" of Scripture. See David Lee, *Luke's Stories of Jesus: Theological Reading of the Gospel Narrative and the Legacy of Hans Frei* (Sheffield: Sheffield Academic Press, 1999), 77-96. But this equation of literal sense with community consensus leaves the role of the present reader's experience still inadequately addressed.

[30] For a highly developed hermeneutic that may point in this direction, see Anthony C. Thiselton, *New Horizons in Hermeneutics*, 8-29.

[31] Wolfgang Iser, *The Act of Reading: A Theory of Aesthetic Response* (Baltimore: Johns Hopkins University Press, 1978), 29.

[32] Ibid., 231.

[33] Umberto Eco, *The Role of the Reader: Explorations in the Semiotics of Texts* (Bloomington: Indiana University Press, 1978), 3-23.

[34] For a more complete discussion of the competing understandings of Genesis 4 in Africa, see McEntire, "Cain and Abel in Africa: Using Competing Hermeneutics as a Pedagogical Method with Ethiopian Students," in *the Bible in Africa,* ed. Gerald West (Leiden: Brill, 2000), 248-59.

[35] See Alan Boesak, *Black and Reformed: Apartheid, Liberation and the Calvinist Tradition* (Johannesburg: Skotaville, 1984), 137-40.

[36] See Itumaleng Mosala, *Biblical Hermeneutics and Black Theology in South Africa* (Grand Rapids: Eerdmans, 1984), 33-37.

[37] Girard's first extended application of his theory of violence to biblical texts came with the publication of *La Violence et la sacre* in 1972. This work was published in English as *Violence and the Sacred,* trans. Patrick Gregory (Baltimore: Johns Hopkins University Press, 1977).

[38] Not all readers will agree that Israel is the protagonist of the Bible. To some extent this is the choice of the reader or critic. A primary premise of Jack Miles's masterpiece, *God: A Biography* (New York: Vintage, 1996; see pp. 9-24), is that God is the protagonist of the Bible. Of course, if Israel is protagonist, then God is the antagonist, and vice versa, so this may simply be a question of point of view.

[39] McEntire, *The Blood of Abel*, 115-26.

[40] This theory is developed thoroughly in *Violence and the Sacred*. It is worked out in even greater detail, particularly in reference to the Bible, in *Things Hidden Since the Foundation of the World*, trans. Stephen Bann and Michael Metteer (Stanford: Stanford University Press, 1987). For a fairly concise and helpful summary of Girard's work, see Robert Hamerton-Kelley, *Sacred Violence: Paul's Hermeneutic of the Cross* (Minneapolis: Fortress, 1992), 13-59.

[41] See Regina M. Schwartz, *The Curse of Cain: The Violent Legacy of Monotheism* (Chicago: University of Chicago Press, 1997), xi.

[42] Hamerton-Kelly, *Sacred Violence*, 196.

[43] For a powerful statement of the impact of such voices, see Justo L. Gonzalez, *Santa Biblia: The Bible through Hispanic Eyes* (Nashville: Abingdon, 1996), 57-58.

Genesis: Striving with God

Oh the mud splattered victims,
Have to pay out all along the ancient highway.
Torn between half truth and victimization,
Fighting back with counter attacks

It's when that rough god goes riding,
When the rough god goes gliding,
And then rough god goes riding,
Riding on in.

—Van Morrison[1]

THE NARRATIVE SHAPE OF GENESIS

Pre-modern readings of Genesis primarily approached the first book of the Bible as a narrative. It is necessary, however, to distinguish those kinds of readings from modern narrative approaches. To insist that modern readers can interact with the story world of Genesis in the same way that ancient or medieval readers may have is nonsense. Two types of barriers stand in the way of modern readers who might attempt to enter into the world of Genesis. First, modern readers recognize immediately, despite the protests of some, that the world of talking snakes, magic fruit, divine wrestling matches, and a conversational deity is not their world. Second, a couple of centuries of critical study of Genesis has found its way to most readers in one form or another. Critical study has had a tendency to divide the text into small units and focus attention on the historical process behind the text. It is hard to escape the influence of source-criticism, whether one accepts or rejects its basic legitimacy or even knows it by name. Even its most ardent opponents often interpret Genesis in reaction to the Documentary Hypothesis. The first kind of barrier will need to be addressed throughout this chapter and assessed at the conclusion. Modern narrative approaches are often an attempt to overcome or sidestep the second barrier.

Establishing a clear beginning point for modern narrative study of Genesis is not possible. Certainly its roots lie in the work of Erich Auerbach and Umberto Cassuto. Auerbach, as the previous chapter indicated, was a literary critic who happened to make use of certain stories in Genesis, alongside samples from Greek epic literature, in order to demonstrate the characteristics of ancient narratives.[2] While he did not produce an extensive narrative description of Genesis, his work has been profoundly influential on many who have. Umberto Cassuto was a conservative Jewish biblical scholar whose commentaries on Genesis appeared in Hebrew in the 1940s and in English translation in 1964.[3] Cassuto's obvious animosity to historical-critical interpretation may have limited his influence for some time, but recent interpreters have begun to recognize him as a brilliant reader of the text in its final form. He was particularly adept at describing the detailed structural patterns present in the narrative that hold it together and make it a whole.

Modern narrative study of Genesis came of age in the 1970s and early 1980s. Shimon Bar-Efrat, Robert Alter, Adele Berlin, Meir Sternberg, and Jacob Licht all produced formative and influential works on biblical narrative in general and frequently drew on Genesis to illustrate specific features.[4] A narrative analysis focused entirely on texts in Genesis first appeared in Jan P. Fokkelman's 1975 work, *Narrative Art in Genesis*.[5] The difficulty of breaking away from historical-critical exegesis is illustrated by Fokkelman's work. After a brilliant introduction outlining his intent to read texts in Genesis synchronically, he proceeded to interpret the "Tower of Babel" story in Genesis 11:1-9. He begins this interpretation with a discussion about the identity of the author and the original historical setting of the story, identifying it as a post-exilic literary response to the destruction of Babylon.[6] Fokkelman did break new ground in the narrative interpretation of Genesis, but the kind of diachronic exegesis he hoped to leave behind is not so easily escaped. The remainder of *Narrative Art in Genesis* and Fokkelman's contributions to *The Literary Guide to the Bible* a dozen years later establish a cleaner break from historical-critical exegesis.[7]

The last two decades have witnessed an explosion of attention to narrative in Genesis, which cannot be fully documented here. Representative samples will appear in the discussion below. More important is the current state of two central issues concerning the narrative shape of the book of Genesis: (1) The relationship between the Primeval History (Genesis 1–11) and the Patriarchal History (Genesis 12–50) and (2) the role of the genealogies in the structure of the book.

The book of Genesis begins with the creation of the universe and ends with the death of Joseph in Egypt. For those who read the book from beginning to end, the shape of a funnel might be the best visual representation of the storyline.[8] The narrowing of focus is a dominating narrative process. At the beginning of Genesis, God creates the world and the human beings within it. By the end, a family, the children of Jacob, has been separated out from all of the other peoples of the world to be the focal point of God's attention. Traditionally, a clear line of division has been drawn between the Primeval Story in chapters 1–11 and the Patriarchal Narratives in 12–50. A number of recent interpreters have effectively emphasized the narrative, stylistic, and theological continuities between these two sections and the somewhat arbitrary nature of the sharp divisions often drawn between them, including the chapter and verse divisions.[9] The patriarchal narratives have often been conceived in terms of cycles of stories—the Abraham cycle, Jacob cycle, etc. Michael Fishbane's early narrative treatment of Genesis, in his 1978 work *Biblical Text and Texture*, labeled Genesis 2:24b–11:27 the "Primeval Cycle" and called attention to the similarity of form and function between this section and the Patriarchal Narratives.[10] Regardless of one's conclusions about possible seams or divisions, the narrative is continuous. Fokkelman has catalogued the "discordant" elements in the book of Genesis. On the surface it seems an odd collection of literary forms with different viewpoints. The connections among them are not always clear. Nevertheless, the elements of discord are overcome by extensive "means of integration." Chief among these are the *toledot*, or genealogies.[11]

The plot of Genesis receives its internal structure from genealogies.[12] This is another aspect of Genesis that bridges the potential gap between 1–11 and 12–50. The five genealogies of 1–11 and the five in 12–50 not only match each other but mirror the structure of the Pentateuch. The genealogies often carry the reader rapidly through hundreds and thousands of years. They also provide the unchosen branches of the family tree some brief acknowledgment. The roots and branches of the genealogies present an understanding of Israelite identity. Here is a place where the modern reader must make clear choices about how to interact with the narrative. The most common choice is probably to skip over the genealogies. They are exceedingly dull and repetitive. The genealogies told ancient Israelite readers who they were and how they fit into the story, but modern readers are left to position themselves. Frei's autonomous, self-referential text fails here. Modern readers must find some sense of correspondence between their lives and the world of the story, because the attempt by the text to tell the reader how to read falls on deaf ears or blind eyes. A simple example of this, aside from the genealogies, occurs in the narratives about Jacob stealing the birthright (25:29-34) and the blessing (27:1-40) of Esau. Surely Israelites were supposed to associate themselves with Jacob, the one receiving the blessing, no matter what the circumstances. Modern readers, however, are quite prone to empathize with Esau, the cheated one. Is this way of reading improper? I suppose that Frei and his followers would have to say that it is not. Such readers are imposing their own set of values, which is seemingly foreign to the text. Nevertheless, this is the reading experience that many, if not most, modern readers have.

The other components of Genesis, the stories,[13] hang on the skeletal framework of the genealogies. The more lengthy narratives function like a zoom lens, giving the reader a close-up view of specific events. These stories often provide detailed accounts of the lives of those who are chosen to receive God's blessing, the winners of the genealogical contests. In telling us these stories, the text depicts a stunningly violent and dangerous world. The recent work of Regina M. Schwartz has drawn significant attention to some of the foundational understandings behind these stories. Schwartz's underlying thesis is that biblical thought is dominated by an "assumption of scarcity."[14] Abel and Jacob are blessed while Cain and Esau are not because there are not enough resources in the world for everyone to be blessed. This assumption sets up a world where chosenness and rejection, blessing and curse, and possession and dispossession are often determined by violent means. Death and danger lurk as constant threats. Thus we enter the world of Genesis, hoping to survive to the end.

TO DUST YOU SHALL RETURN

The setting of the book of Genesis is vague at the beginning, but it becomes clearly focused as the book progresses. Genesis 1 has a universal scope, of course, and Genesis 2–3 has a deliberately ambiguous setting. According to 2:10-15, Eden is the place where the rivers of Mesopotamia, the northern and eastern boundary of the world known to Genesis, meet the rivers of Cush, the known southern and western boundary. Eden is both everywhere and nowhere at the same time. Once Adam and Eve leave the garden, the setting of the Cain and Abel story is unspecified. The text gives only a sense of eastward movement in 3:24 and 4:16.[15] The setting of the flood narrative is again universal, but beginning with the genealogies in chapter 9 and more specifically chapter 10, clear lines on the map finally appear. Geographical names familiar even to most modern readers arise, though they are sometimes listed as the names of the descendants of Shem, Ham, and Japheth. The wandering reader finally begins to get a sense of direction. That sense is delayed one last time by the ambiguous setting of the Tower of Babel incident in 11:1-9, but in the family of Terah the reader finds companions moving in a clear direction through a known landscape.

The first narratives of Genesis are of utmost importance. Genesis 1–3 is the portal through which we enter the world of this book. What kind of world is it? According to the first story of creation in Genesis 1, it is unmistakably an ordered world. Every aspect of the account exhibits this sense of order, from the numbered days to the increasing complexity of the life forms that appear. Not only is creation ordered, but it is designed to maintain this order, each plant producing seeds "according to its kind" (1:12) and human beings "having dominion" over the other life forms (1:28).[16] This feeling of order creates in readers expectations about the nature of the world. Ricoeur, in dialogue with Hans-Heinrich Schmidt and Jon Levenson, links this expectation of order with a desire for justice.[17] The rhythmic quality of Genesis 1:1–2:4a draws the reader into a carefully ordered world. This perfect goodness forms the backdrop against which the rest of Genesis will happen.[18] What the scope of Genesis 1 prevents it from developing, identifiable human characters, will be provided in the more colloquial creation story that follows it.

Some sense of order remains throughout the second story of creation in Genesis 2. Order is brought from the cosmic dimensions of Genesis 1 down to the scale of a man and a woman and a garden. The world of Genesis does not remain idealistic for long, however. In Genesis 3 things begin to fall apart. The orderly world is disrupted by the disobedience of the man and the woman in 3:1-7 and requires reordering by God in 3:14-24. This reordering defines a world much different from either the finely orchestrated universe of Genesis 1 or the paradise of Genesis 2. It is a world containing pain, animosity, unfulfilled desire, arduous labor, and untimely death. As Adam and Eve leave the garden, they move into that larger world created in Genesis 1, and their presence alters that world. They bear God's curse-laden redefinition on their backs as they move east of Eden. This establishes a pattern for the following chapters.

The links between chapters 3 and 4 are extensive. Cain's connection to the ground (4:11-12) reflects Adam's connection (3:17). The pattern of God's dialogue with Cain (4:9-10) follows the dialogue with Adam and Eve (3:9-13). Cain's eastward movement (4:16) parallels that of Adam and Eve (3:24).[19] Things go even more wrong when Cain kills Abel (4:8). These are the first two characters born of a woman as the rest of humanity will be. Their interaction forms the first story in the non-Edenic world. The character of the murder reveals that rivalry is central to human existence.[20] Conflict is inevitable, and it overtakes human beings with sudden ferocity. Sin consumes Cain, Cain consumes Abel, and violence consumes humanity. Once this is established in the first story and magnified by the poem of Lamech (4:23-24), Genesis is able to move on quickly by means of a genealogy to examine the point where violence has infected the whole of creation (6:11), and God is compelled to respond. The end of the Cain and Abel story hangs on to one more essential point. God is still in control of creation. When reordering is required, namely the banishment of Cain, God does it. But this control will not last.

The strangeness of Genesis 1–11 never leaves the modern reader. It is there even in the genealogies, in the extraordinary life spans of the listed characters. This strangeness reaches its greatest intensity, however, in Genesis 6:1-4.[21] The meaning of the story of the "Sons of God" and their illegitimate, half-human children is impossible to fathom. The relationship of this passage to the evaluation that "the wickedness of humanity was great" (6:5) and that "the earth was filled with violence" (6:11) is uncertain. One point of clarity does emerge from this strange fragment. The genealogies of Genesis portray long, healthy life spans. Death comes only as the fitting end of a productive life. With the 120-year limit, death begins to encroach upon life's territory.

The modern reader is likely to be even more shocked and troubled that God chooses to respond to the violence of creation with violence of his own. Alter has called appropriate attention to the observation that the Hebrew word typically translated as "destroy" in 6:13 is the same as the one that appears three times in 6:11-12 and is most often translated as "corrupt." It seems nearly impossible for an English translation to reflect this potential sense of balance between the action of God (6:13) and the actions of humanity (6:11-12). Does God destroy an earth that human beings have already destroyed? Still, such total annihilation seems a drastic alternative. The orderly world that God called "very good" must now be "blotted out" (6:7). This horrifying prospect is muted by a storytelling technique that perfectly matches the content of the story. God chooses Noah as a singular focus. Likewise, the narrator tells the reader only the story of Noah. All else that we might imagine, including the terror of families as flood waters rise and consume their homes and eventually cover the highest points of ground where they have taken refuge, is not placed in our sight. Just as God turns his sight only to Noah, so does the narrator turn the sight of the reader. Only the brief and orderly report of death in 7:21-23 breaks the constant gaze upon Noah and his family. The troubling nature of such devastating punishment did not escape even ancient readers. Ancient interpreters attempted to explain the totality of the punishment in a variety of ways. Even the destruction of the animals was a problem, prompting claims that they too had sinned.[22] Today's readers need not dismiss such misgivings as modern anachronisms.

The sense of order that permeates Genesis 1 returns to prominence in God's dealings with Noah. The reminder of God's order cannot be forgotten, despite the corruption of humanity.[23] The reversal of creation reflected in the language of Genesis 7 is carefully balanced by the rhythmic instructions for preparing the ark.[24] Chaos and order are in conflict here. The violence of humanity brings about chaos, while the violence of God creates the way for a new sense of order. God's pain and anger are unleashed against the world in a torrent, but creation is maintained in a tiny box that moves along the "face of the waters" (7:18) just as God's creative spirit did (1:2). God's response to human violence is to clear the earth for a new start, a second try at creation that will begin from this microcosm of Genesis 1 that God and Noah have carefully constructed in a box. God remembers Noah (8:1).[25] But the tension between destruction and re-creation is not fully overcome. Most troubling is the awareness within the text, and in our own experience, that the flood utterly fails in its purpose. Evil persists. It cannot be drowned. Violence cannot defeat itself. How does God not know this?

In the post-Deluvian world, death and violence are immediately given their proper place. Noah slaughters animals to please God with sacrifice in 8:20, and God recognizes the inherent sinfulness of humans and repents from a destructive response in 8:21. God expands the diets of his creatures to include meat, which will require killing, in 9:3, and places limits on the eating of blood and the killing of human beings in 9:5-6. Even the latter prohibition is stated in vengeful terms. Is God acknowledging here that the punishment of Cain was too light? If Cain had received death as punishment, would that have halted the increase of violence in the world?[26] Danger and untimely death will certainly be part of this new world.

Disharmony and rivalry quickly reenter the human community in another strange story in 9:20-29. This story is filled with disconcerting elements. A son, Canaan, is cursed for the crime of his father, Ham. Unless we are to understand that Ham raped the sleeping Noah, which is a possible euphemistic understanding of "saw the nakedness," there is no apparent, serious wrongdoing. The reader is surely intended to understand that the figures in this story represent groups of people—Semite, Hamite, Canaanite. The world of Genesis quickly divides itself into territories and people groups, among which there are great ethnic animosities. This is the first time one human curses another (9:25) and the first time slavery is mentioned (9:27) in the Bible.

The lines of division are spelled out in the genealogy of Genesis 10. The most troubling aspect of this story and the genealogical result is the racial ordering of society.[27] Modupe Oduyoye correctly identified this as an ideological story.

It explains and justifies the subjection of the descendants of Ham by their white neighbors.[28] Such ideology presents tremendous difficulties for the modern reader, particularly when it justifies violence. To what extent should the reader be drawn into the story? When the story allows or even promotes racism, may a faithful reader assume her or his own autonomy over against the text?[29]

Genesis itself may not be untroubled by such difficulties. Chapter 11 reverses the story and attempts to play it out again. Its first line, "And all the earth had one language," apparently contradicts the three-fold refrain from the preceding genealogy. Genesis 11:5, 11:20, and 11:21 all inform the reader that each group of people has its own language. This has often been cited as an example of sloppy editing in Genesis, but the repetition of Shem's genealogy in 11:10-26 makes it clear that the backtracking is intentional, regardless of the sources of the units. The division of humanity is now provided a more theological explanation. Ethnicity is the result of God's punishment of human sin. All humanity together failed to obey God's command to fill the earth. Instead they stayed in one place and built a tower. Because of their disobedience, God had to scatter them and confuse their language to keep them apart (11:9). Of course, the diversion of some blame for ethnic rivalry from Ham and onto God creates new problems of its own. Nevertheless, the process of separation and differentiation in Genesis truly begins here and is given a stamp of divine purpose. The scene is set for the emergence of God's chosen people in the remainder of Genesis. The appearance of Eber, the father of the Hebrews in 11:15-17, points forward, and the primeval cycle has performed its function.

This cycle was set up by an orderly account of the creation of the universe in Genesis 1. Some sense of this order remains throughout the creation story in Genesis 2:4b-24. In Genesis 3, things begin to go awry. The orderly world is disrupted by the disobedience of the man and the woman in 3:1-7 and thus requires reordering by God in 3:14-24. This establishes a pattern for the following chapters. Things get worse when Cain kills Abel (4:8), when humanity becomes consumed by wickedness (6:5), and when the entire human race attempts to stay together in one place and build a great city (11:1-4). These problems force God to revise creation by banishing Cain further to the east (4:11-16), by flooding the earth (6:7), and by scattering the builders of the tower so that they have no choice but to fill the earth (11:8-9).[30] The disorder in creation is caused by actions that are frequently violent, but God's corrective measures are at least equally violent. Throughout the process, death moves progressively against life, as life spans decrease and the specter of untimely death emerges.

I SHALL NOT LOOK ON THE DEATH OF THE CHILD

Beginning in Genesis 12, or perhaps more properly at 11:27,[31] characters come to the forefront. Adam, Eve, Cain, and Noah are personages about whom we discover some traits, but Abram/Abraham and Sarai/Sarah are the first three-dimensional characters in the book.[32] We learn of their hopes and dreams, their successes and failures, their strengths and weaknesses of character. Indeed, this is one place where the reader, carrying his or her own cultural norms for human behavior, may feel invited to participate in the story. Abraham and Sarah are characters with whom many modern readers can identify. The book of Genesis is notorious for refusing to pass judgment on the actions of Abraham and Sarah. Is it inappropriate for modern readers to condemn the behavior of Abram in 12:10-20 when he passes Sarai off as his sister, thus threatening her life, bringing undeserved punishment onto Pharaoh, and enriching himself? Is it wrong to pass judgment on both Abraham and Sarah for their treatment of Hagar and Ishmael? The world of Genesis becomes a world of moral ambiguity at these points, but modern readers have no problems evaluating these actions as wrong. Such texts have often received less attention than those that portray Abraham and Sarah more positively. Thus, selective readers tend to have a high opinion of these two characters. Awareness of their bad behavior makes the picture more complex. Nevertheless, the good outweighs the bad in these two, and their failings may even make them more human and accessible to modern readers.

The world through which Abraham travels consistently threatens the fulfillment of God's promise in his life. The first threat begins with famine and the possibility of starvation (12:10). The promised land is not so promising. Because of the famine, Abram and Sarai must travel to the land of Egypt, which poses great danger. Abram concocts a lie that protects him from violence but exposes Sarai to the possibility of sexual assault. God comes to the rescue. Using violence again to safeguard his purpose for the word, he afflicts Pharaoh with plagues. Sarai is released and Abram enriched. Would ancient Israelites hearing this story have delighted in this victory over the Egyptians in a way that modern readers cannot?

Once this external threat is over, internal conflict arises. The strife in Abram's household is settled by separation with Lot, but this immediately places Lot in danger from the violence of Sodom (13:11-13). Eventually, Lot is kidnapped by a group of warring kings (14:11-12). Abram goes to rescue him and we learn, somewhat offhandedly, how the great patriarch has survived in this brutal place. He has become a warrior, a leader of an army of more than 300 men (14:14).

The Holy War tradition of Israel finds its humble beginning here as Abraham attributes victory to God, gives an offering to God through Melchizidek, and refuses the spoils of war (14:18-24).

Again, external threat gives way to internal conflict, this time between Abram's two wives, Sarai and Hagar.[33] First, Sarai's resentment of Hagar's fertility drives Hagar away (16:7). She returns, but eventually the conflict between Sarah's son, Isaac, and Hagar's son, Ishmael, brings about a final banishment (21:14).[34] Between these two episodes, Abraham struggles with his calling and the context in which he must live it. Befitting the name of his grandson and the nation of his descendents, Abraham strives with God. He longs for God to choose Ishmael (17:18), but God will have none of it. He pleads for the innocent of Sodom to save them from destruction (18:16-32) but barely slows down God's burning vengeance.[35] The compassion and tenderness of Abraham stand against the wrath of God and lose. It is a harsh world, and a harsh God must make harsh choices. Is it because of such softness that Abraham will have to be tested? David M. Gunn and Danna Nolan Fewell have suggested quite the opposite. Abraham has exhibited a pattern of willingness to jeopardize his own family members to protect himself. Is God testing this moral deficiency?[36] The legitimacy of both of these opposing questions reveals the complexity of Abraham's character and God's interaction with him.

The most difficult test for modern readers lies in the *Akedah* story of Genesis 22. Here the biblical text clearly commends Abraham for an act modern readers find repugnant, the near sacrifice of his son Isaac. We struggle for ways to read this story and find in it a God about whom we can care. Some tantalizing possibilities avail themselves. Does Abraham only think he hears the voice of God in 22:1-2? A narrative reading of the text does not allow such an insertion of psychology. The modern reader ends up at war with a self-referential text, and there is no easy outcome. Maybe everybody, Abraham and Isaac included, knows from the beginning that this is "only a test."[37] Again, the text fights such a reading. The heaviness of the story, particularly in the actions of Abraham, depicts a solemn mood throughout.[38] Close attention to the characters in the story reveals that it is God (*Elohim*) who demands the killing of Isaac and YHWH who prevents it. Is it possible to read these as two different characters, particularly in light of 22:12 where YHWH says to Abraham, "Now I know that you fear *Elohim*"? If we had this story alone, then this would be its obvious meaning, but in the context of Genesis the two names are understood to refer to the same character.[39] A final possibility that holds the most promise comes from our understanding of ancient Near Eastern culture. Child sacrifice was certainly not uncommon.

Sacrifice of the firstborn son may even have been the norm. If this is the case, then the command to Abraham is no surprise at all. The test, then, may not have been whether Abraham would sacrifice Isaac, but whether he could believe that he did not have to. This reading faces at least two major difficulties. First, Genesis contains no other clear references to sacrifice of the firstborn son, before or after Abraham. Second, it depends upon information from outside the text, which raises the difficult question of how much a competent reader of Genesis is expected to know. Alas, there is no easy escape from the horror of the story in which God tells a man to kill the son for whom he has waited 100 years. This sense of horror is not only a modern concern, however. Ancient interpreters also sought a way around the troubling characterization of God in the story. The most common explanation, found in sources like *Juiblees* and the *Mishnah*, was that Abraham's faith had been challenged by an adversary like Job's.[40] In the end, for Abraham and his family, chosenness may bring great benefits, but it does not remove the constant threat of death.

Lest our focus on the harsh and violent aspects of the book of Genesis paint too dark a portrait, chapters 23–24 intervene to tell the quiet and touching story of the death and burial of Sarah and the whimsical and romantic tale of Isaac's marriage to Rebekah. Amid life in a difficult world, comfort and grace appear. Nowhere is this revealed more poignantly than in 24:67 when "Isaac brought her into the tent of Sarah, his mother. He took Rebekah, and she became his wife, and he loved her. Then Isaac was comforted after his mother." There are still timely deaths. Some lives come to a fitting end, having reached fulfillment and attained good remembrance.

The lightheartedness does not last long, however, as Genesis must move on with its purpose. In two terse genealogies, the other offspring of Abraham, the children of Keturah (25:1-6) and Ishmael (25:12-18), are dismissed. Between the two reports, Abraham dies. Isaac has been separated out as the bearer of the promise. The text moves quickly to the conflict between his twin sons. Only a brief aside informs us that Isaac inhabits the same threatening territory as his father had. Famine threatens the life of his family (26:1), causing them to journey to a foreign land. Like his father, Isaac claims that his wife is his sister (26:6-7), protecting himself while exposing her to sexual danger and the people of Gerar to deadly judgment (26:10).

The moral ambiguity of Genesis reaches its high point in the beautifully developed character of Jacob. The entire Jacob cycle is artfully structured to reveal its key themes. It is about God choosing one and rejecting another. The cycle begins immediately after the genealogy of Ishmael (25:12-18), Jacob's rejected uncle, and it ends with the genealogy of Esau (36:1-43), Jacob's rejected brother.[41] Within the cycle are two stories that seem to break away from the main line of the plot. These are the story of Isaac and Rebekah in Gerar (26:1-33) and the story of the rape of Dinah by Shechem (34:1-31). Fokkelman has divided the Jacob cycle into fifteen scenes[42] and observed that these two stories are positioned second from the beginning and second from the end in order to connect the Jacob cycle to the material preceding and following it in Genesis.[43] Fishbane has demonstrated the internal function of these two interludes, which emphasize "the common themes of deception and strife" that characterize Jacob's entire life.[44]

The conflict between Jacob and Esau is revealed immediately as Isaac's genealogy (25:19-20) blends into the story of the early lives of the twin boys (25:21-28). No twins could be more at odds. They struggle in Rebekah's womb, they differ greatly in appearance, they choose opposing ways of life, and they are each the chosen favorite of one of their parents. James G. Williams has aptly labeled them "twins with a vengeance."[45] Girard has pointed to twins as the ultimate threat to a stable order because of their lack of differentiation.[46] On what basis will one be chosen and the other rejected? Genesis never gives us an explicit reason. The closest we may come is the fairly consistent preference for younger sons (25:23). Likewise, there is no reason given for chosenness in general. Schwartz points to the story of Jacob and Esau as the ultimate illustration of the "principle of scarcity," the Hebrew Bible's common assumption that blessing is limited.[47] The working out of this selection process involves violent means and creates great animosity. It highlights the potential confusion created by twins and the differences between the brothers. In the birthright story of 25:27-34, Esau, the hunter who is the favorite of his father because he brings him meat, is starving because he has failed to kill. Jacob, the gentle "dweller in tents" who is favored by his mother, is cooking a "red red" (blood?) stew.[48] After extracting the birthright from Esau, Jacob gives him only lentil soup.[49] In the later story of Isaac's blessing (27:1-40), Jacob kills more quickly than Esau. Rebekah prepares meat for Jacob to take to Isaac and uses the skins of the dead animals to disguise Jacob as Esau.[50] Thus, the twin brothers are confused and then redifferentiated so that the younger may be the chosen one. The narrator of Genesis is maddeningly silent concerning the morality of these actions. Jacob earns well his reputation as a grasper and a cheater, and these elements of his story will play a key role in the cementing of Israel's identity as the life of its great patriarch continues.

The central event in the life of Jacob, and in the defining of the people of Israel in Genesis, is the mysterious encounter at the Jabbok ford in 32:23-33. A meeting with Esau looms the next day, and Jacob's maneuvering to avoid a clash has left him alone on the riverbank. His divisive and deceitful past appears to have finally caught up with him. He engages in battle with a shadowy character and the fight mirrors his life.[51] The identity of the opponent so defies understanding that the uncertainty can only be intentional. It may be Esau who has come to find him. Who better to wrestle with Jacob than the one with whom he has wrestled since the womb?[52] It could be a bandit or a river demon, but neither of these possibilities fit well with the conversation in 32:27-31. Is it a divine messenger or God's own self. This combination forms the best answer, and there is ample precedence in Genesis for confusion between God and God's agents.[53] The narrator calls him a man, but Jacob is convinced he has encountered God in some way. The key point of the story is the change of Jacob's name to Israel. Like the encounter itself, the new name resists interpretation. The supposed etymology in 32:29, like all etymologies in Genesis, is a folk etymology or word play that works only approximately. Our narrative exploration must take "you have striven with God and with humans" more seriously than any hypothetical true etymology of the word *Israel*. Fokkelman's translation "God fights" is appropriately ambiguous, for Jacob both fights against God and with God's help, like the nation that will bear this new name. Likewise, Fokkelman's summary of the name change is fitting: "[Jacob] has been constantly in revolt because he wanted to realize [his] destiny of his own accord and by means of deceit . . . . That obstinate, proud, grim resistance to God is what he now displays on the banks of the Jabbok—and there it is also . . . knocked down."[54]

Richard Elliot Friedman has pointed out an important progression in the narrative of Genesis that takes a large step in the Jabbok ford episode. A shift is taking place in the play between divine and human initiative. In Friedman's words, "Adam disobeys God. Abraham questions God. Jacob fights God. Humans are confronting their creator, and they are increasing their participation in the arena of divine prerogatives."[55] While God called out Abram, Jacob separates himself from Esau by his own trickery. He grasps and demands a blessing, and he receives it. It will be Jacob's own song in chapter 49 that first forms the people of Israel as twelve tribes named for twelve brothers.

The combination of internal and external conflict continues in the texts near the boundary of the Jacob and Joseph cycles.[56] Though Jacob and Esau are reunited in chapter 33 and bury their father together in 35:29, Esau is separated from the chosen family, and his descendents are defined as Israel's enemies in the genealogy of chapter 36. The rape of Dinah in chapter 34 and the revenge carried out by two of her brothers establish animosity between Israel and the other inhabitants of Canaan. Ironically, Simeon and Levi use the identifying mark of

Israel, circumcision, as a ploy to slaughter the Shechemites. Jacob, having learned no good lessons from his own dysfunctional upbringing, shows favoritism toward Joseph; his love for his youngest son is in contrast with the jealousy and hatred of his other sons (37:3-4).

Finally, in Joseph, the modern reader finds a nearly ideal character. Throughout the ups and downs of his life, Joseph remains steadfastly virtuous and God is with him.[57] He is eventually rewarded for his virtue and finds himself in a position to save his brothers from famine, which he does despite their past mistreatment of him. Joseph is a victim of violence early in his life. Again, the violence stems in part from parental favoritism. The interaction between the brothers is complex. Whether Joseph is a completely innocent victim is difficult to tell. When he reports his dreams to his brothers 37:5-11, the reader can detect no tone in his language, but why tell of the dreams at all except to taunt? Of course, the brothers' response far outweighs even this possible offense. The brothers plan to kill him (37:20), and only the persuasion of Reuben prevents the murder (37:22). Joseph's fate is not yet determined as his brothers eat while he waits in the pit. The statement of Judah in 37:26, "What gain is it if we kill our brother and cover his blood? Come let us sell him to the Ishmaelites . . . ," indicates that they still intend to kill him, until they settle on the lesser crime of selling him into slavery. The irony of Judah's statement points to the futility of opposing the selection of the younger brother. Cain was unable to cover the blood of Abel and it cried out to God. A kid goat dies in Joseph's place and secures his reception of God's blessing, as a slaughtered animal did for Abel (4:4), Isaac (22:13), and Jacob (27:16-17). Though Joseph's fortunes rise and fall in Egypt and he suffers at the hands of unjust foreigners, he retains God's favor (39:21) and ultimately triumphs. Once again, famine threatens the lives of the chosen clan with death (42:1 and 43:1), and this time it provides the opportunity for Joseph's dreams of seeing his brothers bow down to him to come true (42:6).

Williams has identified a number of significant patterns in the brother stories of Genesis. Among these are (1) The younger brother is typically a shepherd,[58] (2) the younger brother is favored or chosen, and (3) the younger brother displaces the older. Violence typifies the interaction of the brothers because of all of these factors.[59] Ways of life are in conflict, most noticeably between Cain (farmer) and Abel (shepherd). The favor shown toward the younger creates jealousy and animosity. Cain murders Abel, Esau threatens and pursues Jacob, and Joseph's brothers sell him into slavery. Jacob becomes the father of all Israel, and Joseph's brothers ultimately bow down to him. The conflict is both external, between chosen and rejected brothers, and internal, among the sons of Jacob/Israel. Thus, the brother stories project Israel's future of battle with enemies and strife among tribes. The genealogies delineate the boundaries of the external conflict, and the song of Jacob (Gen 49) defines the contours of internal strife.

The book of Genesis ends with a note on the embalming of Joseph. His dead body and the faithful promise he demands from his family point forward to the exodus and the promised land.[60] Joseph's bones serve as a reminder that though he became the greatest of the sons of Israel, he still died in a foreign land. His body was not returned to Canaan to be buried, as were the bodies of the other patriarchs.

REFLECTIONS

At a number of points during this journey through Genesis, the issue of how God's character is depicted in the narrative has arisen. This subject has been ably and amply treated by W. Lee Humphreys in his recent work, *The Character of God in the Book of Genesis: A Narrative Appraisal*. Humphreys describes three levels of characterization in narrative literature. From least to greatest in complexity, these levels are "agent," "type," and "full-fledged character."[61] Humphreys finds all three levels used extensively to characterize God in the book of Genesis. What is surprising is the order in which the three appear. God first appears in the book of Genesis as a "type." God has a single role to fulfill, that of creator, and God directly and effectively fulfills that role. As the story becomes more complex, God becomes a "full-fledged character" in Genesis 2–36. God demonstrates a sense of internal tension and is involved with other characters in complex relationships. In the final fourteen chapters of Genesis, God becomes merely an "agent," one who is understood to shape events from behind the scenes but is not directly involved through either speech or action.[62] How is God characterized in the modern world? It may depend on who is doing the characterization. For us this is an issue of the use of religious language. The religious language of modern people varies and characterizes God in all of these ways. Our individual ways of thinking and talking about God and thus characterizing God will shape our view of the Genesis story.

Once the scattering of humanity is accomplished in Genesis 11, God chooses one man, Abram, through whom to work his purpose in the world. The purpose is rather vague in the beginning. God will bless Abram and through him all the families of the earth (12:2-3). Tension arises in the plan immediately, however, because God also says, "I will curse the one who curses you" (12:3). The remainder of the book of Genesis is a series of stories of selective blessing. It turns out that not all can be blessed. The potential for competition and death within creation has erupted earlier. When God regards Abel but not Cain (4:4-5), the result is murder (4:8) and cursing (4:11). Noah finds favor in the sight of God (6:8), and God blots out all life on earth (6:7) except for those people and animals that find refuge with Noah. The positive side of God's choosing of Abraham, Isaac, and Jacob is shadowed by the rejection of Lot, Ishmael, and Esau.

In Genesis 12–50, God is actively producing Israel, but this production is accomplished at a price. The cities of Sodom and Gomorrah and their inhabitants are destroyed. Abraham struggles to be a blessing to them (18:22-33), but he fails. Hagar and Ishmael are expelled into the wilderness in order to secure the place of Isaac (21:14). They nearly die before God helps Hagar find water (21:15-19). The "blessing" they receive is minimal at best. Jacob steals the birthright and blessing of Esau, and the two brothers are thrown into conflict. Esau is prosperous, but he and Jacob are unable to live peacefully in proximity to one another (36:6-8). The defining of Israel is accomplished by means that are violent, destructive, and deadly. Even the naming of Israel and the working out of its relationship to God are represented as a violent wrestling match that causes permanent physical injury (32:22-33).

The pattern of conflict does not end once Israel is clearly defined as the twelve sons of Jacob and their families. They continue to fight with their neighbors (34:25-31) and quarrel among themselves (37:18-24). The song of Jacob in Genesis 49 points to differing degrees of blessing. Simeon and Levi are characterized by violent anger and God will ultimately "divide" them because of it (49:5-7). On the other end of the scale of blessing is the tribe of Judah, which will receive the praise of all the other tribes and will rule over them (49:8-12). Not all of the tribes will thrive. This becomes clearer in Moses' reprise of Jacob's song in Deuteronomy 32, in which Simeon is no longer included. Joseph's success in Egypt reunites the family, and the book of Genesis ends with Joseph struggling to maintain family unity in the future through the oath to carry his bones out of Egypt (50:24-26), but the internal and external conflicts of the future are already foretold.

In Western traditions of interpretation, Genesis has most often been conceived as a story of creation, fall, and redemption. My reading of Genesis is not inconsistent with this picture, but it emphasizes other aspects. Perhaps this doctrinal scheme has been extracted too neatly from the disturbing narrative world of Genesis. When the violent and destructive nature of the story is repressed, two diverging movements often appear. One is a tendency to see the world as hope-lessly fallen and lost. Those who view the world in this way long for the order of Genesis 1 and sometimes attempt to reproduce it in small, encapsulated spaces. This tendency extends at least from the community that produced and collected the Dead Sea Scrolls in the first century to the Branch Davidian sect that immo-lated itself in Waco, Texas, in the twentieth century.

A second movement tends to understand the order of Genesis 1 as still pres-ent and often ignores the chaotic nature of the world. Those who assume this understanding commonly explain and accept every event as part of God's will or design. The book of Genesis certainly encourages this tendency, especially in the Joseph narratives (e.g., 45:4-15). For both views, the world depicted in Genesis 4–50 is a frightening place to live. When the real world corresponds to the world of Genesis in its violent and deadly capacities, as it all too often does, people must isolate themselves with walls of brick or ignorant bliss. Both of these approaches to surviving in the world frequently idealize the characters of Genesis, isolating certain traits such Noah's obedience, Abraham's faithfulness, or Jacob's strength for emulation. This ignores the complexity of the stories Genesis uses to develop these characters, who are rarely models of virtue.

When we enter the world of Genesis, we discover that death and conflict are inevitable parts of human existence. They are inextricably woven into our pat-terns of identification and material production. In this world, human beings must struggle to find hope. Moral choices are not clear. Creation is not typically characterized by justice. Yet the world of Genesis is not without hope. Finding and holding on to the thread of hope throughout the long journey from creation to the embalming of Joseph require honesty, diligence, and tenacity. But this final scene points forward to continued existence, blessing, and even deliverance (50:26).[63] Is it appropriate for us to add our modern sensitivities and try to extend this hope to all people and not just chosen groups? Joseph's death in Egypt is a reminder that freedom and prosperity may not always arrive in an individual lifetime. Our struggles to overcome captivity to various cultural forces are communal. This understanding will find an echo in the death of Moses on the edge of the promised land. In our own era, Martin Luther King Jr.'s "I Have Been to the Mountaintop" speech reprises the same theme.

The impact of Genesis on the modern world has too often come from the reading of individual texts. Genesis 1 and 2 provide visions of order and har-mony that characterize the world in its infancy. These visions alternately cause feelings of unrealistic hope and total despair, giving rise to Utopians and prophets of doom. Such counterproductive readings result from a disjointed, non-corresponding experience of the first two chapters of Genesis as narrative worlds in and of themselves, rather than as portals to a fuller world developed in the whole book.

Genesis 3 offers an explanation for the difficult (fallen?) nature of the world. Strong traditions of interpretation have focused specifically on sexual sin as the legacy of this "fall."[64] Whether the Western world's preoccupation with sexual sin is to be blamed more on the text of Genesis 3 or on St. Augustine's reading of it is debatable. Yet, this is certainly a place where readers' assumptions and expectations play a large role in determining their narrative experiences and the impact these narrative experiences have on their lives.

If one reads on from Genesis 4 to 50, however, it becomes evident that violence, not sex, is the sin that so easily besets humankind. Bad habits of fragmentary reading, for which lectionaries and devotional guides are partly to blame, form this misconception. In following Ricoeur more closely than Frei, I must conclude that it is not the Bible that shapes and transforms our world, but our reading of it. Narrative experiences are not unidirectional. Reader and text interact, both bringing something to the moment, and this interaction is most productive when a sense of correspondence is found between our experience and the fully developed narrative world of the text.

It would appear that our increased awareness of conflict and death in our world can create a sense of correspondence between our world and the narrative world of Genesis. We then become more aware of the violent nature of the text. This interplay between the world of the text and the world of the reader may explain the intensified interest in the issue of violence and death in the Bible at the end of the twentieth century. A transformed reading offers possibilities for transforming our world. The difficulty of such a reading creates barriers, but there are signs in modern hermeneutics and in a renewed interest in the book of Genesis that such barriers might be overcome.

NOTES

[1] From the song "Rough God" on the Van Morrison album *The Healing Game* (Polygram Records, 1997).

[2] Auerbach, *Mimesis: The Representation of Reality in Western Literature* (Princeton: Princeton University Press, 1953), 12-23.

[3] Umberto Cassuto, *A Commentary on the Book of Genesis* (2 vols.), trans. I. Abrahams (Jerusalem: Magnes, 1964).

[4] Shimon Bar-Efrat, *Narrative Art in the Bible,* trans. Dorothea Shefer-Vanson (Sheffield: Almond, 1989). Robert Alter, *The Art of Biblical Narrative* (New York: Basic Books, 1981). Adele Berlin, *Poetics and Interpretation of Biblical Narrative* (Sheffield: Almond, 1983). Meir Sternberg,

The Poetics of Biblical Narrative: Ideological Literature and the Drama of Reading (Bloomington: Indiana University Press, 1985). Jacob Licht, *Storytelling in the Bible* (Jerusalem: Magnes, 1978).

[5] Jan P. Fokkelman, *Narrative Art in Genesis: Specimens of Stylistic and Structural Analysis* (Assen: Van Gorcum, 1975).

[6] Ibid., 12-13.

[7] See Fokkelman's "Genesis" and "Exodus" in *The Literary Guide to the Bible*, ed. Robert Alter and Frank Kermode (Cambridge: Harvard University Press, 1987), 36-65.

[8] One problem with the entering of narrative worlds is that repeated reading may make the text too familiar. It may sometimes lose its power to draw us in and to surprise us because of this familiarity. For those who want to experience a new sense of freshness in reading the book of Genesis, the new translation by Robert Alter may prove helpful. This translation is a unique and daring attempt to reproduce in English the literary effect of the Hebrew text. This guiding principle provides Alter's translation with a different feel from many traditional English translations. See Robert Alter, *Genesis: Translation and Commentary* (New York: Norton, 1996). The recent translation of Stephen Mitchell is much less conducive to narrative study because it divides and rearranges Genesis according to source-critical criteria. See *Genesis: A New Translation of the Classic Biblical Stories* (New York: HarperCollins, 1996). Jonathon Kirsch's *The Harlot by the Side of the Road: Forbidden Tales of the Bible* (New York: Ballentine, 1997) retells a handful of Genesis stories with a tremendous amount of imaginative detail, which is neither supported nor directly contradicted in the text. Anita Diamant's novel *The Red Tent* (New York: Picador USA, 1998) moves in a different direction by developing the stories of the women in Genesis in a midrash-like style.

[9] See the discussion of John J. Scullion, "The Narrative of Genesis," in *The Anchor Bible Dictionary*, vol. 2, ed. David Noel Freedman (New York: Doubleday, 1992), 949. The separation of these two blocks of material also involves a supposed shift in theological theme from creation to salvation. See the critique of this easy separation by André LaCocque and Paul Ricoeur, *Thinking Biblically: Exegetical and Hermeneutical Studies*, trans. David Pellauer (Chicago: University of Chicago Press, 1998), 3-8 and 31-34.

[10] Michael Fishbane, *Biblical Text and Texture: A Literary Reading of Selected Texts* (New York: Shocken, 1978), 17-39.

[11] Fokkelman, "Genesis," 36-44.

[12] For a thorough discussion of how the lists of descendents form the literary framework of the book, see Joseph Blenkinsopp, *The Pentateuch: An Introduction* (New York: Doubleday, 1989), 58-60, 98-100.

[13] Labeling the non-genealogical material in Genesis is problematic. The designation I have chosen, "story," is not entirely fair. The genealogies themselves are stories in a way, and the non-genealogical material contains other forms of literature, such as songs and poems.

[14] Schwartz, *The Curse of Cain: The Violent Legacy of Monotheism* (Chicago: University of Chicago Press, 1997), 19.

[15] For an insightful discussion of all the eastward movements in the book of Genesis, see Devora Steinmetz, *From Father to Son: Kinship, Conflict and Continuity in Genesis* (Louisville: Westminster, 1991), 143-44. See also Fishbane's treatment of this pattern in 1–11 in *Biblical Text and Texture*, 36-37.

[16] See Cassuto's symmetric structure, which pairs days one and four, two and five, and three and six. The first day in each pair sees the creation of general spaces and conditions for the specific entities, created on the second day of each pair, which exist in them (*A Commentary on the Book of*

Genesis [Jerusalem: Magnes, 1964], 16-17). Note also Fishbane's further development of this idea in *Biblical Text and Texture*, 10-11.

[17] See LaCocque and Ricoeur, *Thinking Biblically*, 54-61.

[18] Fishbane, *Biblical Text and Texture*, 8.

[19] For a more thorough treatment of this issue, see Steinmetz, *From Father to Son*, 89-91, and Mark McEntire, *The Blood of Abel: The Violent Plot of the Hebrew Bible* (Macon GA: Mercer University Press, 1999), 28.

[20] Girard has gone one step further in asserting that rivalry forms and defines human existence. See *Violence and the Sacred*, trans. Patrick Gregory (Baltimore: Johns Hopkins University Press, 1977), 145-49.

[21] The story is fully elaborated in the extra-canonical book of 1 Enoch. The relationship of Enoch to Genesis is uncertain. Though Enoch may reflect a more complete legend, of which Genesis 6:1-4 is only a fragment, it seems more likely that Enoch exemplifies our mystification by imaginatively completing the story. See James Kugel, *The Bible as It Was* (Cambridge MA: Belknap, 1997), 107-109.

[22] See Kugel's collection of texts and discussion in *The Bible as It Was*, 117-18.

[23] Fishbane has called the order of creation in Genesis a "counterpoint" to the disruptive actions of human beings (*Biblical Text and Texture*, 15).

[24] Alter, *Genesis*, 29.

[25] On the decisiveness of this "turning point" in the story, see Walter Brueggemann, *Genesis*, Interpretation (Atlanta: John Knox, 1982), 85-87.

[26] One tendency in ancient Jewish and Christian interpretation of the early chapters of Genesis was to identify Cain as a demonic offspring. For a survey of these texts, see Kugel, *The Bible as It Was*, 86-87. Some ancient interpreters took this one step further and blamed Cain for the flood (99-100).

[27] It is remarkable that the terms "Semitic" and "Hamitic" are still used by modern anthropologists and linguists. Was the understanding of the biblical writers so precise that its terminology has persisted, or has it been so persuasive that modern social sciences cannot escape its influence? Of course, the placement of Canaanites in the Hamitic group is improper from the perspective of modern anthropology and linguistics.

[28] According to Oduyoye, the text answers the question, "Why are the blacks, who were said to have produced the first empire in human history, everywhere subject to the whites by the sixth century B. C.?" See *The Sons of God and the Daughters of Men: An Afro-Asiatic Interpretation of Genesis 1–11* (Maryknoll NY: Orbis, 1984), 58-60, 99-100.

[29] This is a place where the role of the reader is unclear in narrative theories that claim a self-referential text and that assert that the world of the text is always more real than the world of the reader.

[30] This movement in the book of Genesis has been described as "cracks in the wall" by LaCocque. See *Thinking Biblically*, 3-29. La Cocque has also noted the tendency of readers to recognize themselves in the characters of these stories and the powerful results of this sense of correspondence (29).

[31] See the argument for moving the standard division back a few verses in Blenkinsopp, *The Pentateuch*, 98-102.

[32] Writing about characters whose names change in the midst of a narrative can be tricky and confusing. From this point on when discussing a specific text, I will use the names the individuals have in that text. The dividing line is the name-changing dialogue in 17:1-22. When I refer to these two characters in a general sense, not in relation to one specific text, I will call them Abraham and Sarah.

[33] Many facets of the story of Abraham point forward, both implicitly and explicitly, to the exodus story. Among them are the famine that sends Abram and Sarai to Egypt (12:10), the plagues inflicted upon Pharaoh (12:17), Abraham's dream (15:13-15), and Sarai's conflict with Hagar the Egyptian (16:3-6).

[34] For a careful and passionate exploration of the violent and horrifying aspects of Hagar's story, see Phyllis Trible, *Texts of Terror: Literary Feminist Readings of Biblical Texts* (Philadelphia: Fortress, 1984), 8-35. Alter has noted the strong parallels between the wilderness trial of Hagar and Ishmael and that of Abraham and Isaac in Genesis 22 (*The Art of Biblical Narrative*, 180-81).

[35] The nature of the sin of Sodom is not expressed as clearly in the Bible as some interpreters might lead us to believe. Genesis does not explicitly connect the attempted rape of the travelers in 19:1-11 with God's decision to destroy the city in 18:16-33. See the discussion in Kugel, *The Bible as It Was*, 185-89.

[36] David M. Gunn and Danna Nolan Fewell, *Narrative in the Hebrew Bible* (Oxford: Oxford University Press, 1993), 98-100.

[37] In a popular, recent book Thomas Cahill has stated forthrightly that at least the reader knows from the beginning that the test is contrived and that the killing of Isaac is never a possibility. See *The Gifts of the Jews: How a Tribe of Desert Nomads Changed the Way Everyone Thinks and Feels* (New York: Doubleday, 1998). This conclusion is without support in the text. Of course, repeated reading can bring about this sense. Nevertheless, many readers, myself included, continue to find the story terrifying after hundreds of readings. Surprisingly, the argument that knowing this is a test eases the tension for the reader is supported by Berlin, who claims that ". . . we accept God's actions, knowing that he does not really intend them to be carried out (*Poetics and Interpretation of Biblical Narrative*, 54). Her claim is defeated by her own pairing of this "test" with that in Job, about a man who lost all of his children.

[38] See Licht's discussion of narrative technique in this story in *Storytelling in the Bible*, 115-20.

[39] Of course, the use of these two designations has served as a criterion for source analysis of Genesis 22, but that is of no concern here.

[40] See the summary of such interpretations in Kugel, *The Bible as It Was*, 171-72.

[41] Fishbane, *Biblical Text and Texture*, 40.

[42] Fokkelman, *Narrative Art in Genesis*, 86.

[43] Fokkelman, "Genesis," 39-40.

[44] Fishbane, *Biblical Text and Texture*, 46-48.

[45] James G. Williams, *The Bible, Violence, and the Sacred: Liberation from the Myth of Sanctioned Violence* (San Francisco: Harper, 1991), 39.

[46] Girard, *Violence and the Sacred*, 56-63.

[47] Schwartz, *The Curse of Cain*, 80-81.

[48] The Hebrew words for blood (*dam*), red (`adom*), and Esau's ancestors (`edom*) are all closely connected. See Alter, *Genesis*, 129.

[49] See the thorough interpretation of this story in terms of Girard's thesis in Williams, *The Bible, Violence, and the Sacred*, 40-42.

[50] See Girard's discussion of this text in *Violence and the Sacred*, 4-6.

[51] Fishbane, *Biblical Text and Texture*, 54.

[52] On this possibility, see Jack Miles, *God: A Biography* (New York: Vintage, 1995), 73-75. The one indication of this possibility in the text is Jacob's statement to Esau in 33:10, "I have seen your face like seeing the face of God."

[53] See Richard Elliott Friedman's insightful discussion of this issue in *The Disappearance of God: A Divine Mystery* (Boston: Little, Brown, and Company, 1995), 9-13.

[54] Fokkelman, *Narrative Art in Genesis*, 216.

[55] Friedman, *The Disappearance of God*, 37-38.

[56] This is not necessarily so clear a boundary. Though Joseph does become the main character of Genesis beginning in chapter 37, Jacob lives on through the whole story, and his voice dominates the end of Genesis in grand song in chapter 49.

[57] The nature of God's presence has changed, however. Unlike the face-to-face contact enjoyed by Abraham and Jacob, Joseph receives only symbolic dreams and the reader is merely informed of God's presence in colorless statements (39:2, 21). On this issue in the Joseph narratives see Claus Westermann, *Joseph* (Minneapolis: Fortress, 1996). For more comprehensive discussions of the progressive withdrawal of God's presence throughout the course of the Bible, see Jack Miles, *God: A Biography*, and Richard Elliott Friedman, *The Disappearance of God: A Divine Mystery*.

[58] This pattern extends beyond Genesis to Moses and David.

[59] Williams, *The Bible, Violence, and the Sacred*, 60-66.

[60] Friedman has discussed in significant detail the progressive changes in character development in Genesis (*The Disappearance of God*, 31-35).

[61] Humphreys builds on the work of E. M. Forster and Adele Berlin, identifying these three levels of characterization (*The Character of God in the Book of Genesis: A Narrative Appraisal* [Louisville: Westminster John Knox, 2001], 241).

[62] *The Character of God in the Book of Genesis*, 241-43. These observations are consistent with those made by Miles and Friedman, which are noted earlier in this chapter.

[63] In a recent book, Gareth Lloyd Jones has used the "bones of Joseph" as a metaphor for tradition. This metaphor symbolizes the act of carrying something from the past into the uncertain future (*The Bones of Joseph: From the Ancient Texts to the Modern Church* [Grand Rapids: Eerdmans, 1997]).

[64] See Elaine Pagels, *Adam, Eve, and the Serpent* (New York: Vintage, 1989), xvii-xxviii.

Judges:
Who Shall Go Up?

Let us pause in life's pleasures and count its many tears
While we all sup sorrow with the poor
There's a song that will linger forever in our ears
Oh, hard times come again no more

While we seek mirth and beauty and music light and gay
There are frail forms fainting at the door
Though their voices are silent, their pleading looks will say
Oh, hard times come again no more

'Tis a sigh that is wafted across the troubled wave
'Tis a wail that is heard upon the shore
'Tis a dirge that is murmured around the lowly grave
Oh, hard times come again no more

'Tis the song, the sigh of the weary
Hard times, hard times come again no more
Many days you have lingered
Around my cabin door
Oh, hard times come again no more

—Stephen Collins Foster[1]

THE NARRATIVE SHAPE OF JUDGES

The literary structure of the Book of Judges has received significant attention. The primary focus has typically been on the cycle of stories in chapters 3–16. At first glance, these stories seem repetitive, following a series of steps outlined by the Book of Judges itself in 2:11-23. The intense attention given to the recurring cycle has sometimes obscured the importance of chapters 1–2 and 17–21. These two sections are sometimes characterized as the prologue and epilogue to the body of the story, which is the cycle of stories about the six major judges, but together they constitute about one-third of the book. The repetition of the cycles may also distract attention from linear patterns of movement within the large central section of the book.[2] A narrative approach to this book must give ample attention to its beginning, its progress, and its end.

Attention to the narrative design of Judges has also been diverted by historical concerns, for a number of reasons. The Book of Judges is our only source of written information about the formative period of Israel's history between the arrival in the promised land and the rise of the monarchy. Attempts to mine the book for clues to the anthropology and sociology of the period often have a fragmenting effect. It has also been recognized that the theology and ideology of the book come from a later period. The primary candidate has been the "Deuteronomic" reform period of the seventh century. Therefore, the Book of Judges has frequently been used as a source of information about that period of Israel's history as well. These are all legitimate concerns, and the results of such efforts have been significant. Nevertheless, larger literary concerns have often been neglected.

Tammi J. Schneider is correct in her assessment that feminist concerns have been the primary force behind the increasing attention given to the literary features of Judges.[3] Feminist interpreters noticed, early in the development of their collective work, that female characters play a significant role in Judges. In her groundbreaking work, *Texts of Terror: Literary-feminist Readings of Biblical Narratives*,[4] Phyllis Trible devoted two of her four major chapters to the stories of two women in Judges—the unnamed daughter of Jephthah in Judges 11 and the unnamed concubine[5] in Judges 19. Judges has also received major attention from other feminist critics, such as Mieke Bal, Cheryl Exum, and Susan Ackerman.[6] Because these feminist interpreters have typically used the emerging literary methods of the last quarter of the twentieth century, their work has established new directions in literary criticism of the Book of Judges as well.

Another productive trajectory that has produced a more holistic picture of Judges as a narrative has been the recent attention given to the role of political ideology in the book. Articles by Marc Brettler and Marvin A. Sweeney best exemplify this approach. Brettler argued that one major purpose of Judges is to highlight the virtues of the tribe of Judah and its representatives. At the same time, the book points to the shortcomings of the northern tribes and their members. Judges thus becomes an ideological argument for the Davidic monarchy and against rivals from the north or the Benjaminite family of Saul.[7] Sweeney has carried this emphasis on political ideology further, identifying the condemnation of Ephraim, the Bethel sanctuary, and the northern practice of intermarriage with even greater precision. In addition, his work highlights the significance of the beginning and ending sections of the book, which have too often been confined to prologue and epilogue status.[8] A carefully constructed ideological strategy thus runs through the entire book of Judges that elevates David and the tribe of Judah, while blaming Ephraim and Bethel for Israel's shortcomings.[9]

These two streams of development that emerged from the last quarter of the twentieth century, centered on feminist and political concerns, have been brought together by Tammi J Schneider in the most thorough work on the narrative structure of Judges to date.[10] In all of this work, something of a consensus concerning the narrative shape of Judges seems to appear. The entire book is a carefully crafted, narrative argument in favor of the monarchy in general and the Davidic monarchy in particular. Judges falls fairly naturally into three sections, or movements, based upon shifts in literary style: chapters 1–2, 3–16, and 17–21. This division, however, does not imply a sense of discontinuity in the purpose of the book. Neither does it carry necessary assumptions about origins of different sets of material or the editorial process that produced the book in its present form. Perhaps the two most significant conclusions from these developments can be identified. First, the role played by the middle section is no more significant than that of the first and third sections. It is only greater in quantity, not in significance. Second, while the cyclical nature of the middle section is its most obvious surface feature, the directional qualities are of greater significance. The decline of the tribal system, in terms of leadership quality, military success, and general morality,[11] is a theme that runs through all three sections, producing a narrative continuity that becomes the major focus of interpretation. As Judges presents its six "major" characters, their stories become longer, the times of peace following their successes generally become shorter, and the quality of their personal character becomes more dubious.[12]

Life and death are no longer simply individual or family matters. Between Genesis and Judges, Israel has been constituted as a people. How will this people get along in a new place? Will they survive or will they perish? These are questions the Book of Judges wishes to address.

PERISH ALL YOUR ENEMIES O LORD

The Book of Judges begins in a manner similar to the Book of Joshua. Joshua 1:1-9 reiterates, from Deuteronomy, the death of Moses and the appointment of

Joshua as his successor. Likewise, Judges 1:1 repeats the report of Joshua's death, which was recorded earlier in Joshua 24:29-31. The question raised in the second half of this verse immediately identifies an expectation and a problem. Israel's story, up to this point, has been told around a central, heroic figure, first Moses and then Joshua. Judges naturally looks for the next hero, but none is forthcoming. Perhaps this problem is even foreshadowed by the Book of Joshua, which does not identify a successor for Joshua the way the final verses of Deuteronomy do for Moses. One subtle purpose of this initial story is to elevate the tribe of Judah above the rest of Israel.[13] This move is the first element in the case for the Davidic monarchy, which is so carefully constructed by Judges.[14]

The need for a hero figure is twofold. First, the narrator needs a central hero if the story is to continue in the pattern developed in Exodus–Joshua. Does this narrator know how to tell a story in a way other than following the life of a central figure? Second, the characters in the story have become dependent upon heroic figures for their survival. Moses and Joshua establish a pattern of the leader maintaining the relationship between Israel and God, sometimes even saving the Israelites from death at God's hand. These heroes also lead the way in the struggle for survival. Through the wilderness and into the promised land, they provide food, water, land, and protection. The absence of a hero is a threat to the life of Israel.

Judges wants this kind of individual hero so badly that it attempts to talk about Judah as an individual in 1:3. This confusing image resolves, however, into that of a tribe going into battle to seize land. The account echoes the successes of Joshua.[15] Judah is held up as the leading tribe,[16] and the brutality of Judges is introduced and foreshadowed in the mutilation of Adoni-bezek (1:5-7). This is a tough world, and in the Israelites' perception, they will have to participate in patterns of behavior that include torture and brutal intimidation if they are to survive.

The initial successes of the tribe of Judah quickly give way to mixed results in the military actions of the other tribes. The first chapter of Judges demonstrates the violent nature of land acquisition in the ancient Near East. It is a kill-or-be-killed, take-or-be-taken world. Some tribes drive out their opponents, and others do not. Some subject the Canaanites to forced labor, and some do not. On the whole, Judges 1 moves toward a pattern of coexistence with the indigenous peoples of Canaan. To our storyteller, this pattern seems strangely unacceptable. The pattern of tribe-by-tribe conquest begun by Judah falls apart. Is the survival of the people of Israel in peril?

The ultimate failure of the conquest effort forces an ideological revision at the beginning of Judges 2. Whatever the reasons for the Israelites' failure to destroy the Canaanites, the result will be an ongoing situation of conflict. God's promise of a peaceful existence is replaced by the guarantee of a constant struggle for survival. The ambiguity of the *Bochim* episode in 2:1-5 matches the ambiguity of this story's place in the overall flow of the narrative. *Bochim* is an unknown place in the biblical narrative.[17] Why had the people gathered there? Communication from "the angel of the YHWH" directly to the people seems quite unusual. This highlights further the lack of a leader. These points of confusion in the *Bochim* story are compounded by the mysterious beginning of the next unit in 2:6. Suddenly, Joshua reappears. Was he present at *Bochim* all along? If so, why did the angel not speak through him? How can he be present here when he died in 1:1?

The chronological difficulties of Judges 2 are not easily overcome, but need not be labeled as signs of clumsy editing.[18] Rather, they may be a sign that the narrator needs to start the story over again. The attempt in Judges 1 to tell a conquest story centered on Judah has proven to be a false start. Thus, a narrative resurrection of Joshua allows a new beginning. The recounting of Joshua's death in 2:6-10 is followed by the narrator's presentation of a new pattern for telling the story in 2:11-23. This pattern is typically described as a series of steps. First, the Israelites "do what is evil in the sight of YHWH." This usually involves the worship of other gods (2:11-13). Second, "YHWH's anger is kindled" and the Israelites are "given into the hands of their enemies" (2:14-15, 20-21). Third, the Israelites "are in distress and cry out to YHWH," who has compassion on them "because of their groaning" (2:15, 18). Fourth, YHWH "raises up judges" to deliver the Israelites from their enemies (2:16, 18). Finally, as soon as the judge dies, the Israelites relapse into their idolatrous behavior and the process starts again (2:19). This cyclical process establishes a literary pattern and introduces the characteristic language of the next fourteen chapters of Judges.

Of course, 2:11-23 is heavily freighted with theological language. That aside, this seems like a fairly bland and simple narrative of a people whose fortunes rise and fall over time, just like most any group of people in any time. The conclusion of this section in 2:20-23 insists, however, that the life of this group of people is anything but the result of the ordinary fluctuations of the world.[19] The pain, suffering, and death they experience is the result of the failure of Israel to keep covenant with its God.

The six individual stories of the "major" judges, which are placed onto the narrative template outlined above, are anything but bland and simple. They are among the strangest and most colorful stories in the entire Bible. The main characters are a bizarre and unforgettable collection, to say the least. All of this is fortunate, because we are about to be told what could seem like the same story six times, but it turns out to be anything but the same. The individuality of the stories serves as an apt reminder that behind all of the theological posturing lie the lives and deaths of extraordinary and ordinary people.

The story of the first judge, Othniel, is the simplest of the six. It is as if the Book of Judges needs to warm up, to go through some stretching exercises. The story in 3:7-11 does little more than add the name of the judge (Othniel, a nephew of Caleb) and the name of the enemy (King Cushan-Rishathaim) to the standard language of the template in 2:11-23. All goes well, and the Israelites prevail in war under Othniel's leadership. The forty-year period of rest indicates not only that this pattern of existence can work for Israel, but also that Othniel lived a good, long life and ruled for an appropriate period.[20] The significance of certain other elements of this story will not become clear until seen in the light of the stories that follow.

As Judges tells the story of Ehud, the second major judge, the book is clearly gathering momentum. The episode recorded in 3:12-30 is significantly longer than the Othniel story and is much more vivid in detail. The Ehud story is an ideal piece of biblical storytelling. Most readers have noticed by this time that the Bible is spare in its use of detail. Seldom are we provided with physical descriptions of biblical characters. Thus, the description of Ehud as "left-handed"[21] and of his sword as "two-edged" and "one cubit in length" have an unusual feel about them, as does the description of King Eglon as "fat."[22] As the story develops, however, these physical characteristics become essential to the plot. Modern readers may be significantly uneasy about this story, but it is difficult to imagine that Israelite readers would not have found the story comical. The picture of their stealthy, left-handed hero killing the fat foreign king whose dull-witted bodyguards fail to search his whole body for weapons must have elicited a humorous sense of ethnic pride. On the other hand, this is a brutal assassination, and modern society is becoming appropriately sensitive about laughing at obesity. Nevertheless, my experience is that modern listeners laugh when this story is read aloud to them, though it is typically not without some sense of guilt and discomfort. Eglon is depicted in the story as a brutal oppressor, however, and finding enjoyment in his demise is an attitude that is difficult to judge too harshly. This is a pattern well established in the biblical story. Liberating a people from bondage, thus raising their status, requires the bringing down of another people. The Moabites are reduced by the assassination of their king so that the

Israelites might be free again. The assassination of Eglon opens the door to military victory and the killing of enemies on a much larger scale. The meaning of 3:28 is not transparent, but it seems to report a story of the Israelite army cutting off an attempted retreat out of Israel by the Moabites. The result is the complete slaughter of 10,000 Moabites.

Three unusual features appear at the end of Judges 3. First, there is no mention of the death of Ehud. Of the six "major" judges, only Ehud and Deborah receive no death notice.[23] Second, the eighty-year period of peace described in 3:30 is unparalleled. The ideal period is forty years, as is designated after Othniel, Deborah, and Gideon. We are not told specifically that Ehud judged for all these years. Schneider proposed that the failure to link Ehud explicitly with the period of peace and the failure to designate him specifically as a "judge" may be deliberate slights because of his Benjaminite heritage.[24] The third unusual feature, the first report of a "minor" judge in 3:30, may resolve some of the difficulty.[25] The eighty-year period may be assumed to refer to forty for Ehud and forty for Shamgar. Shamgar receives only a single-verse report. He is credited with killing a large number (600) of Philistines with an unusual weapon, an oxgoad. This minor note is reflected later in the more elaborate story of Samson killing 1,000 Philistines with the jawbone of a donkey in 15:14-17.

Whether the eighty-year notice is connected to the life of Ehud or Ehud and Shamgar combined, it points to two full generations of peace for the people of Israel. They are not oppressed; they live full, prosperous lives, and they die good deaths at appropriate ages. The pattern of leadership established by the judges functions for an extended period of time, even if these times eventually come to an end.

The next disruption in Israel's life arrives with the characteristic language in 4:1, "The Israelites did evil in the sight of the LORD." The appearance of unfaithful behavior here is connected to the death of Ehud. The association of the end of a period of time that represents "the good old days" with the death of a heroic figure produces a point in the narrative that looks like a communal death. The villain this time is a Canaanite king, Jabin of Hazor.[26]

The full cycle of stages plays out until a new hero is identified in 4:4, "Deborah, a prophet, the wife of Lappidoth." Unlike the accounts of the two previous major judges, however, the characteristic language, "the LORD raised up a judge" (3:9 and 3:15), does not appear here. Beginning with Deborah, the introduction of the judges is no longer connected in this simple and direct way to the crying out of the Israelites amid their suffering and the threat to their existence. This shift in language, combined with Barak's leadership failure and the suppression of his character in deference to Deborah's, may be the first significant sign of the decay of the judges pattern.[27] The relationships among the characters in the Deborah story are far more complex than in the previous stories and require careful scrutiny. The story of Deborah is unusual in larger ways. It is the only story in Judges that is told twice. There is a prose account in Judges 4 and a poetic account in Judges 5.[28]

The poetic account is placed in the narrative as a song of victory sung by the heroes, much like the songs of Miriam and Moses in Exodus 15. This elaboration provides a quantum leap in the length and sophistication of the story. The brief, single verse description of a victorious battle in the Othniel story is expanded in the story of Ehud to include a detailed account of a spectacular assassination along with a four-verse account of the ensuing war. The Deborah narrative reverses the order, telling the story of the battle against the Canaanites first, in fifteen verses, followed by a startlingly vivid account of the assassination of Sisera. YHWH, the God of Israel, is more intimately involved in the military victory. YHWH "throws" the Canaanite army into "a panic" (4:15), resulting in the death of all of them. Every soldier is killed by the sword except their leader, Sisera. He escapes only to have a tent peg driven through his head. The unlikely hero of this latter episode is the Kenite woman, Jael. Her guile and deception match that of Ehud. The ultimate result of the Israelite victory is reported at the end of the prose account. The Israelites continue to attack King Jabin until he is destroyed.

The absolute victory, in 4:24, provides the appropriate context for the song of victory in Judges 5. The perspective of the song both adds to and clarifies issues arising in the prose account. The song elevates the role of Deborah as a military hero (vv. 7-9) over that of Barak. Judges 4 had maintained a sense of ambiguity about Deborah's part in the act of war.[29] The poem also expresses some of the hardships and threats to the lives of ordinary people created by warfare (vv. 6-7). The translation of these verses is difficult. The NRSV presents a more positive expression, but most other translations depict a cessation of healthy village life as conditions declined in the period before Deborah arose.[30] Finally, the poem lists eight of the tribes of Israel by name and either praises their participation in the battle (Ephraim, Benjamin, Zebulon, Issachar, and Naphtali) or denounces their failure to do so (Reuben, Dan, and Asher). In Judges, it is often difficult to determine the level of cooperation among the tribes. Chapter 4 mentioned only the participation of Zebulon and Naphtali specifically. By the end of Judges, tension among the tribes will be a major problem that creates the call to abandon this pre-monarchical way of being Israel.

The final verse of the poem, in 5:31, expresses most clearly what is at stake for Israel at this point in its story. Will Israel be God's friend or God's enemy? This is a life-or-death question. God's friends will rise like the sun (5:31), while God's enemies will sink and fall like Sisera (5:27). The forty years of peace attested at the end of chapter 5 indicate that, at least for now, Israel may be counted among God's friends.

The story of Gideon continues a number of important trends in Judges. The length and degree of detail in the story increase significantly. The development of the main character is much fuller and more complex. The portrayal of Gideon is not unambiguously positive, as has been the case with Othniel, Ehud, and Deborah. After his military successes, Gideon's behavior becomes strange and suspicious. Our evaluation of this change depends in part on how we understand the relationship between Judges 6–8 and Judges 9, an issue that will have to wait until after an exploration of the Gideon story proper.

The new enemy, which puts an end to the forty years of peace following Deborah, is Midian. Much of the language in 6:1-9 is that of the familiar cycle, but there are significant additions. Verses 3-6 provide significant detail about the effects of the oppression of Israel's enemies. The livelihood of ordinary Israelites is being destroyed. In response to their crying out, God does not immediately raise up a judge, but sends an unnamed prophet (v. 6) to proclaim a message to them (vv. 7-10), which sounds like 2:1-5. The full identification of Gideon as a judge requires a lengthy process reported in 6:11-40. For the first time, a potential judge must be convinced to take on the role. The story of Gideon "putting out the fleece" (6:36-40) is the most well-known part of the Gideon material. Less familiar, but more important in this study, is his taking down of the Baal altar in 6:25-27. For the first time in Judges, one of God's chosen leaders fears the reactions of his or her own people. The result is that Gideon destroys the altar secretly at night. The story of the people's reaction to this, in 6:28-32, provides an explanation for Gideon's other name, Jerubbaal, which is interpreted as "The Baal contends against him."

Gideon's initial acts as a judge alternate with the signs he requests and receives to confirm his status. He gathers troops from four tribes (Manasseh, Asher, Zebulun, and Naphtali) in 6:33-35 and prepares to fight the Midianites and Amalekites, but then the story pauses to report the episode of the fleece. The resumption of the battle story in chapter 7 raises a new issue. The involvement of God in Israel's victory may become a subject of question. Doubt about this has not arisen thus far in Judges, and this may be another sign of decline in the book. To prevent claims about the great performance of Israel's army, the troops are winnowed down to just 300, in strange fashion, and Gideon devises the bizarre battle strategy involving the torches, clay jars, and trumpets. The confusion of the enemy soldiers and their death by the sword are reminiscent of the battle of Deborah and Barak in Judges 5, while the surrounding of the camp and the blowing of the trumpets and shouting evoke memories of the battle of Jericho in Joshua 6.

The military victory seems overwhelming, but the way it is reported is confusing, and further difficulties arise in chapter 8. Gideon continues to pursue the Midianite army, and conflict arises between him and various groups of Israelites. The confusion of the passage can hardly be accidental, as the direction of the story breaks down entirely. Though Gideon fights and wins another battle in 8:10-12, this victory is not attributed to either God's direction or assistance. In v. 12 it is Gideon, not YHWH, who "threw all of the army into a panic." Gideon's threat against the people of Succoth (8:9) and his executions of Zebah and Zalmunna (8:21) seem to be motivated more by personal vengeance than by obedience to God or concern for Israel's security.[31]

Gideon's words and actions in 8:22-28 become even more confusing. Why does someone so driven by revenge and power in the previous story not accept an offer to become king? For a moment the faithful Gideon reemerges in his assertion "YHWH will rule over you" (8:23), but in the verses immediately following he constructs out of gold what appears to be an idol. This action connects him to two of the great abominations within Israel's story, the making of the golden calf by Aaron in Exodus 32[32] and the making of two golden calves by Jereboam in 1 Kings 12. The downfall of Gideon ends up fitting the pattern of Judges. As a member of the tribe of Manasseh (6:15), Gideon would be an unlikely hero in a book that seems to want to elevate the tribe of Judah over the other tribes, particularly those from the north.

The relationship between the Gideon story in Judges 6–8 and the story of Abimelech in Judges 9 is difficult to determine and will not be fully settled here. The statement that "the land had rest forty years" in 8:28 would seem to bring the Gideon story to a proper close. The additional material about Gideon in 8:29-35 disrupts the ending of the story. Adding to this sense of disruption is the use of a Gideon's other name, Jerubbaal, to refer to Gideon in 8:29-35. This other name had been used previously, once in Judges 6 and once in Judges 7. It appears twice in 8:29-35 and seven times in Judges 9. The sudden increase in the frequency of the use of Jerubbaal may point to a significant shift in Judges. Judges 8:29-35 is an important transitional text, which is tied to the fuller story of Gideon by the references to idolatry and to the story in Judges 9 by the report of Abimelech's birth.

The Abimelech story may be understood as an interlude. It does not fit the narrative pattern of the judges cycle. E. John Hamlin has argued persuasively, however, for understanding Gideon-Abimilech as a single story. A number of recurring motifs tie the story together. These include the identification of trees as sites of key events (6:11, 6:19, and 9:6), the appearance of flames as symbols of power or destruction (6:21, 7:20, 9:15, 9:20, 9:49, and 9:57), and the tearing down of towers, accompanied by the deaths of human beings (8:17, 9:46-49, and 9:51-54).[33]

The vengeful behavior of Gideon/Jerubbaal is magnified in the character of Abimelech. It may be oversimplified to understand the name Gideon as a representation of this judge's positive side and Jerubbaal as a reflection of his negative side, but we have already observed above that the frequency of Jerubbaal increases as the story progresses. In Judges 9, this designation has completely overridden the name Gideon, which never appears in this chapter. Abimelech is the son of Jerubbaal, not of Gideon. He seizes power with a murderous plot (vv. 1-6), he maintains power through fear and intimidation (v. 21), and his vengeful ways finally lead to his downfall. One difficult aspect of this text for modern readers is that an evil spirit sent by God is attributed with continuing the enmity and violent conflict between Abimelech and the lords of Shechem (9:22-25). A tremendous amount of collateral damage is reported in this ongoing conflict at 9:25, 41, 49, and 57. The role of God in providing the motivation for violence and destruction is an abiding question. The idea of an evil spirit coming from God and acting destructively in a person's life will appear more prominently in the discussion of 1 Samuel 16 in the next chapter.

We noted earlier that the statement "And the land had rest forty years in the days of Gideon" (8:28) does not bring the Gideon story to a close. There is an uneasiness about this phrase. The description of the situation in Israel during the reign of Abimelech is hard to perceive as "rest." Two things come to an end with this statement. This will be the last time in Judges that the land will be said to "have rest,"[34] and this is the last time that a period of forty years is attributed to a judge. Gideon/Jerubbaal turns out to be a watershed figure in Judges. The decline of Israelite society into destructive chaos now becomes persistent and rapid.

A brief interlude is present in the notations concerning two "minor" judges, Tola and Jair, in 10:1-5.[35] Other than the barest set of details concerning chronology and geography, there is nothing present in these accounts except for the odd saying about Jair, which sounds almost like a nursery rhyme: "There were to him thirty sons, Riders of thirty donkeys, And thirty towns."

The Book of Judges quickly presses on to the next oppression. The fifth major judge is Jephthah, and though his name will not appear until 11:1, the new round of sufferings experienced by the Israelites begins with familiar language in 10:6: "The Israelites again did what was evil in the eyes of YHWH." The oppressors this time are the Ammonites. As in the Gideon story, Israel's livelihood is threatened as they lose control of their land.[36] The dialogue between the Israelites and YHWH is prolonged in 11:10-16 and places great emphasis on the connection between their idolatry and their suffering. Without the aid of any named intermediary, the Israelites and YHWH arrive at a resolution in v. 16. They put away their idols, and YHWH is moved by their suffering.[37] The pending battle for liberation in 10:17-18 provides the occasion for the introduction of Jephthah in 11:1. This introduction is ominous, as Jephthah, like Abimelech, is an illegitimate son. Like Abimelech, there is also conflict between Jephthah and the legitimate sons of his father. The Israelites must strike a bargain with Jephthah in order to receive his military leadership. What the elders of Gilead offer and what Jephthah accepts during the bargaining in 11:4-11 is a high price. The specific language of kingship is not used here, but Jephthah will literally become their "head," or chief. Phyllis Trible has observed that Jephthah is able to use religious language to avoid promising a victory in exchange for leadership. His statement in 11:9 places the responsibility for victory on YHWH.[38]

The initial actions of Jephthah are somewhat surprising. In 11:12-28 he carries out a lengthy negotiation with the Ammonite king in an attempt to arrive at a peaceful resolution to the conflict. The messages of Jephthah in this section are reminiscent of Moses and Joshua, as he recalls the movement of Israel into the promised land under God's leadership. Jephthah is being developed as an ambiguous character. His parentage is uncertain. His speech varies from manipulative and self-serving to religious and God-fearing. He appears as a warrior (11:1), then acts like a peacemaker. The ambiguity of Jephthah's character sets the stage for the continuation of his story.[39]

The battlefield has become a familiar setting in Judges, and finding Jephthah there in 11:29 feels like the expected. The stories of the various judges vary significantly at the point where we see the hero about to enter into battle. In 3:10, "the spirit of YHWH came upon" Othniel, and the most cursory report of his victory appears in this same verse. In 3:27-29, Ehud speaks one line, but it is the rather unremarkable "Follow after me, for YHWH has given your enemies, the Moabites, into your hand." The report of the victory is slightly longer and more detailed. In 4:14-16, Deborah speaks to Barak at the scene of the battle. Her declaration is similar to that of Ehud, and Barak subsequently leads the army to a victory described in two verses. The story of Gideon breaks from this pattern in elaborate fashion. The entirety of Judges 7 describes his preparations and military exploits. Jephthah's war story possesses the brevity of the earlier battlefield accounts: "The spirit of YHWH comes upon Jephthah." The familiar feel is disrupted with Jephthah's vow in 11:30-31. Nothing like this has appeared in the Book of Judges. The ambiguity of Jephthah's character matches the ambiguity of this vow. Why is it necessary? Why is Jephthah willing to exchange someone else's life for his own success? What is God's response to this vow? Phyllis Trible has addressed such questions with keen insight and makes important observations. There is ambiguity in Jephthah's words themselves. Who does he have in mind as his victim? Jephthah's vow is an unfaithful act. In Trible's words, "Jephthah desires to bind God, rather than embrace the gift of the spirit. What comes to him freely, he seeks to earn and manipulate."[40] When the battle ends as expected, with YHWH giving the Ammonites into Jephthah's hand, we do not know whether the vow has had any effect on the outcome.

The ambiguities of the Jephthah's character, the vow, God's response, and the outcome of the battle all come crashing down onto the head of Jephthah's unnamed daughter in vv. 34-35. The introduction of the daughter emphasizes the contrast between Jephthah and previous judges, such as Gideon, Tola, and Jair, who are extolled for their fecundity.[41] The story of her murder is remarkable in its power. It may be difficult to find characters in Judges with whom to sympathize, but this young woman, whose age is not given, stands nearly alone in the latter half of the book as a figure about whom modern readers care deeply. This story resonates with the *Akedah* story in Genesis 22; thus, it is all the more painful when no ram appears in the thicket to take her place on the altar. She dies young and without children, which the text goes to great lengths to emphasize.

Jephthah has the power that he craves, and his daughter pays the price for it. This power turns out to be an illusion, however, when no period of peace follows his victory. The strife among the Israelites, which first appeared in the Gideon story, is renewed once the external enemy is vanquished. They slaughter each other in massive numbers.[42] The period of Jephthah's rule as judge is unexpectedly short—six years. At the end of his life, it is reported that "he was buried in the towns of Gilead" (12:7). While the plurality of his burial place may be a mistake, which the Septuagint corrects, it is difficult to ignore the possibility of an ambiguous burial, which provides such perfect irony at the end of this life. With no heirs left alive, who would have buried him? Who would have remembered the place where his body was laid to rest?

A literary respite from the civil warfare in Judges 12:1-7 is offered by the final list of three "minor" judges at the end of the chapter. Two details are of note in the brief descriptions of Ibzan, Elon, and Abdon. First, an abundance of offspring is noted for two of these three figures. The ignominy of Jephthah's childlessness is once again highlighted. Second, the numbering of the children of Ibzan and Abdon appears in sayings that sound like nursery rhymes. The result is that the disturbing and painful story of Jephthah is bounded by whimsical lyrics about the children of Jair (10:4) and Ibzan (11:9). These ditties about plentiful offspring stand in harsh contrast to the sound of Jephthah's daughter and her friends "bewailing her virginity" in the mountains (11:37-40). These three minor judges are attributed short periods of leadership, and the Book of Judges moves quickly to the final performance of its repeated cycle in Judges 13.

The final judge, Samson, is the most famous. Following the pattern established in the Book of Judges, he is given the longest story in chapters 13–16. His stories are the most colorful of any of the judges, and his character is the most dubious. Samson is a difficult character with whom to reckon because he is so well known, and perceptions about him are so powerfully forged in our consciousness. The Book of Judges is still looking for a hero, and in many ways Samson seems a good candidate. Mieke Bal has analyzed the Samson story, its use, and its popular reception and she has given significant attention to the matching desire for a hero in the readers of the story.[43] The common perception of Samson as a great biblical hero is called into serious question by a careful reading of his stories.

Judges 13 tells a lengthy story about the birth of Samson. We have not been told about the birth of any of the previous judges. The story of the conception of Samson by a barren mother (13:2-3) takes on a miraculous quality that connects it to the birth of Isaac, Jacob, Joseph, and Samuel. Like the story of Moses, the text skips quickly from infancy to adulthood. Our first glimpse of Samson's personality is in the story of his first marriage in Judges 14. He is portrayed as an impetuous young man who sees what he wants, in this case a Philistine woman, and takes it.[44] The strange story of Samson's wedding feast is the occasion for his first act of violence. This is foreshadowed by the troubling statement in 14:4 that Samson's marriage to a Philistine woman is part of a divine plan to "seek an opportunity" to move against the Philistines, who had oppressed the Israelites for many years. This statement is fulfilled when the episode of the riddle concludes with the spirit of YHWH "rushing upon" Samson, after which he murders thirty

Philistines in order to acquire the clothing he loses in the wager. It is possible to understand that the situation in the Book of Judges has degenerated to a point where the presence of God's spirit provides the power necessary for victory but no longer has any control of the nature of the victory. Samson's actions in 14:19 appear to serve no purpose other than to save him from having to buy the garments himself.[45] With the purpose of Samson's marriage to the Philistine woman dubiously fulfilled, it is seemingly dissolved in 14:20.

In Judges 15, Samson's marriage resurfaces as an "opportunity" for conflict between Samson and the Philistines. Confusion abounds in this story as the conflict between Samson and his father-in-law expands into a conflict between the Philistines and the tribe of Judah. Because of Samson's wanton act of destruction in 15:4, his father-in-law and wife are brutally murdered by their own people in 15:7, and Samson responds by slaughtering an unspecified number of Philistines. The murder of Samson's wife and father-in-law by the Philistines is mirrored by the binding of Samson by his own people in 16:13.[46] Both larger groups seem intent on avoiding large-scale death and destruction, but Samson's strength and spirit of vengeance cannot be contained. They finally overflow in the famous slaughter of 1,000 Philistines with a donkey's jawbone in 15:15. The narrator of Judges maintains some sense of divine involvement in all of this mayhem. We are reminded by the Judahites who speak in 15:11 that they are still subject to the Philistines. The Israelites are still in need of deliverance. As the jawbone incident begins in 15:1, the spirit of YHWH "rushes upon" Samson as it has done before. At the end of the battle, God miraculously provides water for Samson in a manner reminiscent of the provision of water from the rock in the wilderness stories of Exodus 17 and Numbers 20. The enigmatic, concluding note in 15:20 refers to Samson as a judge. The text does not make clear whether Samson fully delivered the Israelites from Philistine oppression, and the twenty-year period is conspicuously half of the full forty-year respites achieved by earlier judges.[47] Nevertheless, for a moment Samson sounds at least like an echo of the earlier pattern.

Surprisingly, the Samson story is resumed in Judges 16. This resumption begins in a similar fashion to the first Samson story in Judges 14.[48] Once again, Samson goes to a foreign city and encounters a woman, or two. The much celebrated story of Samson and Delilah serves primarily to bring his great strength to the center of the text's attention. Samson is ultimately bound, as he was once before, and the story moves toward its climax. Samson dies in a vengeful act of destruction, which surpasses all of the killing he has accomplished in his lifetime up to this point (16:30). The concluding statement concerning Samson's twenty years as judge in 15:20 is reiterated in part in 16:31. The cycle of judges has come to a bitter end, and the leadership pattern it proposes has utterly failed to provide a lasting space where the people of Israel can prosper in peace.[49]

FOR THEY HAVE DONE A WICKED
AND DISGRACEFUL THING IN ISRAEL

With the cyclical pattern in ruins, where will the Book of Judges go? The last five chapters of the book are composed of a collection of loosely based stories, which are filled with death, destruction, and despair.[50] A theme emerges, however, in 17:6 when the introduction of the first of these stories ends with the statement, "In those days there was not a king in Israel. Each did the right thing in his own eyes." This statement appears in identical form in the last verse of the book (21:25), thus bracketing the last five chapters. The first half of the statement, "In those days there was not a king in Israel," is repeated in 18:1 and 19:1, establishing this idea as a framework for Judges 17–21.

The story of Micah and the Levite in Judges 17 may at first seem trivial and even irrelevant to the book as a whole. It is about the making of an idol and the setting up of a place of worship around it, including the installation of a priest. This is one way, however, that the collection of stories in Judges 17–21 matches those in Judges 3–16. It begins with idolatry and the implication that all the trouble that follows is the result of such disobedience. This first story also provides an introduction to the story of the migration of the tribe of Dan in chapter 18. The story of the tribe of Dan contains a number of connections to the book of Joshua. The allotment of land to Dan in Joshua 19:40-48 acknowledges that this tribe would eventually lose its land and would travel to and conquer another territory. Judges 18:1-31 tells this story in a manner reminiscent of the Israelites' arrival in Canaan and conquest of Jericho in Joshua 1–6. Once again, spies are sent ahead who evaluate the territory called Laish in 18:7. The spies again find a house in which to stay. It happens to be the house of Micah, who was introduced in the previous chapter. The Danites eventually send an army, which slaughters all of the inhabitants of Laish and destroys the city, as had been done with Jericho. The acquisition of land requires the murder of unsuspecting inhabitants. On the way to do this, the army stops at Micah's house and steals his idol, his worship implements, and his young Levite priest.[51] The idolatry of this one individual becomes the idolatry of an entire tribe. This story serves to discredit the tribe of Dan, the tribe of Ephraim to which Micah belongs, and the Levites, represented by the young priest and Moses' grandson, who appears as an idolatrous priest in 18:30. The final verse of Judges 18 establishes the idol in Dan as the rival of the house of God at Shiloh.

Judges 19 moves in a somewhat different direction but continues to discredit both Ephraim and the Levites. Along with them, the tribe of Benjamin moves to the forefront as the primary example of wickedness. The tribe of Judah, represented by the woman and her father and indirectly by the city of Jebus, seems to receive a neutral evaluation. This story of the Levite's concubine is perhaps the most brutal and horrifying story in the Bible and therefore has received a great amount of attention.[52] The story begins in the same setting as those in chapters 17 and 18, the hill country of Ephraim. The working out of the conflict between the Levite and his "concubine"[53] provides the setup for the story that eventually begins to follow a biblical type-scene established by the visit of the two travelers to Sodom in Genesis 19. In the Sodom episode, the daughters of Lot are suggested as an appeasement to the mob outside the door, but this proposal is not enacted. The type-scene is extended in Judges 19 when the young woman is sent out of the house and brutally raped and assaulted.[54] Focus is on the Benjaminites as the perpetrators of this crime, but the Levite is no innocent bystander. Not only did he push her out the door, but his words to the brutalized woman the next morning—"Get up. Let us go" (19:28)—are appalling in their lack of concern and compassion.[55] Trible is one of the few commentators to have noticed that the text never explicitly states that the woman is dead before her husband dismembers her.[56]

In Judges 20, the other tribes of Israel, all having received a piece of the woman's body, are outraged and muster a huge army. It is not entirely clear what has them most angry. Nevertheless, the horror experienced by modern readers finds some reflection in the response of the Israelites. The act becomes a pretext for the civil war between Benjamin and the other tribes. The defeat of Benjamin and slaughter of more than 25,000 of its soldiers is attributed to YHWH in 20:35. The language of the war oracle in 20:28 has the sound of those in the earlier part of Judges when the Israelites battled foreign enemies. The destruction of Benjamin is shocking. Like Laish in Judges 18 and Jericho in Joshua 6, the people and animals are slaughtered and the towns burned. Six hundred men apparently escape into the wilderness, and they are all that is left of this tribe.

With the Benjaminites routed, one question remains: can this tribe continue as a part of Israel? The final chapter of the Book of Judges takes up that restoration process. The remaining 600 men need wives if the tribe is to survive. The other tribes have cut them off and will no longer give to them their daughters for marriage. Judges 21:15 reports that the Israelites "had compassion for Benjamin, because YHWH made a breach among the tribes of Israel." But this compassion elicits one final, monstrous act of terror, described in 21:8-12. Because of some religious shortcoming, the people of Jabesh-Gilead are slaughtered, except for 400 virgins, who are given to the Benjaminites as wives. Because this number is not sufficient, the men of Benjamin are also given permission to kidnap women from Shiloh for additional wives. At this point the final word of Judges rings painfully true: "In those days there was not a king in Israel. Each did the right thing in his own eyes."

REFLECTIONS

One of the literary patterns of the Book of Judges observed in this chapter is the decline and disappearance of the periods of rest between a judge's military success and the onset of the next oppression. Initially, it seems odd that even when these periods of rest occur after victories of Othniel, Ehud, Deborah, and Gideon, Judges has no significant interest in them. Why are there no stories from these periods? What would the stories be like if they were there? Complaints are common these days that movies and television, the primary media for story-telling in modern Western culture, contain too much violence and destruction. All stories require conflict in order to function as stories. It is possible to create adequate conflict without violence or the threat of death, but such stories are more difficult to tell and are relatively rare. I am afraid that the book of Judges tells stories of war, murder, sexual assault, destruction, and oppression for the same reasons that modern media do. Such stories are highly "tellable," and they have great appeal to many listeners.

The conclusion that the Bible tells stories preoccupied with conflict and death in order titillate readers raises numerous problems. It is common in the modern world for religious people to object to the use of gruesome themes and images in written and visual media. Movies and video games filled with violence are often blamed for the perceived increase in violence in our world. News media play the same game. The tired maxim "If it bleeds it leads" still seems to operate in the reporting of news. It is difficult to say whether the world we live in is subject to a greater degree of suffering, death, and violent conflict. Certainly, modern technology allows us to see much more of this with our own eyes than any previous generation of human beings has. Indeed, the making of films about the death and destruction of past, present, and future brings the horror of all of human history to bear on our vision of the world, and sometimes it is too much to bear.

The weight of the violence, death, and destruction in Judges is also a heavy load for the reader. While these kinds of stories can sometimes lure our eyes in their direction, they can also have the opposite effect. They can cause us to turn away in revulsion. There is a great temptation to turn away from these images, to ignore the existence of tragedy and pain. We sometimes turn off the television news when we have seen and heard enough. Likewise, there may be days when we might prefer to read a nice psalm than another brutal war story. While its motives may be questionable, Judges keeps us honest about the nature of human existence.[57]

The Israelites depicted in the Book of Judges are obviously in a struggle to maintain their existence. The "promised land" dream of living in a peaceful, productive place where healthy lives are free from the threat of oppression and destruction is not fast becoming a reality for these people. Human beings have never lost their desire, or need, for a hero. They are also desperate for a sense of order in their lives. Like the ancient Israelites, we also search for heroes in modern times. Unfortunately, all of our heroes eventually break down as well. The common perception of our world, like the depiction in Judges, is that everything is becoming more disordered. Old institutions that once provided a sense of stability in our communities are falling apart, and we need something to replace them.

The next chapter of this book examines the story of that new reality, the monarchy, in the book of Samuel. We may ask to what extent the Book of Judges functions as pro-monarchy propaganda. In our society, stories about the breakdown of order are often preludes to new proposals. Every four years in America, we witness two political conventions. The party in power puts the best possible spin on the past four years, and the opposition party retells it in the worst possible light.

The Book of Judges also raises important questions about a people's belief that God is on their side. In Judges, the people of Israel find God to be both for them and against them in alternating moments. This kind of religious language can approach the ridiculous, as a way of attaching the normal ups and downs of life to the whims of a divine being. Such language is as dangerous and fickle as the being it is used to describe. For decades, Jerry Falwell made a living pronouncing God's judgment on various groups of Americans whom he labeled as "sinners." Most Americans either said "Amen" or ignored him, considering him either a righteous man of God or a trivial buffoon. September 11, 2001 so altered the American cultural landscape, however, that when Falwell made statements about the terrorist attacks being God's judgment on America for various sins, the public objection was so strong that he was forced to make a retraction.[58] The shrinking of our world has brought groups making competing claims of divine favor and purpose into close contact with one another. The blending of the rhetoric of divine favor with nationalist and exclusive religious ideologies has become increasingly dangerous. The ongoing struggle of the Bible to work out what such claims mean holds tremendous importance for those who consider these texts sacred.

NOTES

[1] From the song "Hard Times Come Again No More," written by Stephen Collins Foster in 1855.

[2] See Tammi J. Schneider, *Judges*, Berit Olam (Collegeville MN: Liturgical, 2000), xi-xix. Schneider refers to a decline in the status or position of the Israelites at the beginning of each successive cycle. This is roughly equivalent to what I am depicting as linear patterns of development. See also the discussion of Cheryl Exum in "The Centre Cannot Hold: Thematic and Textual Instabilities in Judges," *CBQ* 52 (1990): 410-12.

[3] Ibid., 13.

[4] Phyllis Trible, *Texts of Terror: Literary-Feminist Readings of Biblical Narratives* (Philadelphia: Fortress, 1984).

[5] Schneider, among others, has discussed the problems related to translating the Hebrew word *pileges*. She has opted simply to transliterate the term, rather than translate it, having found no useful English equivalent (Schneider, *Judges*, 16). I have used the traditional translation, "concubine," which is replete with problems. The most significant is the pejorative connotation it carries. While the possible translation "wife" may elevate her status beyond that which the story indicates, it seems no less valid than "concubine," which is inaccurate in the other direction.

[6] Each of these writers has published work on the Book of Judges in multiple places. This work is perhaps best represented in the following: Mieke Bal, *Death and Dissymmetry: The Politics of Coherence in the Book of Judges* (Chicago: Chicago University Press, 1988); J. Cheryl Exum, *Fragmented Women: Feminist (Sub)versions of Biblical Narrative* (Valley Forge PA: Trinity Press International, 1993); Susan Ackerman, *Warrior, Dancer, Seductress, Queen: Women in Judges and Biblical Israel* (New York: Doubleday, 1998). See also the large sampling of readings in Athalya Brenner, ed., *A Feminist Companion to Judges* (Sheffield: Sheffield Academic, 1993).

[7] Marc Brettler, "The Book of Judges: Literature as Politics," *JBL* 108 (1989), 395-418. Brettler's identification of Judges as an "allegorical book" (p. 416) is the one troubling aspect of this essay. He occasionally extends the identification of elements in the stories of Judges with social and historical realities in ancient Israel further than many readers might find comfortable. Nevertheless, his study of Judges as political ideology produced an abundance of helpful literary observations.

[8] Marvin A. Sweeney, "Davidic Polemics in the Book of Judges," *VT* 47 (1997): 517-29. Sweeney's careful grammatical arguments demonstrate the cohesiveness and artistry of the final form of the Book of Judges (see pp. 521-26). The balance between understanding the close connections between 3:7–16:31 and 17:1–21:25 and recognizing a significant literary shift at the end of chapter 16 is difficult to maintain. Sweeney has attempted to maximize the significance of 17–21 by dividing the book into only two sections, 1–2 and 3–21. His argument struggles against the fragmenting efforts of redaction critics who wish to overemphasize the disjunction between 3–16 and 17–21 (see pp. 526-28). Sweeney may have overstated the case here, but he is correct about the significance of 17–21 for what the Book of Judges is doing.

[9] Ibid., 528.

[10] Schneider's work, *Judges*, is part of the series called "*Berit Olam*: Studies in Hebrew Narrative and Poetry." This is the first example of a full commentary-like series devoted primarily to modern literary approaches to biblical books.

[11] Exum has also described a trend of increasing ambiguity in divine involvement as the Book of Judges progresses ("The Centre Cannot Hold," 411). See also Richard G. Bowman, "Narrative Criticism in Judges: Human Purpose in Conflict with Divine Presence," in *Judges and Method: New Approaches in Biblical Studies*, ed. Gale A. Yee (Minneapolis: Fortress, 1995), 34-42. Bowman has found in Judges a demonstration of the limitation of God's power brought about by the misuse of human freedom.

[12] Dennis T. Olson attributes the creation of this downward spiral to a final editor of the Book of Judges, who imposed the scheme on a preexisting set of stories in which it was not present ("The Book of Judges: Introduction, Commentary, and Reflection," in *The New Interpreter's Bible*, vol. 2, ed. Leander Keck [Nashville: Abingdon, 1998], 725-26). Such a possibility is of relatively little concern to a narrative exploration of the final form of the book.

[13] See the detailed discussion of this issue in Barnabas Lindars, *Judges 1–5: A New Translation and Commentary* (Edinburgh: T & T Clark, 1995), 3-14.

[14] For a more thorough discussion between the book of Joshua and the early chapters of the Book of Judges, see Brettler, "The Book of Judges: Literature as Politics," 399-402.

[15] Brettler, "The Book of Judges: Literature as Politics," 399.

[16] Sweeney, "Davidic Polemics in the Book of Judges," 517-18.

[17] For a discussion of the possible associations of this place with Bethel, and the ramifications of such an association, see Schneider, *Judges*, 26-28.

[18] For an extensive discussion of these problems, see Sweeney, "Davidic Polemics in the Book of Judges," 520-23. Sweeney argues that the appearance of the angel at *Bochim* recollects the episode in Joshua 5:13-15, and emphasizes the breaking of covenant (p. 522).

[19] Schneider avoids this more traditional division of the text here, by grouping 2:20-23 with 3:1-4. While this does not follow the paragraph divisions of the Hebrew text, she has demonstrated the transitional nature of 3:1-4, which act either as a conclusion to the material in chapter 2 or as an introduction, along with vv. 5-6, to the stories that make up the bulk of chapter 3 (*Judges*, 32-33). The possibility of such varying positions on the division of the text is ample testimony to the skill of the editor who has woven the Book of Judges together.

[20] It is certainly of significance here that the Bible attributes forty-year reigns to both David and Solomon.

[21] The meaning of the phrase is not entirely clear. Literally it is something like "a man bound [in] his right hand." The connections between the word for "right hand" and the name *Benjamin* are significant. The phrase also appears in another Benjaminite story in 20:16. For a fuller discussion, see Lindars, *Judges 1–5*, 141.

[22] Eglon is the only person described in this way in the Bible. The closest comparison is the description of Eli in 1 Samuel 4:18. But the term used of Eli can be understood as one of respect concerning his "weightiness," which goes beyond mere physical size.

[23] Among other things, this feature indicates that the author of Judges has allowed the various stories, gathered from unknown sources, to retain some of their individual characteristics.

[24] See Schneider, *Judges*, 52. Schneider observed that the Hebrew text does not use the equivalent of "judge" to describe Ehud, while the LXX does use the equivalent Greek term.

[25] The appearance of Shamgar in 3:31 is also puzzling in many ways. The Book of Judges presents brief reports of a total of six "minor" judges. Tola and Jair appear together in 10:1-5. Izban, Elon, and Abdon are grouped together at 12:8-15. It is important to emphasize that the distinction between "major" and "minor" judges is only a literary one, based upon the way their stories are told. There is no data available to evaluate the historical function and significance of these people.

On the difficulties of 3:31, see Schneider, *Judges*, 53-58, and J. Alberto Soggin, *Judges: A Commentary*, trans. J. S. Bowden (Philadelphia: Westminster, 1981), 57-59. Included among these difficulties is that "Shamgar ben Anath" appears to be a foreign name.

[26] The appearance of King Jabin of Hazor in Joshua 11:1-15 among a group of kings defeated and killed by Joshua is problematic. See Schneider, *Judges*, 58-60 and George F. Moore, *A Critical and Exegetical Commentary on Judges* (Edinburgh: T & T Clark, 1895), 110-12.

[27] See Exum, "The Centre Cannot Hold," 415-16.

[28] The poetic account is commonly held to be one of the most ancient texts in the Bible. For a thorough discussion of the history, form, and ancient Near Eastern cultural context of "The Song of Deborah," see Soggin, *Judges*, 92-101. Mieke Bal has appropriately cautioned against the modern tendency to discount poetry in favor of prose because the latter is assumed to be more precise and reliable, while the former is more imaginative in its construction (*Murder and Difference: Gender, Genre, and Scholarship on Sisera's Death* [Bloomington: Indiana University Press, 1988], 131-32). The closest analog to this pairing of prose and poetic accounts of the same event is the pair of accounts of the crossing of the sea in Exodus 14 and 15. Again the poetic account, the "Song of the Sea" in Exodus 15, is generally thought to be the most ancient.

[29] For more on this point, see Ackerman, *Warrior, Dancer, Seductress, Queen*, 31. Ackerman notes that 1 Samuel 12:11 and Hebrew 11:32 list Barak as a military hero and leave out Deborah.

[30] Ackerman, *Warrior, Dancer, Seductress, Queen*, 35-36.

[31] For further discussion of these issues, see Schneider, *Judges*, 123-31.

[32] The use of collection and use of golden earrings by Gideon makes the connection to this story particularly powerful.

[33] E. John Hamlin, *At Risk in the Promised Land: A Commentary on the Book of Judges* (Grand Rapids: Eerdmans, 1990), 90-91. Hamlin recognizes that a diverse collection of materials has been woven together to form this complex story. Note particularly Hamlin's observation that if Judges 6–9 are taken together as a single unit, they comprise about one-fourth of the entire Book of Judges.

[34] Hamlin, *At Risk in the Promised Land*, 90.

[35] The other list of minor judges in 12:8-15 contains three. It is easy to imagine that Shamgar might have been part of a three-name list here, but mention of his name in the Song of Deborah (5:6) required the moving of his note to the end of chapter 4. See the discussion of the difficulties with the current placement of Shamgar above.

[36] For a well-developed discussion of the meaning of loss of land, see Hamlin, *At Risk in the Promised Land*, 108.

[37] See the discussion of this scene in Exum, "The Centre Cannot Hold," 421-22.

[38] Phyllis Trible, *Texts of Terror*, 95.

[39] For more on the ambiguity of Jephthah's character, see Trible, *Texts of Terror*, 93-94.

[40] Trible, *Texts of Terror*, 97.

[41] Exum, "The Centre Cannot Hold," 421.

[42] Ibid., 423.

[43] Mieke Bal, *Lethal Love: Feminist Literary Readings of Biblical Love Stories* (Bloomington: Indiana University Press, 1987).

[44] Robert Alter has noted that the marriage story breaks away from the norm, omitting the standard betrothal story, and emphasizes Samson's impatience (*The Art of Biblical Narrative*, 62-63).

[45] On the complexity of the interaction of the divine spirit and the free action of human beings in the Samson story, see Bowman, "Narrative Criticism: Human Purpose in Conflict with Divine Presence," 34-39.

[46] Concerning the many ways that the Samson story in Judges 14–15 parallels the one in Judges 16, see Exum, "Aspects of Symmetry and Balance in the Samson Saga," *JSOT* 19 (February 1981): 3-9.

[47] On the differences between Samson as a judge and the earlier judges, see Schneider, *Judges*, 216-17.

[48] See Exum, "Aspects of Symmetry," 3-4.

[49] Schneider, *Judges*, 226-27.

[50] For more on this idea, see Olson, "The Book of Judges," 863-66.

[51] This story should probably remind the reader of Genesis 31, where Jacob's family flees the house of Laban, having stolen the household gods of Laban. Jacob's party is then pursued by Laban.

[52] The most thorough and insightful treatment is that of Phyllis Trible in *Texts of Terror*, 64-91.

[53] The Hebrew term here, *pileges*, is difficult to translate and understand. See the discussion in Schneider, *Judges*, 246-49.

[54] The virgin daughter of the host is also part of the proposal in 19:24, reminiscent of the Sodom story, but she is apparently not sent out.

[55] Jack Miles has observed that it is her husband who utters the most brutal words in the story (*God: A Biography*, 158-59).

[56] See Trible, *Texts of Terror*, 80. As Trible has observed, the Greek text indicates some discomfort with this idea and resolves this discomfort by inserting the phrase "she was dead" in 19:28.

[57] On this theme, see Annie Dillard, *A Pilgrim at Tinker Creek* (New York: Quality Paperback, 1974), especially 1-2 and 241-42, among others.

[58] See the discussion of this specific event and the larger issue in Charles Kimball, *When Religion Becomes Evil* (San Francisco: HarperSanFrancisco, 2002), 46-52.

Samuel:
Like the Other Nations

Maybe there's a God above,
As for me, all I've ever seemed to learn from love
Is how to shoot at someone who outdrew you.
Yeah but it's not a complaint that you hear tonight,
It's not the laughter of someone who claims to have seen the light
No it's a cold and it's a very lonely Hallelujah. Hallelujah . . .

I did my best, it wasn't much.
I couldn't feel, so I learned to touch.
I've told the truth, I didn't come all this way to fool you.
Yeah even though it all went wrong
I'll stand right here before the Lord of Song
With nothing on my lips but Hallelujah. Hallelujah . . .

—Leonard Cohen[1]

THE NARRATIVE SHAPE OF SAMUEL

An attempt to look at and talk about the book of Samuel as a unified literary work must take into account at least three major issues in the history of interpretation of this book. First, for reasons we may never know, this book was long ago divided into 1 Samuel and 2 Samuel.[2] For the purpose of the exploration of Samuel in this chapter, it will be important to maintain the idea of a single unified work, even if it does appear in two volumes in Christian Bibles. Whoever was responsible for the division recognized a major shift in the story at the point of Saul's death, which ends 1 Samuel, but the development of David's character bridges any potential gap in the story at this point. Many interpreters have noted that it is odd to have a book called 2 Samuel in which the character named Samuel never appears. Maintaining the unity of the book serves to retain an important sense of Samuel's presence throughout the book.

A second major issue is the inclusion of the book of Samuel in the larger work typically labeled the "Deuteronomistic History." This term is used to designate the four books Judaism calls "the Former Prophets"—Joshua, Judges, Samuel, and Kings. The thematic and ideological connections between these books and the book of Deuteronomy have been recognized by interpreters for centuries. The rigorous formulation of the idea of a Deuteronomistic History is best attributed to the work of Martin Noth during the middle of the twentieth century.[3] If the book of Deuteronomy serves as the theological backdrop for the Deuteronomistic History, then it does so for the book of Samuel. In his recent work on 1 Samuel, David Jobling has revitalized a proposal originated by Martin Noth and further developed by Dennis McCarthy. Because the canonical division of the Deuteronomistic History into four books is a later development, Jobling proposes an alternative division based upon the "theological summaries" that appear in Judges 2:11-23, 1 Samuel 12, and 2 Samuel 7. If these points are taken as the more significant beginnings and endings, then the Deuteronomistic History and the book of Samuel within it communicate their message differently. A reading of Samuel as a unified literary work and the idea that it forms part of a larger work may stand in some tension with each other. This tension threatens to pull parts of the book of Samuel away from the whole. The approach of this reading will be based upon an attempt to place enough emphasis on the unity of Samuel to hold its components together.

A third difficulty is the common practice, particularly in academic circles, of reading 2 Samuel 9–1 Kings 2 as "The Succession Narrative." This idea was formulated in the influential work of Leonhard Rost.[4] Rost understood this entire section as a unified story of the working out of the struggle for the throne following the death of David. Up to this point in the Bible, it has been common for books to end with the death of a major character or characters. Genesis ends with the deaths of Jacob and Joseph, Deuteronomy with the death of Moses, Joshua with the death of Joshua, and 1 Samuel with the death of Saul. The death of David in 1 Kings 2 thus seems a bit unusual. In the case of Joshua, however, there is a brief reappearance at the beginning of the next book. Thus, David's brief appearance in 1 Kings is not unprecedented. Rost's proposal seems to solve the problem of the continuation of David' life into the book of Kings, but it disrupts the attempt to read the biblical books of Samuel and Kings according to their traditional boundaries. A serious challenge to Rost was raised by David Gunn in 1978 with the publication of his *The Story of King David: Genre and Interpretation*.[5] Gunn argued particularly against the division between 2 Samuel

8 and 2 Samuel 9 because this division breaks up the story of the most important character in this part of the Bible, David.[6]

More lengthy and seemingly more sophisticated literary treatments of the book of Samuel have appeared since Gunn's. The most significant of these may be the works of Robert Polzin and Jan Fokkelman. Polzin published his work on 1 Samuel, *Samuel and the Deuteronomist*, in 1989 as a follow-up to his 1980 work, *Moses and the Deuteronomist: Deuteronomy, Joshua, Judges*. These were then followed in 1993 by a volume on 2 Samuel called *David and the Deuteronomist*. Each of these volumes provides a close, careful reading of the final form of the Deuteronomistic History. The titles reveal that Polzin recognized the significance of the development of characters in the literary shaping of these books.[7]

Fokkelman has produced an even more massive analysis of the book of Samuel—four volumes with more than 2,000 pages. Fokkelman's attention to literary detail in these works can be helpful when it is not overwhelming, but even the titles of his four volumes reveal his sense of dissatisfaction with the final shape of the text, which he divides and reorders for his own treatment.[8] This also reveals the continuing influence of Rost's Succession Narrative on his work.

Robert Alter followed his translation and commentary on Genesis, which was mentioned earlier in this study, with a similar volume on Samuel called *The David Story: A Translation with Commentary of 1 and 2 Samuel*. In the title of his introduction, Alter expanded the book's title to "The Story of Samuel, Saul, and David." While acknowledging the composite nature of the book of Samuel, Alter insisted that the interlocking development of these characters forms a powerfully unified story. He continued to argue, however, for the inclusion of the first two chapters of Kings, which tell of David's death. Translation and commentary on these two chapters are included in his book. Alter made this somewhat puzzling inclusion without insisting upon an originally independent Succession Narrative.[9]

The work of Gunn probably provides the most constructive direction toward a literary map of the book of Samuel. Along with *The Story of King David*, Gunn has also published another small volume called *The Fate of King Saul*. Gunn has recognized most clearly that the book of Samuel is a character-driven story. It develops three major characters, Samuel, Saul, and David, and depicts the intense relationships among them.[10] The story begins with the birth of Samuel in 1 Samuel 1–2 and ends with a summary of David's kingship in 2 Samuel 21–24. While David lingers into 1 Kings, the story there is not about him but about Solomon. The shape of the book of Samuel, therefore, must be determined by the development of its primary characters. One step backward must be taken at this point in order to begin the story properly with its first major character, Eli. A further note of complexity is added by the relationship between Eli and the ark of the covenant. This person and object are so closely related that in 1 Samuel 4 they essentially die together. Therefore, I will follow the contours of overlapping character development in my organization of the book of Samuel:

1 Samuel 1–7	Ark/Eli and Samuel
1 Samuel 8–15	Samuel and Saul
1 Samuel 16–2 Samuel 4	Saul and David
2 Samuel 4–24	David[11]

The boundaries of such organization are fuzzy, of course, but the book of Samuel does not have the abrupt shifts of many other biblical books. This further emphasizes the overlapping quality of its character developments. I have extended the first section beyond the death of Eli, because the ark continues to be significant through 1 Samuel 7. I have ended the second section before the death of Samuel, because he virtually disappears from the story after he anoints David. I have extended the third section beyond the death of Saul, because Ishbosheth and Abner continue to represent "the house of Saul" after his death.

Of course, David is the most significant character. The discussion of 1 Samuel 2 below takes up questions concerning the extent to which David presides over the whole book of Samuel. Thus, it is appropriate that the overlapping development of characters outlined above eventually resolves into a singular focus on the great king.[12]

1 SAMUEL: THE BOWS OF THE MIGHTY ARE BROKEN

Readers of any version of the Bible begin the book of Samuel with great monarchical expectations. The last portion of the book of Judges offers the hope of a king as a solution to lawlessness, disorder, and death. For Christian readers, the Davidic genealogy at the end of the book of Ruth heightens this sense of expectation. The beginning of the book of Samuel is, therefore, somewhat unexpected. Opening with a miraculous birth story is fine, but this is the birth of someone who will not become king. The circumstances of this birth point backward to similar births in the past, particularly in the patriarchal narratives, but to what it points in a forward direction is less certain.[13] The motif of barrenness serves two purposes. The death represented by childlessness hangs over the narrative, providing the first conflict that must be resolved, but the memory of God's deliverance of barren women in the past provides a reason for hope.

The Song of Hannah in 2:1-10 celebrates this hope, while its specific source remains uncertain. Hannah sings of a future when the threats of oppression and death that have terrorized Israel for so long might finally be overcome. Her words are characterized by statements of reversal that reflect the turn of good fortune in her life in the previous chapter. Fokkelman correctly identified power as the primary theme of the poem. The image of the horn in v. 1 and v. 10 effectively brackets the whole poem, which is filled with images of power and strength.[14] The poem sets the stage for the entire book as a story of the power dynamics of Israel's monarchy. The song specifically mentions the king in 2:10, and so it is anachronistic. Does this poem have Saul or David specifically in mind, or the monarchy in general? Why is it sung at the birth of Samuel? The difficult statement in 1:28 compounds the confusion. In what sounds like a typical name etymology, Hannah says something like, "So, I have lent him to YHWH all the days that he exists, he is lent to YHWH." The difficulty is that the word translated "lent" is from the same root as Saul's name.[15] This entanglement of personalities may reflect major problems in the formation and transmission of the text, but it also foreshadows the nature of the entire book of Samuel, which will struggle to work out the relationships between these characters and God.

As the boy, Samuel, matures, the story prepares to dispose of the family of Eli in 1 Samuel 2. The oracle pronounced by the mysterious "man of God" in 2:27-36 is harsh and deadly in its impact. YHWH breaks the covenant with Eli and his family (2:30) and pronounces a future of death and destitution. Eli's two sons, Hophni and Phinehas, are mentioned specifically in 2:34 as objects of the divine wrath: "On one day, the two of them shall die." The family of Eli is about to be replaced, and Samuel has clearly been established as the rising star. All of this is confirmed in the story of the calling of Samuel in chapter 3.

In 1 Samuel 4, the Deuteronomistic narrative returns to the familiar ground of a battlefield. The Philistines, the enemy that first emerged in the Samson stories and brought an end to the occasional success of the Israelite judges, resurface here as the symbol of all that stands in the way of Israel's quest for well-being. The defeats come in waves and overwhelm Israel in this story. The report of the messenger to Eli in 4:17 reflects this progression—the army destroyed, the sons of Eli dead, the ark of the covenant lost to the Philistines, and finally, Eli himself dead. All seems lost, and the agonizing, deathbed lament of Eli's daughter-in-law in vv. 21-22 appears to sum up Israel's hopelessness. Much depends, however, on where we choose to let this story begin. If all of 4:1 goes with this story, and the emergence of Samuel is included within it, then it is not really about the departure of God's glory from Israel, but a shift in the personality of Israel's human leadership.[16] YHWH now relates to Israel through Samuel. The old Eli/ark/Shiloh era is over.[17]

First Samuel 5–7 is something of a diversion, but a necessary one. The ark of the covenant will never again be the greatest symbol of God's power and presence in Israel. The book of Samuel must clear the way for the king to assume this position. Nevertheless, the ark cannot remain in the hands of the Philistines. Not only is it a source of plague and death for these foreigners, it is a significant distraction for the narrative. With the return of the ark to Israel in 6:10-18, the narrator brings the eye of the reader back onto Israel, and eventually onto Samuel in chapter 7. When the ark goes under cover in Kiriath-jearim and Samuel speaks to the people, the focus of the story is back in the right place and ready to continue in 1 Samuel 8.

Israel's response to the threat to its existence is the demand for a king. Here, as elsewhere in the Bible, multiple reasons for establishing the monarchy are offered. First Samuel 8 brings the personality of the new character to the center. Samuel dominates this chapter. The first reason given for a change in leadership is that Samuel is getting old and his sons are not "going in his ways" (8:3). How quickly Samuel begins to look like Eli, but Samuel proves to be a much greater theological and political force than his predecessor. The triangular speech pattern that develops among the people, Samuel, and YHWH is reminiscent of the Israel-Moses-YHWH relationship in the wilderness traditions. The verbal interchange fittingly gives rise to an old and horrifying threat. Samuel's catalogue of the ways of kings moves the conversation toward a more honest articulation of motives. Ironically, Samuel introduces the list with the words, "This will be the judgment (*mishpat*) of the king . . ." (8:11), using the same word root that describes the period of the Judges in Israel. The ultimate threat, finally expressed in 4:17, is that the Israelites will again be slaves. Having regressed backward through the period of the Judges and the wilderness experience to the oppressive conditions of Egypt, the Israelites will find that when they "cry out" amid this threat to their existence as a people, as they did in Egypt (Exodus 2:23-24), YHWH will no longer hear them as he did there. The truth comes out in their response to Samuel in 8:20. What the people want is military power.[18] The massive defeat at the hands of the Philistines seems to have taught them that if they want to compete on the battlefields of the ancient Near East, they will need a well-funded, well-trained, professional army led by a king, and they are willing to pay whatever price is necessary to have one. In 8:22 the conversation is concluded and the deal is done.

First Samuel 9 begins the next major shift toward a new personality, but this time the transition will not go so quickly and easily. Samuel does not stay in the spotlight by himself for long, but he continues to be a more powerful and persistent character than Eli was. Saul first appears in the story in odd fashion. The bizarre story of the search for the donkeys hardly sounds like the introduction of a king. Moreover, the end of the book of Judges has predisposed readers of the Bible against the tribe of Benjamin. It hardly seems appropriate that the first king would come from this tribe. This predisposition may be balanced somewhat by the description of Saul in 9:2-3, but contradictions abound.[19] The narrator tells us that Saul was "better" (NRSV says "more handsome") than all other Israelites. The enigmatic final phrase literally says, "from his shoulder and from upon it was higher than all the people."[20] These statements are typically understood as compliments about Saul's physical appearance, but rarely is Saul depicted as acting in such grand fashion. One must begin to wonder if these comments are satirical in nature. Indeed, the donkey story immediately following shows a somewhat weak and bumbling Saul.[21] Alter has argued that 9:11-12 is a disrupted betrothal type-scene. When the hero in a foreign land encounters young women at a well, the young women should run home with news of the stranger, and the leading character among them should marry him. This is what happens with Jacob and Rachel in Genesis 29:1-20 and with Moses and Zipporah in Exodus 2:15-21. In 1 Samuel 9:11-12, the young women simply give Saul directions and send him on his way. The disruption of this pattern in Saul's case may serve as a signal to the reader that his life and his reign as king will not go as planned. Saul seems doomed from the beginning of his story.[22] The relationship developing between Saul and Samuel is deeply complicated, and the narrator is skillfully bringing us into that complexity. W. Lee Humphreys has produced an outline of 1 Samuel 9–31 that falls into three acts. Each act begins with an encounter between Samuel and Saul. In each of the first two acts, this encounter is followed by a period of success for Saul. All three acts end with Saul's failure, including his death in the final scene in 1 Samuel 31.[23] The discussion below reflects this pattern of rise and fall in Saul's reign and Samuel's role in Saul's fortune.

The traditions concerning Saul's ascent to the throne are obviously diverse in perspective. The narrator of Samuel manages to weave them together in 1 Samuel 9–11. Amid this section is a report of brutal oppression of the Transjordan tribes by an Ammonite king. The story of Nahash's threat to gouge out the right eye of all the inhabitants of Jabesh-gilead underscores the sense of "disgrace" and humiliation suffered by the Israelites.[24] Saul's reaction to these events plays a significant role in his public rise to power. Yet, even as Saul is delivering Israel from this threat, the story still undermines his success by recording his act of dismembering oxen and sending the pieces throughout Israel as a call to battle (11:7). This palpable reference to the story in Judges 19 reminds the reader once again that anointing a Benjaminite king is an ill-fitting beginning to the Israelite monarchy.[25] This negative reminder of Saul's unfitness is balanced by the portrayal of Saul as a peacemaker in 11:13. He does not seek vengeance against those who opposed his kingship. Saul's inevitable demise, which is already being foreshadowed at this point, is difficult to comprehend fully. J. Cheryl Exum has correctly noted that a proper reading of the Saul tradition requires a careful balancing of the "dark side of God" and Saul's own self-destructiveness.[26]

With Saul installed as king, Samuel moves out of the leadership picture in chapter 12. Samuel reminds the people of all that YHWH has done in the past to deliver them (vv. 6-11) and warns of the deadly consequences of disobedience (v. 15 and v. 25). The interplay of threats and promises in vv. 19-25 sets the stage for Samuel's continuing role in the story. The new king becomes the primary focus of the text's attention in chapters 13–15, but Samuel will remain as an advisor and manipulator of Saul. The dubious nature of Saul's position as king is revealed immediately by the Hebrew text as it refuses to provide Saul's age of ascension and provides a problematic figure of "two years" for the length of his reign in 13:1.[27] The manner in which the text of the book of Samuel seeks to undermine Saul's kingship may be subtle, but the parallel efforts of the character named Samuel become overt in chapter 13.[28] In what looks like a setup, Samuel suddenly appears on the scene in 13:10 at just the right time to catch Saul desperately, but inappropriately, offering a sacrifice. As a result of this "mistake," the text finally says plainly that Saul will not establish a dynasty for himself and his family (vv. 13-14). Saul and his son, Jonathan, overcome this setback and defeat the Philistines in chapter 14, but, once again, Saul's success as king is undermined by a personal error. The "rash oath" of Saul in 14:24 places the Israelite army and Jonathan in danger, in a story reminiscent of Jephthah and his daughter in Judges 11.

At the end of 1 Samuel 14, Saul's reign takes another upturn with a striking series of military victories. The well-being of the Israelites is enhanced as their enemies and oppressors are defeated. This victory sequence extends into chapter 15 with the account of Saul's brutal and devastating defeat of the Amalekites. The story in 15:1-9 contains many elements that serve as a vivid reminder of Joshua 6. These include the victory and annihilation of the city using the language of the "ban" in 15:8, the prior arrangement to rescue the Kenites because they had assisted the Israelites when they came from Egypt, and the improper collection of spoils after the battle. Saul is left looking like Achan and his doom is sure.[29]

First Samuel 15–16 is the nexus where all of the powerful personalities of the book begin to converge. The emotions are gut-wrenching and impossible to identify clearly. What does it mean for God to "regret" in 15:11 and 15:35? At what or whom is Samuel angry in 15:11? What is the point of Samuel "grieving over" Saul in 15:35? Why are the desperate, penitent pleadings of Saul in 15:20-25 not acknowledged by God? All of this emotional turmoil erupts in Samuel's brutal slaying of Agag in 15:33. The last person hacked into pieces in the Bible was the Levite's concubine in Judges 19. This act was used to call for an uprising against the Benjaminites. Again, the dismemberment signals the defeat of the Benjaminites, this time personified in Saul. The uprising here will be much more subtle but of far greater importance.

There are obvious chronological problems in 1 Samuel 16–17.[30] For the sake of this study, it is much more important to recognize that the writer of 1 Samuel wants to introduce David in a particular way than to attempt to reshape the narrative chronologically. Readers see his private anointing before he gains public attention. David comes into private contact with Saul before he becomes a public hero. The rejection of Saul has a powerful impact on him. Though he will live until the end of 1 Samuel, we see him begin to die the moment David is anointed. The writer portrays two kinds of spirits, both of which come from God. The spirit that comes on David in 16:13 brings life and power to this emerging personality. The "evil spirit" that comes on Saul in 16:14 will torment him until he kills himself.

The anointing of David by the divine spirit of monarchy causes him to grow quickly as a person of power. While we get a first, brief glimpse of David as a musician in 1 Samuel 16, the image of David as a warrior is the one that endures. The women of Israel recognize this in 18:7, just as Michelangelo did when he forever engraved into the human imagination the figure of David as a powerful giant of a man. The story of David's slaying of Goliath is perhaps one of the most carefully and intensely crafted stories in the Bible.[31] Polzin has counted thirty-six verbs in the seven verses that depict the battle scene (vv. 48-54).[32] It is possible to miss the sense of replacement in v. 54. David grows in stature with the decapitation of Goliath, and stows away his armor, though the reason for this action is not revealed. Does he hope one day to fit into it? The ambiguity of "his armor" in v. 54 leaves open the possibility that this is Saul's armor (see 17:38) that David keeps and reminds us of the more significant replacement that is occurring.[33] Whether this is a proper reading or not, Saul properly senses that he needs to watch out for David. David's reception of Jonathan's robe, armor, and weapons in 18:4 develops this theme of clothing and replacement even further.[34]

First Samuel 18–21 is a large section of this story that is significantly repetitive.[35] It is bounded by the two occurrences of the saying "Saul has killed his thousands and David his ten thousands" in 18:7 and 21:11. Within this section, David binds himself closer and closer to Saul, while Saul's fear and mistrust of David intensify. Twice, under the spell of the "evil spirit from the LORD" Saul attempts to impale David with a spear (18:10-11 and 19:9-10). Saul and Jonathan have two intense interactions concerning David. In the first (19:1-7), Jonathan convinces Saul not to kill David and brings the two back together. In the second (20:30-34), Jonathan is unable to dissuade Saul and must tell David to flee. Amid this sequence of stories, David becomes betrothed to two of Saul's daughters, first Merab and then Michal. Only the marriage to Michal appears to be completed, in 18:27. All of the potential bonds that might bring Saul and David together, however, eventually repel them from each other, and the series of episodes in 1 Samuel 18–21 ends with David fleeing to Gath, taking Goliath's sword with him (21:8-10). Unable to become Saul, for the moment, David becomes Goliath.

The theme of madness has played a significant role in the story since the "evil spirit from the LORD" first came upon Saul in 16:14. It is a great irony that while Saul's real madness threatens David in the spear incidents, it also forms the pretext for his entry into the royal court (16:16-23) and provides him a means of escape from Saul's murderous intention in 19:18-24. It is a further irony that David's madness in 21:10-15, which, in contrast to Saul's, is feigned, also saves David's life and provides him a safe exit from the court of Saul.

First Samuel 22–27 contains the collection of stories of David as a fugitive. At this point in the story, David moves into the foreground alone, and Saul moves into the background. It is not unusual in the Bible for a key figure to flee or be driven or carried away to a foreign place or a life of wandering for a time before returning to his proper place. This tradition links David with Jacob, Joseph, Elijah, and Moses.[36] There is a double-sided nature to this portion of the narrative. David may be described as a bandit or a mercenary in these stories. The response of readers to this set of events varies tremendously. Some may be troubled by David's close association with the Philistines, while others see him only as a victim of Saul's murderous jealousy. The ambiguity of David's character is displayed in the incident involving the priests at Nob. This episode is first introduced in 21:1-8 when David manipulates the priest, Ahimelech, into giving David the holy bread for him and his followers to eat. The text does not inform us precisely who these other men are. David vouches for their purity in order to get the bread. His explanation hardly seems plausible. Either there are no men meeting him or they are the mixed band described in 22:2. David seems be able to play fast and loose with priestly regulations, in contrast to Saul, who has been judged severely for such behavior in 13:23.

The result of David's acquisition of the bread is the slaughter of all the priests and their families and livestock. This is the first occasion on which other people suffer for the transgressions of David, while he escapes with only a passing sense of remorse (22:22), a theme that will recur numerous times as David's story continues. The destruction brought by David, though indirectly, onto the inhabitants of Nob is balanced by the succeeding story of David's rescue of the people of Keilah from the oppression of the Philistines (23:1-14). The thanks David receives is another attempt on his life by Saul, with the apparent aid of those he has just rescued. An element that had been lurking in the background of the David narrative comes into full view here. David has access to knowledge from the LORD. Four times in 23:1-14 David is able to ask questions and receive answers. He is thus able to reassure his men that they will be successful in their defense of Keilah (v. 5) and escape Saul's subsequent attempt to kill him.[37] David's abundance of knowledge contrasts with Saul's inadequate knowledge. Saul does learn that David is at Keilah, though we are not told how he acquires this knowledge, but David's superior knowledge allows him to escape. In the continuing struggle between the two anointed kings, David's superior knowledge will insure his survival.[38]

The subsequent stories in 24:15–25:22 intensify the contrast between David and Saul. Saul continues to pursue David in an effort to kill him. David, on the other hand, when provided a perfect opportunity to kill Saul in 24:1-7, refuses to do so. Saul's pursuit of David comes to a temporary end in the strange meeting between the two men in 24:8-22. The conversation is filled with a strange mixture of emotion and deception. David pleads innocence and even calls Saul "my father" in v. 11, but David knows that he has been anointed to take Saul's place. He sounds genuinely weary of being "hunted." In response, Saul weeps and calls David "my son" in v. 16.[39] The two seem to come to some kind of settlement of the feud between them before they each go their separate ways, but the truce will not hold for long.

The text uses (or creates?) this pause in the conflict between Saul and David to take care of some important, unfinished business. First Samuel 25:1 reports the death of Samuel. The old prophet has been an absent presence within the narrative all along. The book of Samuel itself seems uncertain what to do with this character while it works out the drama between Saul and David. The story unofficially disposes of him in 15:34–16:13. Once he has anointed David, Samuel has little if any role to play. The text keeps sending him to Ramah (15:34 and 16:13) and claims that he and Saul did not see each other again "until the day of his death" (v. 34). Nevertheless, Samuel reappears in 20:18-24 and is present for one of Saul's flights into prophetic frenzy. Samuel apparently travels and lives with David for a while in Naioth (29:18-19). In 25:1, Samuel dies at Ramah. We are told that "all Israel assembled and mourned him." The text does not specify that Saul attended the funeral, though 15:34 would assume so. The last clause of 25:1 seems to imply that David was there as well, so the great triumvirate of our story may have come together one last time. The narrative continues to find it difficult to let go of Samuel, however, and his ghost will appear one last time when conjured up by the medium in 28:3-25.

Meanwhile, Saul's pursuit of David and David's wandering life as part bandit, part fugitive, and part mercenary begin again. The two stretches of such narratives in 1 Samuel 22–24 and 25–27 mirror each other in their report of Samuel's death. The episode in which David again passes up the opportunity to kill Saul in 26:1-25 is a reflection of the cave episode in 24:1-7. Again, David takes something of Saul's, this time his spear and water jar, to prove his unwillingness to kill Saul. Again there is a protracted conversation between Saul and David, with significant differences. David seems to keep a greater difference this time, and while Saul still calls David "my son" (26:17), David does not call Saul "my father."[40]

The remainder of 1 Samuel 25, the story of Abigail and Nabal in vv. 2-42, also serves as an instructive center amid the two stories of David sparing Saul's life that revolve around it. By itself, the story of Abigail and Nabal is of little consequence. It would serve only to explain how Abigail came to be David's wife, but 25:43 also notes David's marriage to Ahinoam with no story provided for background to the marriage. The significance of the story must be in Nabal's resemblance to Saul. Nabal is the one other person besides Saul who resists David's rise to the throne. David also has opportunity and motive to kill Nabal. Only the wisdom and quick action of Abigail prevent this. The LORD strikes Nabal dead in 25:38, and this provides assurance to both David and the reader that God will take care of Saul. Abigail is not suitably matched to Nabal, whose name literally means "fool," just as the throne is not suitably matched to Saul. Upon Saul's death, David will take the throne as surely as he takes Abigail to be his wife after the death of Nabal. The specific note in 25:38 that Nabal dies within ten days is a sign that Saul's death is not far off.[41]

In the sequence of stories in 1 Samuel 27–30, David and Saul part for the last time. David joins the Philistine army and Saul decides to leave off his pursuit of David (27:4). David's activity with the Philistine army and his association with Ziklag will need to be accounted for at some point,[42] but for now the text of 1 Samuel is surprisingly forthright about David's status as a mercenary bandit. In between two sets of stories about David leading raids and being raided lies the mysterious story of Saul and the medium at Endor in 28:3-25. Saul is falling apart before our eyes. For once, the great warrior is afraid of the enemy (v. 5), and he is no longer able to communicate with God. The list of possible means of communication in v. 6 emphasizes the extent to which Saul is cut off from divine assistance. In an act of desperation, Saul decides to use a forbidden means of gaining information, but because he has removed all the mediums from Israel he must travel to Endor. The conjuring of Samuel's ghost brings Saul in close contact with the world of death and brings back for one final appearance the figure with whom this book began. Samuel only reminds Saul of all that was said about Saul's eventual death and loss of the throne (vv. 16-19). At first it appears that Saul will choose to die in Endor rather than go on to meet this fate, but eventually he eats and goes back to face the Philistines in battle.

Before the final battle between Saul and the Philistines, the text must separate David from the Philistine army, which it does by means of the story in 1 Samuel 29. For the moment David is a liminal figure, fighting on the side of neither the Israelites nor the Philistines as the climax approaches. The destruction of Ziklag and the kidnapping of David's wives and children serve as distractions to keep him away from the battle that will pave his way to the throne. The story walks a delicate path, providing a place for David to be skillful and victorious in battle while power slips away from Saul, but not by David's efforts. After David defeats the Amalekites in 30:16-20, providing one more reminder of Saul's failure to be obedient in his own battle against them,[43] David is able to begin to reconcile himself with the people of Judah by presenting them with part of the spoil he has taken from the Amalekites (vv. 26-31).

At the beginning of 1 Samuel 31, the attention of the text swings abruptly to Mount Gilboa. The death of Saul provides an occasion for a final evaluation of this character. There is no doubt that, on the whole, the biblical account portrays Saul negatively, but there is significant debate over whether he is a villain or a tragic hero. Humphreys has argued that the earliest version of the material in 1 Samuel 9–31 is a story primarily about Saul as a tragic hero figure. This story has been reworked twice, first by adding a "prophetic" layer in which Samuel is given priority, and then a "royalist" layer extolling David.[44] Exum has countered that the final form of the text need not be hypothetically divided into sources to identify Saul as a tragic hero. Reading the text as it stands, Exum sees Saul as a tragic hero. Of Saul at Endor, she says, "Not content to let his tragic destiny unfold, the tragic hero stalks it."[45] Of Saul's journey through the final chapters of 1 Samuel, Exum adds, "In pursuing their nemesis, tragic heroes usually take a course that isolates them from others."[46] Thus, we find Saul on Mount Gilboa, nearly alone. Gunn calls Saul "one of God's own victims" and notes that he ends his life in a heroic manner.[47] While accepting that Saul is a tragic figure, W. Boyd Barrick has objected to these readings of Saul as a "martyred hero." He finds their root in Josephus's portrayal (*Antiquities* 6:343-50) and compares them to modern attempts to make George Custer a "martyred hero."[48] This struggle among interpreters over how to perceive Saul is surely affected by the lives of those who are doing the reading, but it also reflects a struggle within the text itself. This struggle continued as the book of Chronicles omitted Saul from its retelling of the story of the monarchy, while Josephus saw him as "noble" in the moment of his death.

A final issue arises in the story of the death of Saul, and it is one that will carry us into the first chapter of 2 Samuel. In the story in 1 Samuel 31, Saul commits suicide.[49] Surprisingly, the legal material in the Bible makes no statement about the act of suicide. Saul and his armor bearer are two of the three clear cases of suicide, along with Ahithophel in 2 Samuel 17:23. Other cases, such as Samson and Lot's wife, are debatable. Because of the disruptive effects and raw emotions surrounding the act of suicide, it is not surprising that 2 Samuel 1 offers two additional views of the death of Saul, one in the report of the Amalekite in vv. 1-10 and another in David's lament in vv. 19-27. Though the men of Jabesh-Gilead put an end to the physical shame of the dead king by rescuing his body, burying him, and mourning his death, the text is not finished remembering Saul yet.

2 SAMUEL: FROM THE BLOOD OF THE SLAIN

It will take David seven years and the first four chapters of 2 Samuel to consolidate his kingship over Israel. Though he is the only powerful personality left in the story, his treatment of Saul's memory and Saul's descendents must be careful. Brueggemann has pointed out significant parallels between 2 Samuel 1–4 and 1 Samuel 24–26. In both sequences of stories, David's cause is advancing at the expense of Saul's, but the narratives carefully guard against any accusation of blood guilt against David. This ideological protection of David becomes more difficult in 2 Samuel 1–4 because David is in power, and the murders of Abner and Ishbosheth (Ishbaal) could be considered his responsibility, even if he did not directly commit or order them. Ultimately, the defense of David may not be entirely successful.[50]

The report of the Amelekite in 2 Samuel 1:1-10 is in obvious conflict with the narrator's description of Saul's death in 1 Samuel 31. Further, these two reports stand on either side of the gap that is now perceived between 1 Samuel and 2 Samuel. It is customary for biblical books to end with the deaths of major characters. Genesis ends with the successive deaths of Jacob and Joseph, Deuteronomy with the death of Moses, Joshua with the death of Joshua and Eleazar. It is also common for biblical books to begin with a recollection of those who died at the end of the previous book. The beginning of Exodus recalls Jacob and Joseph, the beginning of the book of Joshua recalls Moses, and the beginning of Judges recalls Joshua. Death provides both a sense of closure and a new beginning in the biblical story. How should we evaluate these conflicting reports of Saul, however? Should we decide that one of the two is false, or that there were differing traditions about the death of Saul? The book of Samuel provides us with these two very different accounts, without the need or ability to evaluate them as true or false. The most common understanding is that the Amelekite lies to court David's favor. A moment of irony then enters the story when the act he thinks will get him a reward actually gets him executed. Adele Berlin has added additional nuance to this view by arguing, first, that the words of the Amelekite reveal his report as false[51] and, second, that the two reports accomplish a significant shift in the point of view of the story. As we hear the Amelekite's report and witness David's response, the focus of the story shifts entirely to David, ending the alternation of attention on David and Saul that characterized 1 Samuel 16–31. The division of the book of Samuel into two books at this point, regardless of when and why it happened, is thus an appropriate dividing point.[52]

The portrait of David is complicated by his execution of the Amelekite and further by his singing of the lamentation called "The Song of the Bow" in 2 Samuel 1:19-27. The song glorifies Saul and Jonathan and expresses intense grief at their deaths. To what extent is David's sorrow feigned as a political expediency? Obviously, David benefits from the death of Saul, but it is not unrealistic for him to have mixed emotions about both Saul and his family. Regardless of David's true feelings, the official position of the people of Judah and their leader is that Saul and Jonathan were heroic and that their deaths are a great loss to be mourned. The mourning is brief, however, and the resulting struggle for power takes place immediately after it in 2 Samuel 2. The portrayals of David and Ishbosheth[53] in this chapter are sharply different. The divine guidance David receives in 2:1 immediately reminds the reader of the David of 1 Samuel who overcame Saul because of knowledge received from God. Ishbosheth is passive, a puppet controlled by Abner in 2:9. The introduction of David as King of Judah is followed immediately by his overtures of blessing to Jabesh-Gilead in 2:4-7. Ishbosheth's introduction as king of Israel is followed by the report of his short reign in 2:10. The text reveals, from the beginning, that David will outlast Ishbosheth; then it brings the armies of these two contenders together for battle in 2:12-32. After David's first victory in the civil war is reported, the elegant summary statement in 3:1 gazes both backward and forward. The houses of David and Saul have been at war since 1 Samuel 16, and they have been growing stronger and weaker, respectively, since then. There is no doubt left about who will be victorious, and the listing of David's sons in 3:2-5 points toward the coming of a dynasty.

David's consolidation of power is recorded in 2 Samuel 3-10. Amid the necessary internal assassinations and external wars stands the "eternal covenant" between the God of Israel and the house of David in 2 Samuel 7. The grandeur of royal ceremony and the glory of war often obscure the deaths that lie in their wake, especially the small ones, but the storyteller manages to slip them in occasionally. David's killing of 22,000 Arameans in 8:5 is a statistic without emotion and is the kind of report expected in such a text, but the final story of Michal comes as a surprise. Among his many wives, David has reclaimed this daughter of Saul who had be given to him then taken back. With Saul dead and David on the throne, however, Michal becomes a liability rather than an asset. Second Samuel 9:1 shows David making certain that the house of Saul is under his control and no longer poses a threat. Its only apparent survivor, the crippled son of Jonathan named Mephibosheth, is brought under the watchful eye of David's court, in the guise of kind remembrance. Michal's childlessness (6:23) assures that she can produce no new Saulides as rivals to the Davidic monarchy. Exum has described the dull pain of Michal's fate: "A woman's tragic fortune is to survive, watching as others benefit from her family's losses."[54] In strange ways, the family of Saul will linger in the text. The downturn of David's fortunes in 2 Samuel 9–20 includes three texts involving Mephibosheth—near its beginning (9:1-13), its middle (16:1-4), and its end (19:24-30).[55] The final major section, 2 Samuel 21–24, opens with the story of a famine that is resolved by the executions of seven of Saul's descendents (21:15).

With all of the issues surrounding David's reign settled, it hardly seems that the story can go on much longer. The uncertainty about monarchy expressed in 1 Samuel 8–10 seems forgotten. As the shadow side of David, Saul has carried away the negative aspects of kingship, clearing the way for the eternal reign of the house of David. But just when it seems that the story no longer has either a villain or tragic figure, the shadow emerges again within David's own character.[56] David's life takes a sudden turn with the familiar story of his affair with Bathsheba and the resulting conspiracy to kill Uriah in 11:1-27. The sudden appearance of this side of David's character is a shock, and it is not surprising that in the retelling of David's story in the book of Chronicles, this story is completely omitted.[57] David has taken away a man's wife before, but 1 Samuel 25 was careful to keep Nabal's blood off of David's hands and to delay David's involvement with Abigail until after Nabal's death. Nabal was also portrayed as a foolish and despicable man. Uriah, on the other hand, though a foreigner, is noble, loyal, and heroic. These character traits actually contribute to his death. David has killed and manipulated people before, but always in ways that were necessary to promote his rise to power. As this shadow emerges within David's life, destruction and death begin to enter David's house. Issues of character and power are perhaps best summed up in John Dominic Crossan's poignant observation, "What was a bandit but an emperor on the make, what was an emperor but a bandit on the throne?"[58]

David's affair with Bathsheba is difficult to characterize. The account is bracketed by the story of the Ammonite war in 11:1 and 12:26-31.[59] Eventually, Bathsheba becomes a woman of influence significant enough to assist her son in his claim to the throne (1 Kings 1), but in 2 Samuel 11 the imbalance of power between David and Bathsheba is so great that a lack of explicit resistance on her part can hardly be assumed to indicate a willing complicity. Indeed, it is even possible to understand David's action as rape, but the narrator provides insufficient information to remove the ambiguity. The final evaluation of this issue likely depends upon the perspective and experience of the reader. Exum has characterized the event as rape, both by David and, to some extent, the narrator, who violates Bathsheba by exposing her to the reader.[60] Exum's reading has been effectively countered by George G. Nicol, who recognized the ambiguity of the text and demonstrated that the author could not have been more delicate or modest in the telling of this story. While Nicol has successfully defended the narrator here, the ambiguity he found in the text leaves the question of the motives of Bathsheba and David unresolved.[61] The biblical text will eventually judge David most severely for his role in the death of Uriah.

The parable told by Nathan and his pronouncement of judgment on David in 12:1-15 characterize David's behavior primarily as theft. In the parable the beloved lamb, which apparently represents Bathsheba, is killed, so the story does not match the situation perfectly. The more poignant element is the punishment for David's crime, which falls upon his children. The death of the infant child, in 12:15-23, begins a tortuous spiral of tragedy within the house of David. The king's reaction to the sickness and death of the child born to Bathsheba is puzzling, both to the reader and the other characters in the story. David fasts and mourns for the seven days that the child is ill, but ends his mourning at this point.[62] The episode closes, in 12:24-25, with the notice that Bathsheba conceived another child, Solomon, by David.

The conclusion of the Ammonite war, which began in 11:1, appears in 12:26-31. As stated earlier, the Ammonite war encloses the David and Bathsheba story. This latter portion also raises significant questions about David. Why does he go to join the battle now, unlike in 11:1? Why is it permissible for him to take the material spoils of war, when Saul was judged harshly for doing this? Is it acceptable for David to enslave an entire nation?[63] Ironically, these strong actions of David come at a time when he is in his weakest and most vulnerable state, a point when his kingdom is about to explode internally.

The eruption within David' house, which was predicted by Nathan in 2 Samuel 12:11, is ignited by the Amnon-Tamar-Absalom episode in 13:1-29.[64] Amnon's actions toward Tamar are reminiscent of his father's toward Bathsheba. This event is explicitly described as a sexual assault, which may or may not shed light on David's earlier behavior. Most surprising is David's lack of action in response to the behavior of his children. In what may be an intentional parallel, David begins to resemble Eli in the early chapters of 1 Samuel, who was also a recipient of a prophecy of death and destruction within his family. A great deal of time passes, as 13:1 and 13:23 note. The book of Samuel is not interested in other aspects of David's reign. The relationships within the royal family take center stage. The effect of this is that in narrative time Absalom's revenge in 13:23-29 swiftly follows Amnon's abominable acts. In a stunning reversal, David begins to take on the role of Saul, and Absalom the role of the young David. The relationship between the aging king and the potential usurper becomes complex when Absalom flees to a foreign country for refuge. The false accusation made against Absalom in 13:30, that he had killed all of David's other sons, is the kind of charge David struggled to avoid in relation to the heirs of Saul.

The convoluted story of reconciliation between David and Absalom in 2 Samuel 14 is also filled with echoes from the past. The woman of Tekoa plays the part of Nathan, telling David a story that connects with his own life such that David's judgment about the woman and her son commits him to a course of action in his own life. The woman's story also connects the Absalom-Amnon conflict more explicitly to the long biblical tradition of conflict between brothers. The woman of Tekoa could easily be Eve telling the story of her two sons. At this point, it is difficult for the reader to know how to feel about Absalom. Is he a hero who avenges his beloved sister? The narrator goes to great length to extol his heroic stature in 14:25-27. He has even named his own daughter for the sister whose honor he valiantly defended. Yet, Absalom's position in the brother tradition is ambiguous. He is the younger brother, like Abel, Isaac, Jacob, Joseph, and David, but he has killed his brother as Cain did, as Esau and the brothers of Joseph wanted to do. In the end, the reconciliation between David and Absalom seems forced, and it is brief. The rebellion is on.

While the conflict among David's children fulfills the prophecy of Nathan in part, the specifics of 2 Samuel 12:11 require a much greater development. It turns out to be David's own son who will overthrow him and take his wives (16:20-23). The divide within the house of David erupts and the whole nation is thrown into turmoil. The threat of death hangs over everyone (15:14), and they are forced to choose sides. The disruption brings old feelings to the surface and the story reveals that the placid surface of the reign of David is a façade. The curse of Shimei, in 16:1-8, exposes the old Saulide rift. This story is preceded by the middle of three references to Mephibosheth (16:1-4), the remaining Saulide threat. Doubt is cast upon Mephibosheth's loyalty in 16:3 when the servant, Ziba, accuses him of treason amid Absalom's uprising. The question of Mephibosheth's loyalty to David is resolved in 19:24-30,[65] after Absalom has been defeated. In an ironic twist, the account of rebellion from within David's own house is encompassed by the intriguing stories of Mephibosheth's ultimate fidelity to the king.

This civil war comes to an end with the death of Absalom and the defeat of his army in 18:1-18. The agonizing response of David shows the mixed emotions and the hollow nature of this victory. David is undone (18:33–19:2), and the people of Israel are confused in their response to the restoration of his reign (19:8-15, 41-43). The story cannot end in such agony and grief, and it does not have to. Fortunately, the narrator has the story of another rebellion to tell. The quelling of the rebellion of Sheba, in 20:1-22, provides something of a bandage to cover the wound left by Absalom's uprising. The nation and army are reunited in this effort. Though the fault lines between Judah and the other tribes are still visible in this story,[66] the throwing of Sheba's head over the wall (20:22) brings at least a temporary sense of calm over Israel's troubled story as the end of David's reign approaches.

That the story of David's reign has reached an end is indicated by the listing of his officials in 20:23-26. This list is similar to the one in 8:16-18, and the two lists form what Alter has called "bookends to David's reign in Jerusalem."[67] This observation leaves the last four chapters hanging, awaiting some sort of definition. This need has been amply filled by Brueggemann, who labeled 2 Samuel 21–24 "An Appendix of Deconstruction."[68] Having traveled through the long story of the development of Israel's monarchy that leads through the reign of David, we now pause upon the summit to look back at this king. A close examination of these chapters reveals an intricate structure that points toward a distinctive purpose. There are six elements present in these chapters:

21:1-14	A narrative about a famine
21:15-22	A list of warriors and their exploits
22:1-51	A poem about God' faithfulness to David
23:1-7	A poem about David's royal status
23:8-39	A list of warriors and their exploits
24:1-25	A narrative about a plague

These elements are obviously arranged chiastically, but there is also a significant sense of forward movement.[69] Most significant is the understanding of the causes of the famine in 21:1-14 and the plague in 24:1-25. The famine in the first story is blamed on Saul's slaughter of the Gibeonites. This act is avenged and the famine ends when David hands over seven descendents of Saul to be executed. Once again, we are reminded of how David manages to dispose of potential rivals without appearing to be self-serving. The elaborate burial David provides for these seven, along with the acquisition and burial of the bones of Saul and Jonathan, exhibit David's magnanimity to the house of Saul one last time. In 24:1-25 David is the cause of the plague. The story of the census is difficult to understand.[70] How is it that YHWH can incite David to sin? We are reminded of the evil spirit from YHWH that possessed Saul. The deft alteration in 1 Chronicles 21:1 indicates that not only modern readers are troubled by this understanding of evil. Why do tens of thousands of Israelites die because of David's sin, while David and the whole city of Jerusalem are spared? This final story raises serious questions about heroes and villains and the source of power.[71] The image of David is undermined here, and the last we see of him is a desperate figure struggling to maintain some semblance of control in his kingdom. Brueggemann has argued that this story and the story of Hannah in 1 Samuel 1 form an *inclusio* concerning power. In the end, David is like Hannah, "empty-handed, utterly needful, utterly trusting."[72]

REFLECTIONS

The book of Samuel turns out to be a struggle for power among its major personalities. This power has three components: religious, political, and military. Samuel expresses religious power and seems politically astute, but the rise of the monarchy takes political and military power away from him. Saul is a giant of a man, in military terms, but seems politically inept, and religious power is withheld from him. It is left to David to be the one who unites all of these components within one personality. Brueggemann has labeled David a "sport of nature."[73] What is it that makes David so golden and, at the same time, dooms Saul to failure? The power of life and death is at work in the lives of these leaders. The book of Samuel understands this power of life and death in terms of the divine spirit. This spirit is bipolar. The spirit of monarchy that is with David is opposed by an evil spirit from the LORD that torments Saul.

In our own world, power over life and death is often accompanied by claims of access to the divine spirit. Enemies are typically described using the language of evil. They are an "evil empire" or an "axis of evil." The flow of power is difficult to understand and human beings are desperate to assign some sense of purpose to it. The literature of the Bible provides a potent template for establishing such a pattern. In the story of Saul and David, every subtle shift in the flow of power is associated with a divine choice and linked to the movements of the bipolar, divine spirit.[74]

The modern use of this ideology is of great significance. Modern leaders generally realize that the ability to unite political, military, and religious power can increase the magnitude of power exponentially. The question for anyone who recognizes the potential of such manipulations of power is whether to make use of them or expose them. This is perhaps the ultimate issue for the modern church. Should the church seek to align itself with political power or should it resist power? Of course, the church is divided on this issue, and the various positions interact with a book like Samuel in differing ways. Those who favor the use of political and military power by religious communities often read David as a flat, purely heroic character. A more nuanced reading of the entire book of Samuel reveals not only the complexity of David's character, but of all the characters and the interplay of power among them. Awareness of these complexities ought to make readers of the Bible at least skeptical of the alignment of political and military power with religious authority. In the great modern parable of power, J. R. R. Tolkien's *Lord of the Rings*, only a humble hobbit such as Frodo has a chance to resist the temptations of power and destroy the ring. Yet, even for Frodo, the closer he gets to destroying the ring, the heavier it becomes.

The book of Samuel is also acutely aware of the damage that surrounds power. David is the archetype of the powerful leader. The huge mechanism that surrounds him, both the elements, characters, and events within the narrative and the structure of the narrative itself, serve to support his status. At times it seems that David can do no wrong. All of his rivals mange to get killed without his direct complicity. The dirty work of climbing onto the throne and expanding an empire gets assigned to those around him, while he plays whatever role suits his political purposes, whether it be court musician, war hero, fugitive, or public mourner. When David does slip, he is always able to right himself and others pay the penalty for his sins, from his own children to a nameless mass of 70,000 Israelites. This phenomenon occurs in all hierarchical endeavors. As potent figures make their way to the top, their path is littered with those who suffer the cost. Second Samuel may or may not be a "deconstruction" of David. The question it poses for modern readers is whether we can muster the courage and imagination for the deconstruction of power. Such work can never be finished because power is so hungry and the world wants a hero so badly that even an attempt at deconstruction like this one is almost completely subsumed within a larger canonical enterprise that cleans up and presents David afresh as the great psalmist and ideal king. The book of Samuel only avoids becoming part of the mechanism of power if, as Brueggemann and others have suggested,[75] the end points us back to the beginning. David is exposed as one who is as powerless as Hannah, and all of those whom David has climbed over, from Saul to Absalom, are remembered.

Our own world is littered with those broken by the movement of power. It is always their fault, of course. They are either possessed by evil like Saul, ungrateful like Michal, foolish like Nabal, weak and lazy like Mephibosheth, in the way like Uriah, expendable like Tamar, or unrealistic and unwilling to play along like Absalom. Is it possible to read the book of Samuel for and with these broken ones, both ancient and modern?

NOTES

[1] From the song "Hallelujah," different versions of which appear on several of Leonard Cohen's albums.

[2] See the discussion in Hanz Wilhelm Hertzberg, *1 and 2 Samuel*, trans. J. S. Bowden (Philadelphia: Westminster, 1964), 17-20.

[3] Noth published his influential work *Überlieferungsgeschichtliche Studien* (Halle: Niemeyer) in 1943. A major portion of this book developed the concept of the Deuteronomistic History. That portion has been published in English as *The Deuteronomistic History* (Sheffield: Sheffield Academic Press, 1981).

[4] See Leonhard Rost, *The Succession to the Throne of David*, trans. Michael D. Rutter and David M. Gunn (Sheffield: Almond Press, 1982). This is a translation of Rost's *Die Überleiferung von den Thronnachfogle Davids* (Stuttgart: W. Kohlhammer, 1926).

[5] See David Gunn, *The Story of King David: Genre and Interpretation* (Sheffield: JSOT, 1978).

[6] Ibid., 65-84. Gunn, however, is still more interested in finding boundaries for his "David Story" than in the final shape of the canonical book of Samuel.

[7] Robert Polzin, *Moses and the Deuteronomist: A Literary Study of the Deuteronomistic History: 1 Samuel* (San Francisco: Harper & Row, 1980); *Samuel and the Deuteronomist: A Literary Study of the Deuteronomistic History: 1 Samuel* (San Francisco: Harper & Row, 1989); and *David and the Deuteronomist: A Literary Study of the Deuteronomistic History: 2 Samuel* (Bloominton: Indiana University Press, 1993).

[8] See Jan P. Fokkelman, *Narrative Art and Poetry in the Books of Samuel: A Full Interpretation Based on Stylistic and Structural Analyses*, vols. 1-4 (Assen: Van Gorcum, 1981–1993). Volume 1 carries the subtitle "King David (2 Samuel 9–20 & 1 Kings 1–2)," volume 2 "The Crossing Fates (1 Samuel 13–31 and 2 Samuel 1)," volume 3 "Throne and City (2 Samuel 2–8 and 21–24)," and volume 4 "Vow and Desire (1 Samuel 1–12)." Fokkelman treated 2 Samuel 9–1 Kings 2 at the beginning of his work because he thought this section fit his reading method best (vol. 1, p. 1).

[9] See Robert Alter, *The David Story: A Translation with Commentary of 1 and 2 Samuel* (New York: W. W. Norton, 1999), ix-xxiv. Alter argued, contra Polzin, that the additions of the Deuteronomistic editor were minimal (xii). While hedging on the existence of an independent Succession Narrative, Alter does seem to favor Rost's other proposal, that 1 Samuel 4ff. and 2 Samuel 6 form what was an independent Ark Narrative. Nevertheless, his focus is still primarily on the final form of the story (x-xi).

[10] See David M. Gunn, *The Fate of King Saul: An Interpretation of a Biblical Story* (Sheffield: Sheffield University Press, 1980).

[11] The lack of a paired character here will be addressed later in the exploration of David's internally divided character in this section.

[12] The puzzling nature of the name of the book is revealed in the Septuagint. Naming the entire book "Samuel" seems an odd choice. The Greek tradition avoided this oddity by using the titles 1 and 2 Kingdoms to designate the books typically called 1 and 2 Samuel. This resulted in the use of the titles 3 and 4 Kingdoms to designate the books more commonly called 1 and 2 Kings.

[13] See the discussion of Walter Brueggemann in "1 Samuel 1–A Sense of a Beginning," in *Old Testament Theology: Essays on Structure Theme, and Text*, ed. Patrick D. Miller (Minneapolis: Fortress, 1992), 219-34.

[14] See Fokkelman, *Narrative Art and Poetry in the Books of Samuel,* vol. 4, 100-107. The horn image is typically obscured in English translations, which interpret the metaphor by translating it as "strength" or "power." Literally, the second line of the poem says, "My horn is made high by YHWH," and the second to last line says, "He will give a horn to his king." This concentric feature is part of a pattern in the poem that Fokkelman has analyzed to excessive extremes (73-99).

[15] For a thorough and creative discussion of issues surrounding this and related problems in 1 Samuel 1–2, see Marc Brettler, "The Composition of 1 Samuel 1–2," *JBL* 116 (Winter 1997): 601-12.

[16] There is confusion about where the division between chapters 3 and 4 should fall. See my discussion of this issue in *The Blood of Abel: The Violent Plot of the Hebrew Bible* (Macon GA: Mercer University Press, 1999), 78-79.

[17] For a somewhat different, but related way of understanding the function of 1 Samuel 4–7 to the surrounding material, see Polzin, *Samuel and the Deuteronomist,* 55-60.

[18] See Alter, *The David Story,* 44.

[19] On the shaping of biblical characters generally, and Saul specifically, see Shimon Bar-Efrat, *Narrative Art in the Bible,* trans. Dorothea Shefer-Vanson (Sheffield: Almond, 1989), 47-92.

[20] The similar statement in 10:23 may be somewhat clearer.

[21] Alter, *The David Story,* 47.

[22] See Robert Alter, *The Art of Biblical Narrative* (New York: Basic Books, 1981), 60-61. There are additional, early indications of Saul's ultimate failure. For a thorough discussion see Polzin, *Samuel and the Deuteronomist,* 101-108.

[23] W. Lee Humphreys, *The Tragic Vision and the Hebrew Tradition* (Philadelphia: Fortress, 1985), 23-27.

[24] On the significance of this aspect, see Alter, *The David Story,* 60. Alter also discussed the similar effect of the report about the lack of ironsmiths in 13:19-22 (74-75).

[25] See Polzin's discussion of the extensive literary connections between Judges 19–21 and 1 Samuel 11 in *Samuel and the Deuteronomist,* 111-14.

[26] See J. Cheryl Exum, *Tragedy and Biblical Narrative: Arrows of the Almighty* (Cambridge: Cambridge University Press, 1992), 17-18. In her treatment of Saul as a tragic hero, Exum has utilized a careful comparison between Saul and Samson, who also seems doomed from the beginning by a mixture of his own character and an ambivalent divine choice.

[27] Early manuscripts of the Septuagint omit 13:1 entirely. Some later manuscripts contain the verse and give Saul's age of ascension as thirty. The Syriac text puts Saul's age of ascension at twenty-one, but omits any mention of the length of his reign. In the Christian tradition, this textual problem is exacerbated by the statement in Acts 13:21 that Saul reigned for forty years.

[28] On the story of Saul's failures and their interpretations throughout Jewish and Christian history, see the brilliant analysis of Gunn in *The Fate of King Saul,* 23-56.

[29] Polzin has noted the connections between 1 Samuel 14:36-46 and the story of Achan in Joshua 7 (*Samuel and the Deuteronomist,* 137-39). Perhaps this further predisposes the reader to see Saul in the light of the villain of Ai (Achan) rather than the hero of Jericho (Joshua).

[30] The David of 16:18 (man of valor, warrior, etc.) can hardly precede the unrecognized stripling of 17:56. Kyle McCarter addresses these problems from a text-critical and source-critical perspective. See *1 Samuel: A New Translation with Introduction and Commentary* (Garden City NJ:

Doubleday, 1980), 298-306. See also the lengthy discussion of Polzin (mostly in endnotes) in *Samuel and the Deuteronomist*, 161-62.

[31] Enormous textual problems surround 1 Samuel 17–18. The Greek text lacks thirty-nine of the eighty-eight verses that make up the Hebrew text of the story. Because the additions in the Hebrew text create many of the internal contradictions of the story, textual critics argue two opposing positions. Some say that the Hebrew text reflects the original, while the Greek translator has removed difficult and contradictory passages to make the story smoother. Others counter that the Greek text reflects an earlier Hebrew text, before an editor wove into it additional material from another version of the story, thus creating a longer, more conflicted text. This issue cannot be settled here, but it provides a good illustration that any interpretation must make a choice about which text to read. The reading offered here will follow the longer, Hebrew text, but readers should be aware that there is an ancient version of the story that is significantly different and that would produce different interpretive results. For a detailed description of this textual problem, see Emanuel Tov, *Textual Criticism of the Hebrew Bible* (Minneapolis: Fortress, 1992), 334-36.

[32] See Polzin, *Samuel and the Deuteronomist*, 171. Note Polzin's thorough description of the literary features of the entire chapter on 163-76.

[33] On the importance of clothing and the transference of the kingship, see Gunn, *The Fate of King Saul*, 80.

[34] Exum describes Jonathan's role as "mediating" the kingship from Saul to David (*Tragedy and Biblical Narrative: Arrows of the Almighty*, 75).

[35] See Polzin's discussion of the functions of repetition in 1 Samuel 19 in *Samuel and the Deuteronomist*, 181-82. Polzin has demonstrated that repetition serves both to link events to each other within this section and also to link them to events elsewhere in the Deuteronomistic History. Exum has shown that the second element of repeated pairs often provides clarification of the first occurrence (*Tragedy and Biblical Narrative: Arrows of the Almighty*, 27).

[36] Lesser biblical characters who fit this motif are Jephthah, Ezra, and Nehemiah. Outside the Bible, see Mohammed, Oedipus, Simba in *The Lion King*, and Luke Skywalker.

[37] In the middle of these four responses, Abiathar, the only remaining survivor from Nob, brings the priestly ephod to David. The ephod seems to be the source of the third and fourth answers, by some means of divination. The third and fourth questions, in vv. 11-12, are yes/no questions answered in a single Hebrew word. The means of receiving answers to the first and second questions in vv. 2-4, before the arrival of the ephod, is not specified. Polzin has argued that the responses here are of a more prophetic, rather than priestly, nature because they are longer, consisting of five and eight Hebrew words respectively (*Samuel and the Deuteronomist*, 200-201). The first two questions are yes/no questions, however, and perhaps this distinction should not be pressed too far. David has access to information from many sources, some divine and some not, as v. 9 reveals.

[38] For more on the contrast between Saul's knowledge and David's knowledge in this section of 1 Samuel, see McCarter, *1 Samuel*, 367.

[39] See the discussion of this curious conversation in Alter, *The Art of Biblical Narrative*, 72-73.

[40] See the discussion on the nature and function of doublets in Alter, *The David Story*, 162.

[41] For a more detailed discussion of the relationships between these stories that has many points of contact with this one, see Polzin, *Samuel and the Deuteronomist*, 205-15.

[42] Tony Cartledge has argued that David is portrayed as a "double agent" here. David manages all at once to evade Saul, play the Philistines for fools, destroy some of Israel's other enemies, and buy

the favor of local Judeans by giving them the spoils of his victories (*1 & 2 Samuel* [Macon GA: Smyth & Helwys, 2001], 309-14).

[43] For more on the painful poignancy of this point, see Gunn, *The Fate of King Saul*, 110-11.

[44] See Humphreys, *The Tragic Vision and the Hebrew Tradition*, 23-41.

[45] Exum, *Tragedy and Biblical Narrative*, 22.

[46] Ibid., 39.

[47] Gunn, *The Fate of King Saul*, 111. Gunn's reading is similar to that of Northrop Frye, who identified Saul as "the one great tragic hero of the Bible" and also argued that "the suggestion of malice within the divine nature" is "the one element that makes the story of Saul genuinely tragic" (*The Great Code: The Bible and Literature* [San Diego: Harcourt Brace, 1981], 181).

[48] See W. Boyd Barrick, "Saul's Demise, David's Lament, and Custer's Last Stand," *JSOT* 73 (1997), 25-41.

[49] The vocalization of the verb in 31:3b in the Masoretic Text may indicate a translation such as "and he quaked with fear" (see Alter, *The David Story*, 189). Most translations opt for "and he was badly wounded." How one translates this phrase may have an impact on the character of Saul's suicide.

[50] See Walter Brueggemann, *Power, Providence, and Personality: Biblical Insight into Life and Ministry* (Louisville: Westminster, 1990), 66-78.

[51] See Adele Berlin, *Poetics and Interpretation of Biblical Narrative* (Winona Lake IN: Eisenbrauns, 1994), 80-81. This point is obscured in most English translations. In 1:6 the Amalekite literally says ". . . and, behold, Saul was leaning on his spear, and, behold, the chariots and horsemen approached him." The double use of "behold" is highly unusual in such a report and indicates a lack of veracity in his report. Polzin has pointed out that the narrative gives us no apparent indication whether David thought the Amalekite was lying. This is part of the narrator's consistent pattern of not revealing David's inner life (Polzin, *David and the Deuteronomist* [Bloomington: Indiana University Press, 1993], 3).

[52] See Berlin's entire discussion of the reports of Saul's death within her treatment of the subject of "point of view" in biblical narrative (*Poetics and Interpretation of Biblical Narrative*, 79-82).

[53] Ishbosheth means "man of shame." Many versions of the Bible present the name of this character as Ishbaal, which means "man of Baal." The book of Chronicles calls him Ishbaal, and the assumption, probably correct, is that this is the real name of Saul's son. The book of Samuel is perhaps reluctant to use a name containing the name of a foreign God. I will refer to him by the name that the book of Samuel calls him, because this name plays a role in his characterization in this book.

[54] Exum, *Tragedy and Biblical Narrative*, 92. Exum also pointed to the problematic text in 2 Samuel 21:8-9, which contradicts 6:23 by listing children born to Michal. This is often understood to be a textual error, and Michal's name is replaced by Merab, another of Saul's daughters. The uncertainty of Michal's status as a mother and the parentage of these children may be understood as further injury to this woman who defies and poses a threat to David.

[55] For an extensive discussion of these three passages and their relation to each other, see Fokkelman, *Narrative Art and Poetry in the Books of Samuel*, vol. 1, 23-40. The possible narrative functions of these texts will be taken up later in this study.

[56] In recent decades, much work has been done relating biblical stories to the psychological theories of Carl Jung. It is not surprising that one of the places to which Jungian biblical interpretation

most often gravitates is the story of Saul and David. For examples of these kinds of readings, see John Sanford, *King Saul, the Tragic Hero* (New York: Paulist Press, 1985), and Edward Edinger, *The Bible and the Psyche: Individuation Symbolism in the Old Testament* (Toronto: Inner City Books, 1986), 77-92. Both of these works deal with the psychological process of "individuation" or "self-realization" and recognize in Saul and David the kind or vivid character portrayals that shed light on this process.

[57] For a discussion of David as his own nemesis, "an enemy he cannot defeat," see Cartledge, *1 & 2 Samuel*, 495.

[58] John Dominic Crossan, *The Historical Jesus: The Life of a Mediterranean Jewish Peasant* (San Francisco: HarperSanFrancisco, 1991), 172.

[59] On the effects of embedding the story of David's adultery within a story of war, see Cartledge, *1 & 2 Samuel*, 496, and Fokkelman, *Narrative Art and Poetry in the Books of Samuel*, vol. 1, 41. Fokkelman noted that this is the one place in the book of Samuel where the narration moves between ". . . two scenes of action far removed from each other and maintains the tension between them both."

[60] See J. Cheryl Exum, *Fragmented Women: Feminist (Sub)versions of Biblical Narratives* (Sheffield: JSOT Press, 1993), 170-201.

[61] See George G. Nicol, "The Alleged Rape of Bathsheba: Some Observations on Ambiguity in Biblical Narrative," *JSOT* 73 (1997): 44-48.

[62] See the comments on this passage in Alter, *The David Story*, 260-62. On the contrasts between David's mourning of this child and Absalom in 2 Samuel 19 and other issues in this text, see Cartledge, *1 & 2 Samuel*, 523-26.

[63] On these questions and others, see Cartledge, *1 & 2 Samuel*, 528-29. Cartledge has also acknowledged the difficulty of 12:31 (p. 528). Literally, it says, "The people that were in it he brought out and put in/on the saw and the iron picks and the iron axes." Most translations read something like ". . . brought out and put to work with . . . ." While this meaning is plausible, it silently evades the possibility that David tortured his captives using these implements.

[64] For a brilliant discussion of the internal structure of this passage, see Bar-Efrat, *Narrative Art on the Bible*, 239-82.

[65] See the discussion of this difficult passage in Fokkelman, *Narrative Art and Poetry in the Books of Samuel*, vol. 1, 23-40. This final Mephibosheth story is also found in proximity to the story of David's pardoning of Shimei (19:16-23), another Benjaminite and Saul loyalist.

[66] Note the appearance in 20:2 of the warcry that will ultimately divide the kingdom after the death of Solomon (1 Kgs 12:16).

[67] Alter, *The David Story*, 328.

[68] Walter Brueggemann, "2 Samuel 1-24—An Appendix of Deconstruction," in *Old Testament Theology: Essays on Structure, Theme, and Text*, ed. Patrick D. Miller (Minneapolis: Fortress, 1992), 235-51.

[69] For more extensive discussions of these features, see Brueggemann, "2 Samuel 21–24—An Appendix of Deconstruction," 237-46, and Fokkelman, *Narrative Art and Poetry in the Books of Samuel*, vol. 3, 271-331.

[70] The ancient taboo against counting people, or even possessions, is fairly widespread. For a discussion of this taboo in African culture and its implications for this story, see Sammy Githuku, "Taboos on Counting," in *Interpreting the Old Testament in Africa*, ed. Mary Getui et al. (New

York: Peter Land, 2001), 113-18. For a connection between this taboo and a psychological understanding of human development, see Edinger, *The Bible and the Psyche*, 90-91.

[71] See the discussion in Fokkelman, *Narrative Art and Poetry in the Books of Samuel*, vol. 3, 308-11, 363.

[72] Brueggemann, "2 Samuel 21–24—An Appendix of Deconstruction," 250.

[73] Walter Brueggemann, *Power, Providence, and Personality: Biblical Insight into Life and Ministry* (Louisville: Westminster John Knox, 1990), 41-48.

[74] Biblical scholars typically describe this view as "Deuteronomic." The idea that obedience to God brings success and disobedience elicits curse is spelled out in Deuteronomy 28 and many other places. This ideology is politicized in the book of Judges. The book of Samuel refines it into a fully developed means of explaining Israel's fortunes, both internally and externally.

[75] See the discussion in Brueggemann, "2 Samuel 21–24—An Appendix of Deconstruction," 250-51.

Ezra–Nehemiah:
All Who Trembled

Our path is worn, our feet are poorly shod.
We lift up our prayers against the odds,
and fear the silence is the voice of God.

—Emmylou Harris[1]

THE NARRATIVE SHAPE OF EZRA-NEHEMIAH

The books of Ezra and Nehemiah are typically treated as a single unit for a number of reasons. Among them are the appearance of the character named Ezra in both books and the central theme of rebuilding in both books; these similarities create a strong narrative connection between them. Despite numerous problems related to history, chronology, and text,[2] these books do tell a coherent story that begins with the departure of the exiles from Babylon and ends with the reading and application of the Law of Moses by Ezra in a restored Jerusalem. Between these two events lies the perilous story of a beleaguered group struggling to reestablish a lost way of life.

Historical and literary concerns are not always easy to separate. Among the points of controversy in the interpretation of these two books is the chronology of the two main characters, Ezra and Nehemiah. The argument that they must actually have appeared in Jerusalem in the opposite order of that in the text has been influential. Its primary assumption is that the biblical writers have confused Artaxerxes I and Artaxerxes II.[3] This historical issue is of relatively little importance for a narrative treatment of the books. Of significance, however, are some of the literary incongruities that contributed to the proposed reversal. Two examples illustrate the point. Ezra 9:9 indicates that Ezra comes to Jerusalem and apparently finds the city wall already built. The building of the wall then occupies the early chapters of the book of Nehemiah. Ezra 10:1 seems to portray a more developed and populated Israel than does Nehemiah 7:4. The recognition of these two problems does not require information from outside the text. They may be acknowledgments within the text that chronology has been overridden by ideology in the organizing of the material. From a narrative perspective, however, it may be more appropriate to say that multiple points of view are represented in the text and that they disagree in their evaluation of the progress made in the rebuilding.

The books of Ezra and Nehemiah are filled with obvious source documents. There are decrees, letters, lists, and personal memoirs. This aspect of the books has caused attention to focus on smaller units of text and their inherent problems. A broader, narrative portrayal of these books has, on the other hand, received relatively little emphasis. Recent interpretation has begun to overcome this problem but has not entirely succeeded.

Gordon F. Davies has produced a fairly extensive rhetorical analysis of texts from Ezra and Nehemiah. His study reveals much about the literary function of many passages, but the emphasis on the rhetorical effect of individual texts has limited the attention given to narrative flow and the overall structure of the books.[4] Lester L. Grabbe's recent work presents a "Literary Analysis" in its first half, the bulk of which consists of a "close reading" of Ezra and Nehemiah. Grabbe has produced a more cohesive reading, which points to two decisive factors about the books of Ezra and Nehemiah. First, these books are carefully and skillfully constructed works of literature. A wide variety of material has been put together to tell a coherent and relatively simple story. Second, a close reading reveals that the internal tensions created by this diversity of materials are still present in the books.[5] Both of these elements are part of the narrative shape of the books. The books of Ezra and Nehemiah tell stories of conflict. This conflict is reflected in the literary fabric of the story. Together, both of these aspects of conflict likely reflect a situation of real conflict out of which these books arose, but this is primarily a historical or sociological question and will not be addressed here.

The following exploration of the books of Ezra and Nehemiah will assume that there is a deliberate narrative design to the whole, regardless of the compositional history of all of the components. The books of Ezra and Nehemiah are roughly parallel to each other. Both begin with a lengthy building scene in which the protagonists (the Golah group) persevere despite intense opposition. Ezra 1–6 reports the building of the temple in Jerusalem and Nehemiah 1–7 the building of the wall around the city. The two rebuilding scenes are linked by the inclusion of the list of returnees near the beginning of the building scene in Ezra (ch. 2) and near the end of the building scene in Nehemiah (ch. 7). The second part of both books narrates the reforming programs of the primary characters,

Ezra in Ezra 7–10 and Nehemiah 8–10, and Nehemiah in Nehemiah 11–13. Two features serve to link these parts of the two books most overtly—first, the mysterious appearance of Ezra in the book of Nehemiah and, second, the expulsion of foreign wives from the community in Ezra 10 and Nehemiah 13:23-30. A number of other features serve both to link Ezra and Nehemiah together as a unified narrative and to increase the sense of parallel structure between them.[6]

The narration found in Ezra and Nehemiah is unusual in two ways. First, this is the only place in the Hebrew Bible, outside of the prophetic books, where first person narration appears. The first person portions are only part of the story, in Ezra 7:27–9:15 and much of Nehemiah 1–7.[7] The assumption in this study, again, is that these portions play an integral part in the narrative design of the books. Meir Sternberg has identified the second unusual feature of these narratives, which is their lack of omniscience. For the most part, the narrators in the Hebrew Bible are omniscient. This is certainly the case with the narrator(s) of Genesis–2 Kings. Therefore, omniscience is undeniably the dominant mode of narration in the Hebrew Bible. The narrator(s) in Ezra and Nehemiah, however, does not speak from the same "God's-eye" view.[8]

EZRA: BECAUSE THEY WERE IN DREAD

The book of Ezra, as stated earlier, is a complex combination of story material and documentary elements, such as decrees, lists, and letters. The imbedded documents contribute to the narrative flow of the book and will be treated here as integral elements. Their purpose, however, is not always readily apparent. The exiles in Babylon are set free by the Decree of Cyrus in 1:1-4. This group's authority rests in its possession of the cultic implements, which are listed in 1:6-9. The boundaries of the group are established by the list in 2:1-67. In this manner, the documents serve to define the group in terms of its center, possession of cultic authority, and its extent, those included in the list. The presence of the list indicates activities of inclusion and exclusion in the forming of community. Exclusion appears explicitly in the text in 2:61-63.[9] Enforcement of this act of exclusion is carried out by imperial power in 2:62, as the governor[10] informs those who are excluded of their "unclean" status. The end of Ezra 2 sees the authorized group of returnees, with its membership fixed, settled in Jerusalem and Judah. The text does not describe the degree of violence necessary to accomplish these goals. Neither does it inform us of the ultimate fate of those who are excluded. The book of Ezra is not forthright about internal conflict within the returned community. Only small traces of such conflict are present in the narrative.

Ezra 3 continues the story at a later point. Under the leadership of Jeshua and Zerubbabel, the community begins offering sacrifices. Ezra 3:3 reports that the reason for beginning the burnt offering rituals, which naturally involve the killing of animals, is that the returnees are "in dread of the peoples of the lands." A precise identification of these people is neither necessary nor possible.[11] The purpose they serve in the story is to provide adequate motivation for the resumption of the sacrificial cult. The returnees find themselves in a vulnerable and dangerous position. These new residents of Judah apparently feel the need to secure divine protection against the neighboring peoples. The narrative implies that their actions are successful, because the returned community manages to organize a building project and to begin laying the foundations of the temple in 3:8-10.

The end of chapter 3 contains another example of internal conflict portrayed in a subtle manner. When the foundations of the temple are completed in 3:10, the people respond in two different ways in 3:11-12. Some "shout for joy" while others weep. It is possible that the elderly who remembered the first temple wept out of disappointment because the new temple was much smaller, and this is a frequent interpretation,[12] but this is not necessarily so. This visible reminder of the former temple, which had been destroyed, would seem to be enough to cause such emotion regardless of how the two buildings might have compared. In any case, the situation brings a mixed response, and the sound of this mixed response in 3:13 summons the attention of the adversaries in 4:1. Elsewhere in the Hebrew Bible, the "great shout" of the Israelites is an element of holy war intended to discomfit the opponents, but that is neither the intent nor the result here.[13] The situation of the returnees is far too tenuous for such a possibility. Ultimately, it has the opposite effect of rallying opposition.

Conflict quickly erupts in Ezra 4:1-3. The shout of the people at the laying of the foundations of the temple summons the attention of another group. In 4:1, the narrator immediately identifies them as adversaries, though their expressed intention is to join the returned community and assist in the building. Again, the Golah party invokes the power of the Persian Empire in order to exclude this group (4:3). In 4:4, another group of adversaries, which may or may not be related to the first, acts to halt the building project. The environment in which the returnees find themselves is hostile. Opponents are all around. The narrative is unable or unwilling to identify them clearly, contributing to the portrayal of a chaotic and threatening situation. These adversaries in 4:4 are called "the people of the land" in the singular form of the expression that appeared earlier in 3:3.[14] The narrator of Ezra places great emphasis on external conflict. The mention of Cyrus and Darius in 4:5 points to the distant imperial power hanging over the confused and frightening social context in which the returnees find themselves. The returnees appear to be completely dependent upon this power for their sense of safety and survival.

It must be noted here that Ezra 4:5–6:19 appears in the Aramaic language within the Hebrew Bible. The potential reasons for this switch in language are many and complex. Within this section are a number of documents that would logically have been written originally in Aramaic, but this observation fails to explain entirely the switch to Aramaic, for two significant reasons. First, not only do these letters and decrees appear in Aramaic, but also the narrative material around them. Second, the writer of Ezra has already rendered in Hebrew at least one document, the Decree of Cyrus in 1:1-4, which would certainly have been originally in Aramaic. From a narrative perspective, this switch of language, regardless of other purposes, transports the reader into the world of Babylonian/Persian political power. Within the story, the Golah group must cooperate with Persian power in order to accomplish its purpose. In strikingly reflective fashion, the text must speak the language of empire if it is to come to the conclusion of the story.[15]

At Ezra 4:6, the narrative takes a complex turn. Ezra 4:6-23 presents the details of a lengthy conflict. The narrator reports the sending of three letters but includes the text of only the third letter. In each case, opponents of the Judahites in Palestine write the letter to the Persian king. Curiously, these letters come from a time after that of the temple building activity.[16] The report demonstrates a long record of antagonism on the part of the opponents, leading up to the time when the narrative was actually written. Why does the narrator include this material? The apparent answer is that it justifies the exclusion of these people from the returned community because of their repeated actions of opposition.[17] The argument of the text is somewhat illogical. In essence, it contends that these people deserved to be treated as adversaries because after the returnees treated them like adversaries (4:1-4), they acted like adversaries. This section reveals the attitude the narrator either wishes to impart to the audience or assumes the audience already shares. The narrator understands conflict to be inevitable. Oddly, the returned community that rebuilds the altar, begins offering sacrifices, and lays the temple foundations because of their fear of the surrounding population (3:3) ceases the building project because they are afraid of the neighboring people (4:4). Being the people of God is a tricky and dangerous proposition. Proper attention to purity and separation from other groups creates conflict, which threatens the restoration process. Yet, the progress of the restoration project offers the prospect of greater safety.

The narrator of Ezra brilliantly develops the way out of this dilemma in the story. The record of future tension between the returned community and the surrounding peoples assures the reader that compromising the purity of the community is not an option. The stalemate must ultimately be settled by imperial power. Of course, this threatens the understanding of God shared by the narrator and the audience. This tension is not completely resolved in the book of Ezra. The people of God are both restored by God and dependent upon Persian sponsorship. This is why the book of Ezra must begin with the Decree of Cyrus, which makes the daring claim that YHWH acts through the Persian king (1:1).[18] The narrative returns from the future, back to the present situation in 5:24.[19] The halting of the building of the temple in the days of Darius is analogous to the later problems encountered in the construction of the wall during the reign of Artaxerxes.

The building of the temple is taken up again in 5:1-2. This time the prophetic leadership of Haggai and Zechariah combines with the political and priestly leadership of Zerubbabel and Jeshua. The narrative does not note any actual progress in 5:1-2, only that they "set out to rebuild." At this point the Persian Empire officially enters the scene. The governor, Tattenai, inquires about the authority of the builders. In 5:5 a definite note of progress in the building does appear, and abruptly the scene shifts to the Persian court. Another letter is recorded in 5:6-17. This time the present building of the temple is in question. The narrator reports the confrontation in the form of a dialogue within the letter. That the response of the Golah group to the challenge of their adversaries (5:11-17) fills the bulk of the letter and describes their purpose in such detail reveals the function of this letter in the narrative. The letter serves to plead the case of the Golah group, both to Darius and to the reader. Perhaps most important, both are reminded that the desire of the Persian Empire, originally stated in the Decree of Cyrus (1:1-4), matches the divine plan. This view is emphasized further by the repetition, in somewhat different wording,[20] of the Decree of Cyrus in 6:1-5. The narrator treads a thin line here, struggling to give due credit to imperial power and to the divine will. As the temple-building episode moves toward an end, the point of view of the narrative becomes apparent. God's purpose for Israel is accomplished through the application of human power. In the past, that power had been Israel's own as a nation. In the narrative present of the book of Ezra, that power is the Persian Empire's.

With the external conflicts resolved through appeals to Darius, the story returns to issues of internal conflict. Two reports of sacrificial ritual conclude Ezra 6. First, the Golah group celebrates the dedication of the new temple with the ritual killing of 712 animals (6:17).[21] Israel is defined here as the ones who participate in this ritual and only the returnees are included (6:17). Second, the Passover is celebrated. According to 6:20, the lamb is killed for the Golah group, but in 6:21 others are admitted and share in the eating of the lamb. Those who now join the Golah group are required to separate themselves from "the nations of the land." The settling of internal conflict and maintenance of community boundaries is accomplished by ritual killing. The dedication sacrifice identifies the acceptable members of the community. The settling of external conflict is signaled by the reversion back to the Hebrew language at the end of the temple dedication. Persian involvement, reflected by the use of imperial language (Aramaic), is no longer necessary. With the temple community identified and stabilized, the inclusion of new members becomes possible, but must be accompanied by the shared ritual killing in the Passover celebration.[22]

Finally, in chapter 7, the character for whom the book is named appears. Ezra leads a new group out of Babylon to return to Jerusalem. This group is authorized by the same elements as the original group in Ezra 1. They go with the protection of imperial power (7:14) and funded by imperial wealth (7:15, 21-22). They carry holy vessels for use in temple worship in Jerusalem (7:19). Ezra 7:11-26 is a letter from Artaxerxes granting all of this imperial weight to the journey of Ezra and his companions. It is clearly reminiscent of the royal decrees and letters sprinkled throughout Ezra 1–6.

Two additional elements have been added here, however. First, the Ezra group takes with them money designated for the purchase of sacrificial animals. Second, the letter from Artaxerxes specifically endorses the "law of your God," the enforcement of which is to be backed by Persian imperial threat (7:25-26). These elements perform a variety of critical narrative functions.[23] Why does Ezra delay his return to Jerusalem? The original Golah group has been back in Judah for some time, struggling amid hardship and danger. The delay is explained as necessary for Ezra to prepare for the implementing of God's *torah* in Jerusalem (7:10). Once again, the purposes of the Persian Empire are one with God's will. Those who break God's law will be subject to death, banishment, or financial punishment. Once external conflicts are settled and community boundaries are set, internal conflict can be addressed, and the threat of violence is used internally to enforce adherence to community standards.

An additional problem stands in the way, however. The Golah group has been firmly established in Ezra 1–6, with the temple as its center. How can the members of the Ezra group become insiders? The answer to this question lies in the dynamics of Ezra 1–6. The Ezra group must follow this same pattern in order to be assimilated. Thus, in chapter 7, they travel from Babylon with full Persian sponsorship and bring implements of worship with them. Chapter 8 continues the process of identifying the Ezra group with the earlier group by carefully listing them (8:1-14), affirming the priestly credentials of some of the members (8:15-20), and exposing them to danger from external enemies (8:31-34). Their survival of this final hardship acts as a sign of God's blessing on their mission.

The status of the Ezra group members as legitimate returnees has been carefully established in Ezra 7–8. All that remains is the appropriate public signal of their acceptance. Ezra 8:35-36 portrays this event in brief but careful fashion. As in the Passover celebration in 6:19-22, sacrifice is required in order to incorporate new members into the group. Participation in sacrificial ritual signifies membership. Ezra 8:35 reports that the Golah group (literally, the sons of the Golah) offers an extensive sacrifice. The designation of those offering the sacrifice is sufficiently ambiguous. This text sits amid what is commonly labeled "The Ezra Memoir." Ezra speaks of himself and his group as "we" in vv. 31-34. Whether the ones offering the sacrifice in v. 35 include Ezra's group or just those who were already settled in Judah is appropriately difficult to determine. The two groups have been merged in a subtle manner.

The openings and closings of group boundaries in Ezra 6:19-22 and 8:34-35 present situations of great potential for conflict and danger. In both cases, this potential is resolved by the killing of surrogate victims as part of a sacrificial ritual.[24] Hanging over these processes of community formation at all times is the power of the Persian Empire and its blanket of protection. Ezra 8:35b appropriately closes the stories of inclusion with a note that the imperial officials approve the result.

At the beginning of Ezra 9, the person of Ezra is firmly established as an authority figure. His voice continues to tell us the story, and when a problem arises the officials come to him. Observing the story through the eyes of Ezra, the reader occupies a position of power with him.[25] An old and fearsome specter reappears in 9:1-4. The theme of "failure to separate themselves from the peoples of the lands" echoes back through Ezra 3:3, through the failures of the monarchy, through the condemnations in Judges 2:1-5, and to its point of origin in Deuteronomy 7. This is the failure that doomed the original nation of Israel to death before it even began. Little wonder that Ezra tears his clothes. He laments a past death and the possibility of another one in the future.

The death of an animal signals Ezra's shift from mourning to action. The first act he must perform is to bring God around to his way of thinking, so he prostrates himself in prayer.[26] It is easy to lose patience with Ezra here, and ultimately I will, but 9:12 reveals the core of his concern in such a way as to invite some sympathy.[27] Ezra's group is struggling to survive. The generosity of the Persian Empire (9:9) is not limitless. It can only support the survival and success of a limited number of people. Thus, the potential expansion of the group brings with it the threat of death (9:12).

Ezra's problem is that points of torah are in conflict. The kind of purity and separation demanded in Deuteronomy 7 does not fit easily with the generosity urged in Deuteronomy 10:17-19 and 24:17-22.[28] Promises of survival and threats of death are wedged into the religious language of covenant. The Persian Empire may sponsor the restoration of Israel, but God has brought it about by transferring God's own favor of the Israelites to the eyes of the Persian king (9:8-9). Nevertheless, only justice can maintain this favor (9:15), and the presence of God remains a deadly threat.

At the beginning of Ezra 10, the view of the reader is expanded. The text no longer speaks in the first person, and we see through the eyes of the narrator a crowd surrounding Ezra. Is Ezra aware of this audience? It is possible to read the rhetorical and homiletical nature of Ezra's prayer as an indication that he knows he has an audience and that he intends to persuade them.[29] It is now no longer only God whom Ezra has brought around to his way of thinking. It is the whole community. In the voice of Shecaniah (10:2), this crowd agrees with Ezra about the source of the problem and its remedy.[30] Survival requires a paring down of the community along ethnic lines. The agreement to put away foreign wives and children (10:3) will create a new group of widows and orphans who will be exposed to danger outside the community, but this is the perceived cost of survival. The completion of this process of separation would be difficult and painful. Ezra's resumption of mourning in 10:6 reveals that the accomplishment of his goal is by no means assured. To his posture of mourning he adds the act of fasting. Bringing all of the Golah community into line will require the exertion of power. The threat of economic deprivation and exclusion in 10:8-9 forces compliance. The message to the men of Judah and Benjamin is clear. They must send part of their families away destitute or they will all be sent away destitute. Of course, this is no simple course of action. It requires official actions of divorce, adjudication, and appeal.

The ultimate exposure of women and children to starvation and acts of brutality is an element of the story that the narrator chooses not to show the reader. The results of the mass divorce are presented to us in a list, thus ending the book of Ezra in a way similar to its beginning. A list served to determine community boundaries at the end of Ezra 1–2, and another list completes the process in Ezra 10. Again, the death of an animal (10:19) signals the successful reconfiguring of the community boundaries. The reader is left only to imagine the suffering and potential death of the abandoned women and children.

The story in the book of Ezra concludes without informing us whether this act of blame and exclusion improves Israel's fortunes. Ezra has taken the easy road of blaming and excluding the least powerful members of society. That the marginal are sacrificed for the sake of the survival of those at the center comes as no surprise, for this is the way of the world. Two hard questions remain. First, does the Bible commend such behavior by telling the story and by bringing God in to participate through the prayer of Ezra in 9:6-15? Second, if I were placed in Ezra's position, having to choose between the survival of some and the potential death of all, would I choose differently? How does my modern concern for inclusion interact with the ancient story? With these questions asked but unresolved, we move on to the book of Nehemiah, which will replay many of the issues raised in the book of Ezra.

NEHEMIAH: IN GREAT EVIL AND SHAME

The introduction to this chapter illustrated the parallel literary design of the twin books of Ezra and Nehemiah. Nehemiah 1–7 reports a building project like Ezra 1–6, but the commencement of Nehemiah's building project also serves to link the beginning of the book of Nehemiah with the end of the book of Ezra. The prayer of Nehemiah in 1:5-11 is not identical to the prayer of Ezra in Ezra 9:5-16, but the connections are considerable. The posture of mourning and act of fasting (Neh 1:4) present the same visual image of each of the two leaders.

While fear motivates the rebuilding of the altar and temple in Ezra 3, shame seems to motivate the rebuilding of the walls in Nehemiah (1:3). It seems odd that a temple would be built for safety and a wall for status. The reverse certainly seems more logical. This illogic, however, matches the narrative illogic already noted, that the temple is constructed before the walls. The books of Ezra and Nehemiah thus demonstrate a sense of consistency here, even if it is an odd one. Nehemiah's maneuverings, which succeed in transporting him back to Jerusalem with a royal mandate, are carefully bounded by identical evaluations of the city's condition. In 1:3, the representatives of the Golah group in Jerusalem travel back to Susa to report to Nehemiah that Jerusalem and its inhabitants are "in great evil and shame." After his midnight ride around the city in 2:11-16, Nehemiah speaks to the officials, and this same evaluation proceeds from his own mouth in 2:17. The highlight is the repetition of "evil" and "shame."[31] The community is in serious danger. The situation had been reported to Nehemiah and thus to the reader in 1:3. Both Nehemiah, the first person narrator, and the reader have now traveled to Jerusalem and confirm the evaluation firsthand, based upon the nocturnal tour on which he takes us.

Lists function in Ezra-Nehemiah to delineate community boundaries in times of trouble. The list of builders in Nehemiah 3 confirms the participation and inclusion of those listed. This list, however, serves another function in the narrative. It takes us on a tour of the wall, one full circuit, as it is being constructed.[32] This expanded view is accompanied by a diversion from the first person narration of Nehemiah.[33] Among the factors indicating the urgency of the building task is the participation of the daughters of Shallum (3:12). The sense of shame and threat imposed by the circuit ride around the broken wall in 2:11-16 is matched and balanced by this tour of the wall being rapidly rebuilt.

The plan to rebuild the walls creates immediate opposition (2:10, 19-20). The potential opponents come to the site, just as in Ezra 4. While in this case no offer to join the effort is made, such a possibility is rebuffed in Nehemiah 2:20 just as in Ezra 4:3. The actual beginning of the building in Nehemiah 3:33 causes the direct acts of opposition. This feature of the Nehemiah story is in close parallel to Ezra 4:4-5. In both stories, the building project that would bring security and stability becomes a threat, and the resolve of the Golah community is tested.

The passage following the construction tour is difficult for a number of reasons. First, the verses that appear as 4:1-6 in the English Bible are designated as 3:33-38 in the Hebrew Bible. Second, it is not clear who is narrating. Have we returned to the first person narration of Nehemiah or not? This latter ambiguity may function as part of a gradual move back to explicit first person narration in 4:6.

The beginning of Nehemiah 4 serves to continue the pattern of opposition and threat. At each step in the progress of rebuilding the wall, Sanballat and his companions have appeared as an obstacle. Sanballat's appearances at 2:10 and 2:19 are mirrored by those at 4:1 and 4:7.[34] The powerful prayer in 4:4 stands between these two references to opposition. Sanballat and his allies "hear" the Judahites building. Now the voice of this one praying[35] asks God to hear. The prayer asks God to "turn back their shame (see 1:3 and 2:17) upon their heads."

Nehemiah solves the problem by dividing his workers into groups of builders and guards. The image of armed workers watching constantly for potential attacks on the wall project reveals the paradox of their situation. To build a wall for protection, the Israelites must expose themselves to danger. The continuing success of the project is attributed to the help of God (4:14-15), but external threats still loom over it.

As chapter 5 begins, the narrator turns our gaze inward. External threat has been at least tentatively thwarted, but internal tension within the Restoration community persists. Difficult economic conditions threaten the lives of the lower classes. Some in the upper classes choose to take advantage of this situation. Some of the acts of economic oppression portrayed here are clearly condemned by the law (see Lev 25 and Deut 23). Nehemiah understands that this internal economic division exposes the community to external attack (5:9). With a threat of divine curse, Nehemiah puts a halt to the charging of interest and the taking of pledges. Further, he claims his own acts of generosity (5:10, 14-19) as an example of the kind of behavior that will keep the people united and safe.

The threat of danger continues to hang over the wall project as it nears completion. Nehemiah is able to dodge a final threat against his life or reputation in chapter 6. Shemaiah's warning comes in carefully veiled form. The Hebrew text arranges 6:10 as poetry, and it has a song-like quality. Verse 12 refers to this message as a "prophecy," albeit a false one, so the oracular form is fitting. Nehemiah determines that the goal is not to kill him or protect him from being killed, but to make him look bad, and he again invokes a divine curse upon his enemies in 6:14.

The wall is finally finished and the story of the building project is brought to completion with a list, which fills chapter 7. This list, nearly identical to the one in Ezra 2, draws a boundary around the citizens of Judah just as the wall surrounds Jerusalem. The two appearances of the list surround the two building projects, which bring the security of temple (center) and wall (boundary) to the endangered and beleaguered community in Jerusalem. As in the book of Ezra, the event of completion brings the appearance of the character named Ezra (Neh 8:1-12) and the celebration of a festival (8:13-18).

Chapter 9 recounts the perilous and painful story of Israel. Ezra reminds his readers of the times when God protected the Israelites from suffering and death (v. 9, v. 15, and v. 21), killed enemies on their behalf (v. 11 and v. 24), and punished them with death for their own iniquities (v. 27 and v. 30). With the threat of repeating this sinful and deadly past in full view, these Israelites sign their names to a new covenant with God. Those who sign are representatives. They are identified in 9:38 as "our officials, our Levites, and our priests." Thus, this list, like previous ones, also serves multiple functions.[36] Most significantly, it draws a boundary around these significant groups of leaders. The language of inclusion and exclusion continues in Nehemiah 10:28-31, which echoes Ezra 3:3, 6:21, and 9:2. Being the people of God in Ezra-Nehemiah's world requires separation from others and the placing of a curse on outsiders. Such actions are accepted as necessary to secure God's blessing and avoid destruction at God's hand. Previous death and destruction is recalled in the promise to keep the land Sabbath in Nehemiah 10:31. Second Chronicles 36:21 had identified this as the specific purpose of the death of the nation of Israel. The exile had been a forced observance of the accumulated land Sabbaths, which had been neglected. This group of Israelites will not risk such a death again, regardless of the cost.

With the covenant renewed, the book of Nehemiah enters again into a flurry of list making. Modern readers can hardly be expected to care about the details of such lists, but the significance of list making for the determination of community boundaries cannot be ignored. This activity in the text, and my discussion of it, may seem painstakingly repetitious, but the maintenance of community identity is an ongoing, repetitive task. In the world of Ezra-Nehemiah, those making such lists understand them as part of the task of survival in a perilous setting, like the building of the walls themselves. Lack of community identity is a deadly danger.

This perception of danger leads to the troubling ending of the book of Nehemiah. The final episode of the book of Ezra arose out of recognition that the drawing of a boundary was not enough to secure ethnic and cultic purity. There are also foreigners within the boundary that Nehemiah draws, and they must be rooted out. Again, the foreign wives are identified as the culprits. Amid a frenzy of social house-cleaning and enforcement of Sabbath law in Nehemiah 13, Nehemiah expels these foreign wives.[37] He brutally punishes the Jews who violated the prohibition against foreign marriage (13:25). The primary reason offered for this action is the expected claim concerning the danger of cultic impurity brought by this group. The foreign marriages of Solomon are recalled as an instructive example. Nehemiah maintains the presumption of Ezra, that all of Israel's difficulties, past, present, and future, are the fault of foreigners.[38]

Just as in the final episode of the book of Ezra, the narration of Nehemiah 13, which has returned to overt first person form, keeps the eye of the reader on the Judahite community. The continuing lives and ultimate fate of those not included in the lists all along and those who are expelled at the end are not brought into view.[39] Prayers are sprinkled into the final chapter, as they have been throughout Ezra-Nehemiah, in order to position God on the side of Nehemiah's cause.

REFLECTIONS

In the chronological line of the biblical narrative,[40] the end of the book of Nehemiah is the final word on Israel's story. The survival and presence of the Bible itself may be understood as a testimony to the success of the Ezra-Nehemiah program, but the Bible contains no statement describing such success. The reader is left hanging, wondering how to emerge from the world created by this book. Perhaps this tension, and the many tensions present in Ezra-Nehemiah, reflects the modern concern with community identity and survival. Part of the biblical assumption of scarcity[41] is the belief that survival depends upon some limitation of community. The modern need and desire for boundaries resonates with the biblical story in some ways. While attitudes about racial and ethnic purity may be shifting as the world shrinks, and as science overturns the assumptions behind our attitudes on these issues, a desire for geographical, political, and economic boundaries persists. Roderick Nash has written eloquently on the connection between modern American and ancient Israelite attitudes toward wilderness.[42] An unbounded world is perceived as dangerous in both settings. In modern America, this perception results in demands for more secure national borders and in the proliferation of gated communities. We are not certain whether to understand Nehemiah's wall building and list making as acts of courage or acts of fear. Is his establishment of Jerusalem a program of renewal or retrenchment?

The shrinking modern world brings questions about the role of culture into sharp relief. More and more, we are abandoning the seemingly noble notion of a "melting pot" of cultures because of its effect on identity. The survival of cultures, of ways of life, is now understood as a life and death issue for individual human beings. The deadly impact of loss of identity and purpose is revealed by the high rates of suicide in the Western world. Individuals make tragically destructive decisions as part of a search to belong to something. Charismatic leaders find this need to belong an easy target for manipulation. Ezra and Nehemiah play with these same fears and insecurities. We are left uncertain how to evaluate the positive and negative sides of this characteristic of human experience. There is nothing more fulfilling than belonging to a healthy community and nothing more devastating than being in an unhealthy one. Is the Jerusalem community described in the book of Ezra-Nehemiah healthy or unhealthy? In what ways should modern religious communities emulate the community in this book, and what features ought to be avoided?

Ezra-Nehemiah says something important about how we perceive outsiders. Caring for our needs for boundaries and belonging, even in healthy ways, creates a sense of "us and them." There are real threats in the world to our health and well-being. Survival requires attention to the borders and centers of our identity. Ezra-Nehemiah portrays for us the complex nature of this human task. If we do not always like the way that the characters named Ezra and Nehemiah and their followers perform, then this book is a call to do better.

NOTES

[1] From "The Pearl" on the Emmylou Harris album *Red Dirt Girl* (Nonesuch, 2000).

[2] Efforts to solve these problems fill many volumes and have been the primary focus of academic study of these two books.

[3] The arguments concerning the reversed chronology are best summarized by H. H. Rowley in "The Chronological Order of Ezra and Nehemiah," in *Ignace Goldziher Memorial Volume*, vol. 1, ed. D. S. Lowinger and S. Somogyi (Budapest: Globus, 1948), 127-40.

[4] Gordon F. Davies, *Ezra and Nehemiah*, Berit Olam (Collegeville MN: Liturgical Press, 1999).

[5] Lester Grabbe, *Ezra-Nehemiah* (New York: Routledge, 1998), 183-85. Grabbe is interested in an additional line of inquiry. The "discordant notes" in Ezra and Nehemiah create an avenue for comparing these books to the historical events that lie behind them. This issue occupies most of the second half of his book but is not of direct interest to the present study.

[6] For additional discussion of these elements, see Lester L. Grabbe, *Ezra-Nehemiah*, 94-99. Grabbe has argued that these features of the two books point to a unity of narrative composition, despite what he understands as the independent origin of the materials found in the two books.

[7] Of course, there has been significant historical-critical attention given to these Ezra and Nehemiah memoirs. For a well-developed review of this discussion, see Williamson, *Ezra-Nehemiah*, Word Biblical Commentary (Waco: Word, 1985), xxiv-xxxi.

[8] Meir Sternberg, *The Poetics of Biblical Narrative: Ideological Literature and the Drama of Reading* (Bloomington: Indiana University Press, 1987), 12-13, 86-87.

[9] A narrative approach to the list does not reveal all of the internal tension and conflict that diachronic approaches might. On these, see Wilhelm Rudolph, *Esra und Nehemiah* (Tübingen: J. C. B. Mohr, 1949), 19-20, and Daniel L. Smith, *The Religion of the Landless: The Social Context of the Babylonian Exile* (Bloomington IN: Meyer Stone, 1989), 106.

[10] This character is a good test case for narrative analysis. To what extent should historical investigation provide information about Persian governance, which the original readers would likely have known, to modern readers? How much historical inquiry should be allowed in the effort to identify characters, a literary concern?

[11] See Ernest W. Nicholson, "The Meaning of the Expression `m h'rts in the Old Testament," *JSS* 10 (1965): 66. In this definitive article, Nicholson concluded that the expression "people of the land" (`m h'rts) had "no fixed and rigid meaning, but is used in a purely general and fluid manner

and varies in meaning from context to context." Nicholson did not specifically address the plural expression "peoples of the lands" found here in Ezra 3:3.

[12] See, for example, Williamson, *Ezra-Nehemiah*, 48-49. Jacob M. Meyers offered the possibility that both the weeping and the shouting were responses of joy (*Ezra-Nehemiah: Introduction, Translation, and Notes*, AB [Garden City NY: Doubleday, 1965], 29).

[13] The use of sound as a narrative device has precedent in the Hebrew Bible. The most important example is probably 1 Samuel 4:5 where the shout of the Hebrew army at the arrival of the ark of the covenant carries the narrative to the Philistine camp. In that case, the sound of the shouting is related to a specific element of holy war, "the great shout," prescribed in Deuteronomy 7:23 and most powerfully demonstrated in Joshua 6:20. In Ezra, rather than transporting the reader, the shout pulls new characters, the adversaries, into the next scene. See my discussion of the use of this device in 1 Samuel 4 in Mark McEntire, *The Blood of Abel: The Violent Plot of the Hebrew Bible* (Macon GA: Mercer University Press, 1999), 81.

[14] See note 11.

[15] For a powerful discussion of the practice of language imposition as a tool of empire and its relation to the Tower of Babel story, see José Míguez Bonino, "Genesis 11:1-9: A Latin American Perspective," in *Return to Babel: Global Perspectives on the Bible*, ed. John Levison and Priscilla Pope-Levison (Louisville: Westminster John Knox, 1999), 13-16.

[16] This is another place where the tension between literary methods and historical methods arises. If the narrator and implied readers are unaware that the Persian kings to whom the letters are sent (Ahasueras and Artaxerxes) come after Darius (4:5), then there is confusion in the narrative that is revealed only by historical analysis. On the other hand, if both narrator and implied reader are aware of the order of the Persian kings, then the insertion of future material is a literary device of which modern readers ought to be conscious. I am assuming the latter explanation and, therefore, include awareness of this achronological nature of the text in this narrative study.

[17] See Williamson, *Ezra-Nehemiah*, 65.

[18] This perspective is shared by Isaiah 45:1, which calls Cyrus God's "anointed one" (messiah).

[19] Williamson refers to the literary device in 4:24 as a "resumptive repetition." Its purpose is to bring the reader back to the primary story line (*Ezra-Nehemiah*, 57).

[20] The second appearance of the decree is in the Aramaic section. It is, therefore, obviously different. Perhaps the reader, aware of the language change, is led to believe that this Aramaic version is the true original.

[21] Note the disparity between this number and the 142,000 animals slaughtered during the dedication of Solomon's temple in 2 Chronicles 7:4-5. For a discussion of the significance of these numbers, see Mark McEntire, *The Function of Sacrifice in Chronicles, Ezra, and Nehemiah* (New York: Mellen Biblical Press, 1993), 66-68. Judson R. Shaver has demonstrated that the Passover celebrations here in Ezra and in Chronicles combine the various legal traditions concerning Passover in the Torah. See *The Torah and the Chronicler's History Work: An Inquiry into the Chronicler's Reference to Laws, Festivals and Cultic Institutions in Relationship to Pentateuchal Legislation* (Atlanta: Scholars Press, 1989), 116-17.

[22] McEntire, *The Function of Sacrifice*, 68-72.

[23] For a discussion of the rhetorical aspects and resulting impact of Ezra 7, see Davies, *Ezra and Nehemiah*, 41-48.

[24]This understanding of the story being told in the book of Ezra is consistent with the sacrificial theory of Girard. For his summary, see *Violence and the Sacred*, trans. Patrick Gregory (Baltimore: Johns Hopkins University Press, 1977), 8. Girard elaborated on this basic understanding in much of the rest of this book.

[25] The apparent gap between Ezra 8 and 9 has been something of a problem. To what does "these things" in 9:1 refer? Should we read into this gap some of the events described in Nehemiah 8? See Williamson's discussion of this issue in *Ezra-Nehemiah*, 127-29. The first person form serves to link chapters 8 and 9, while chapter 10, which shifts back to third person, is closely linked thematically to chapter 9. Thus, the places where these chapter divisions appear are visible seams in the text rather than gaps. The resulting narrative garment becomes the focus of our attention rather than any scraps that may have been cut away.

[26] See Walter Brueggemann's discussion of "prayers of complaint" in *Theology of the Old Testament: Testimony, Dispute, Advocacy* (Minneapolis: Fortress, 1997), 219. Brueggemann contends that prayer formulas like those in Psalm 85:5 and 85:15 serve to "remind Yahweh [*sic*] of who Yahweh is." The goal here appears to be similar. This prayer seeks, at least, to remind YHWH of who Ezra thinks YHWH is.

[27] On issues of exclusion and power dynamics, see Mark McEntire, "Letters in Stories and Stories in Letters: An Intertextual Exploration of Ezra 4–5 and Galatians 1–2," *Perspectives in Religious Studies* 27 (Fall 2000): 249-61.

[28] On the role of creativity as opposed to legalistic rigidity in Ezra's solution, see Johanna W. H. van Wijk-Bos, *Ezra, Nehemiah, and Esther* (Louisville: Westminster, 1998), 45-46.

[29] See Blenkinsopp, *Ezra-Nehemiah* (Lousiville: Westminster, 1991), 181-85, and Mark Throntveit, *Ezra-Nehemiah* (Louisville: Westminster, 1992), 48-58. Blenkinsopp has noted that the effect of weeping in drawing a crowd at 10:1 reflects this same effect in 3:13–4:1 (188). On this occasion the crowd is sympathetic rather than adversarial.

[30] For further discussion of this issue, see van Wijk-Bos, *Ezra, Nehemiah, and Esther*, 43-44. Van Wijk-Bos has correctly noticed that Shecaniah uses the wrong designation for these women. According to standard biblical practice, they should be characterized as "strangers" or "sojourners," not "foreigners (44). Ezra later adopts the same terminology as Shecaniah (46).

[31] The standard Hebrew word for "evil" used here could easily be translated in smoother ways, such as "difficulty" or "trouble." I utilize this more awkward translation to emphasize the potential theological nature of this evaluation. The word I translate as "shame" might also be rendered as "reproach" or "disgrace." Note the inexplicable choice by the NRSV to use "shame" in 1:3 and "disgrace" in 2:17, thus disguising this important verbal connection. The ancient social categories of honor and shame have begun to receive attention in the field of biblical studies. For an introduction to the role of honor and shame in Israel's relationship with YHWH, see Saul M. Olyan, "Honor, Shame, and Covenant Relations in Ancient Israel," *JBL* 115 (Summer 1996): 201-18.

[32] For a discussion of the details and difficulties involved in the list, see Blenkinsopp, *Ezra-Nehemiah*, 227-42.

[33] Whether this passage refers to Nehemiah in the third person is a matter of dispute. The reference to "their lord(s)" in 3:5 is ambiguous and may or may not refer to Nehemiah. See Williamson, *Ezra-Nehemiah*, 201.

[34] Williamson, *Ezra-Nehemiah*, 215-17.

[35] There is no narrative introduction to this prayer. It suddenly interrupts the insults of Tobiah the Ammonite. It may be the voice of Nehemiah, but there is no indication.

[36] Davies, *Ezra and Nehemiah*, 111.

[37] For a thoughtful critique of Nehemiah's ideology and actions, see van Wijk-Bos, *Ezra, Nehemiah, and Esther*, 94-98.

[38] Davies argues that these acts of separation are reminiscent of Genesis and are necessary for defining God's people. Thus, they are not subject to claims of racism and genocide (*Ezra-Nehemiah*, 128-29). More difficult questions, however, must be raised about the power dynamic present in these two different worlds.

[39] On this aspect of the story, see Grabbe, *Ezra-Nehemiah*, 196-97.

[40] Of course, this statement excludes the additional books that are part of some biblical canons.

[41] On the relationship between the concept of scarcity and the issue of foreigners in the Bible, see Regina Schwartz, *The Curse of Cain: The Violent Legacy of Monotheism* (Chicago: University of Chicago Press, 1997), 83-91.

[42] Roderick Nash, *Wilderness and the American Mind*, 3rd ed. (New Haven: Yale University Press, 1982), 8-43.

Matthew:
Not Peace but a Sword

Hell's brewin', dark sun's on the rise.
This storm will blow through by and by.
House is on fire, viper's in the grass.
A little revenge and this too shall pass.
This too shall pass, I'm gonna pray.
Right now, all I got's this lonesome day

It's all right . . .

Better ask questions before you shoot.
Deceit and betrayal's bitter fruit.
It's hard to swallow, come time to pay.
That taste on your tongue don't easily slip away.
Let kingdom come, I'm gonna find my way
Through this lonesome day
Lonesome day . . . .

—Bruce Springsteen[1]

THE NARRATIVE SHAPE OF MATTHEW

For most readers an ideal narrative approach to any of the Gospels is difficult, if not impossible. Imbedded in the minds of most Bible readers or hearers is a harmonized gospel that cannot be suppressed without great effort. Luke's stable Nativity scene in a December churchyard looks somewhat empty unless Matthew's Magi are present. It is startling how consistently unaware ordinary readers are that many literary units appear in only one or two of the four Gospels. Specialists in biblical studies are also hindered in their attempts to read the individual Gospels as complete narratives. So attuned have we become to the parallel passages in the other Gospels that comparisons and judgments about redactional concerns are a knee-jerk reactions. If ordinary readers have their narrative view blocked by a preformed harmony of the Gospels, then "expert" readers have theirs obscured by the disharmony of the Gospels. Nevertheless, both groups, with some awareness and practice, can make reasonable headway in this effort to read an individual Gospel as a story.

The Gospels offer an initial challenge to the mode of reading proposed in this volume. A fair sampling of biblical books would seem to demand their inclusion, but which and how many should be included? For reasons best kept secret until the proper time in this chapter, I have chosen to explore the Gospel according to Matthew as a narrative world.

Narrative criticism of Matthew, and the Gospels in general, has been the object of intensifying efforts over the last quarter-century. The beginning of this process was the work of Jack Dean Kingsbury. Kingsbury began by taking on a formidable foe, the influential Bacon hypothesis concerning the structure of Matthew.[2] Benjamin Bacon proposed, a half-century ago, that the Gospel of Matthew is built on a framework provided by its five major discourses. Kingsbury effectively argued that Bacon's structure gave inadequate place to key elements of the Gospel, specifically the birth and death of Jesus. In addition, Bacon and his followers appeared to be trying too hard to read Matthew as a new Pentateuch and, therefore, had failed to read the first Gospel on its own terms.[3] Kingsbury proceeded to offer his own structure for Matthew's Gospel based primarily on the narrative transitions in 4:17 and 16:21.[4] He described this narrative structure in a more detailed and deliberate fashion in his later work.[5]

More recently, F. J. Matera and Warren Carter have adopted the narrative theory of Seymour Chatman as a means of understanding Matthew's plot structure. Chatman proposed that plot is an organization of events based on varying degrees of importance. He is perhaps best known for the categories he called kernels and satellites. Kernels are the major events on which the plot turns and from which the overall story receives its shape. The confirming test is that these units cannot be removed without disrupting the plot. Satellites are less important events placed around the kernels to fill out the story. A kernel and its associated satellites form a "narrative block," which is then a major component of the story as a whole.[6] Of course, there is no unanimity concerning the identification of kernels.[7] This method has both the strength and the weakness of allowing each reader to determine which events merit the status of "kernel." Matera and Carter agree that there are six kernels, forming six narrative blocks in Matthew. They disagree significantly on the identification of the kernels and the precise boundaries of each of the blocks. Surprisingly, neither interpreter chose the crucifixion as a kernel, and only Carter chose the resurrection.[8] They seem not to have escaped the influence of Bacon entirely. I will not be operating with a precise ranking of events according to their importance or centrality. The general concept of narrative blocks is helpful and has led to a better picture of Matthew's structure, but a precise application of this model has led at least two excellent interpreters to the indirect conclusion that removing the crucifixion from the Gospel of Matthew would not "destroy the narrative logic"[9] of the book.

Blocks are a rather clunky image that need to be supplemented by an understanding of literary structure that focuses on threads running through the Gospel. In this respect, the recent work of Janice Capel Anderson is most helpful. She has highlighted the use of verbal repetition in the Gospel of Matthew and the role such repetitions play in the operation of the narrative.[10] Many previous interpreters have called attention to Matthew's repeated use of formulas and other elements, but Anderson has provided a thorough cataloging and analysis of all types of verbal repetition.[11] She has also argued persuasively against the structural schemes of Bacon, Kingsbury, and Lohr[12] because their work has not given adequate attention to "internal structural devices" and the role they play in the plot of the Gospel.[13]

In addition to the enlightening conclusions produced by the recent narrative analyses discussed above, productive proposals concerning the role of the reader in the Gospel of Matthew have begun to appear, particularly in the work of Carter and Anderson. Carter focused on the ways in which the reader recognizes and responds to the "narrative conventions" of the narrator.[14] By the use of certain literary devices, the narrator attempts to guide the reader to desired conclusions. Of course, this requires what Carter and others have called "a competent reader." Following the foundational works of Wolfgang Iser and Umberto Eco,[15] Carter has emphasized the need for the reader to "fill in the gaps" left by the text.[16] Eco has demonstrated that not only does a text assume a competent reader, but it also plays a role in creating such a reader.[17] It was Iser who coined the phrase "implied reader," emphasizing the ability of the text to establish the reader's role and to maintain some control over the reading process.[18] Iser's view of the reader's role in a narrative informs our understanding of the operation of a narrative world. The potential world may exist in the text, but it is the reader's job to "animate the meaning of the text as a reality."[19] Anderson has illustrated, more specifically, the need for the reader of Matthew to recognize repetitive cues and draw the appropriate connections.[20] Her image of Matthew as a "narrative web" is a poignant one.[21] The interaction of text and reader and debates about the amount of control each might exert are highlighted by this image. Through the use of many literary techniques, including repetition, Matthew does weave a web that becomes a narrative world. At the same time, by the intuitive reception and overt recognition of these techniques, the reader assists in the spinning of the web. At the risk of pushing this metaphor too far, I will end this discussion of narrative criticism of the Gospel of Matthew with a pair of questions: Who might get caught in this web? And what is the ultimate fate of those who do?

RACHEL WEEPS FOR HER CHILDREN

The Gospel of Matthew has a distinctive beginning. The beautifully structured genealogy may in fact be the reason it was chosen as the first Gospel in the New Testament. The full story of Israel, from Abraham to the moment of Jesus' birth, is established as the literary framework of the Gospel. It thus opens up the narrative world of the rest of the story. The obviously stylized succession of three fourteen-generation periods creates what at first appears to be a deliberate, well-planned foundation. At the same time, the genealogy is disrupted by the unexpected appearance of five women.[22] Because women are not typically mentioned in genealogies, the reader's attention is captured by the mention of Tamar, Rahab, Ruth, Bathsheba (named only as "the wife of Uriah the Hittite"), and Mary. For those who know the traditions of Israel, the female lineage of Jesus is shocking—prostitute, prostitute, foreigner, adulteress, unwed pregnant teenager. For those who already know the story of Jesus, however, the shock is reassuring. God's purpose was accomplished in the past through these scandalous women. If so, then God's purpose can be accomplished through the little boy that the neighbors must have known as Mary's bastard child.

The disruptive elements of the genealogy point forward to the disruptive impact of Jesus' birth. The scandalous pregnancy threatens to destroy Mary's life (1:19-21). The impact is softened first by Joseph's character. He decides to reject her privately rather than publicly. It is only his faithful response to a dream that keeps the holy family from being torn asunder. This Joseph follows the example of the first great dreamer of the Bible, Joseph son of Rachel and Jacob. The next threat is from Herod. The birth of Jesus has caught the attention of the world,[23] as the Magi indicate, and Herod's fearful response brings death to Bethlehem. The slaughter of the innocents (1:16-18) is the most horrifying passage in the Gospels, and it is one of the major reasons I have chosen to explore Matthew here. Matthew is the only Gospel that records this savage act. In stark contrast to the joyful singing in Luke's infancy narrative, Matthew knows that when God's presence comes into the world (1:22-23), the result is terror, disruption, violence, and death. The writer of Matthew deftly leads the reader into this frightening world. The life of the Immanuel child is spared by divine intervention, but it is altered as Joseph's third and final dream-warning directs the family to Galilee to avoid further threat (2:22). The childhood of Matthew's Jesus is shaped in response to human violence. The childhood of some of those around him is ended. The steady drumbeat of the fulfillment citations,[24] the most apparent narrative thread running through Matthew, ties this event into the fabric of God's purpose.[25] Margaret Davies has emphasized the pattern of suffering as "the prelude to God's deliverance," which is well established in Israel's tradition and is played out one more time here.[26]

In Matthew 3, the narrator moves immediately to Jesus' adulthood. He is introduced by John the Baptizer, and the wild-eyed desert prophet knows how violent and disruptive will be the clash between God's presence and the human world. John's image of the "thresh and burn" Jesus (3:12) is juxtaposed with the calm, obedient Jesus coming to be baptized and the peaceful, heavenly image of the descending dove. The Gospel of Matthew has established a pattern of portraying a calm surface with events flowing in a steady direction, periodically disrupted by a roiling, bloody undercurrent. This reveals a major weakness of structural schemes like Bacon's, which focus almost exclusively on the placid, catechetical surface of the Gospel. A continuing test of any narrative approach will be its ability to take account of the echoes of violence, disruption, and danger in Matthew.[27]

Jesus' emergence from the safety of Galilee into John's world of confrontation is short-lived. The Herodian threat still lurks. Again, only a passing mention in 4:12 informs us that Jesus' return to Galilee and his settling in Capernaum are the results of John's arrest by Herod Antipas. The life of Jesus is further shaped by the threat of violence. The Galilean ministry brings relief to that troubled region. The afflictions of the people there are catalogued in 4:24, and Jesus quickly becomes famous as one who delivers people from the ravages of the natural and supernatural worlds.

The response to the healing miracles of Matthew 4 sets up the Sermon on the Mount. For those who look to Jesus as a promoter of nonviolence, the sermon is the centerpiece. Readers who have followed Jesus to this point are struck by the stark contrasts in Jesus' teachings, from boundless blessings for the downtrodden (5:1-11) to the harsh demands of discipleship (5:20, 48; 7:13-14, 19, 23). It is difficult to understand 5:38-41 as advocating anything other than absolute pacifism. The sermon takes for granted that those who follow Jesus will live in a world of persecution (5:11-12), assault (5:39), and inequity (5:45).

When Jesus comes down off the mountain after the sermon, he and his followers begin to encounter the conflicts that he has largely avoided to this point. At first Jesus is victorious over the violent forces of the world. He calms the sea (8:23-27) and subdues the demoniacs who "were so fierce that no one could pass" them (8:28-34). The Gadarene crowd is perhaps the first to glimpse the coming storm that Jesus himself will bring. They beg him to leave. He has upset their world and the distinctions that have defined their lives, and they are rightly afraid.[28] The calming presence of Jesus and the disruptive intrusion of the kingdom of heaven tend to arrive in tandem.

Matthew 9 brings Jesus into direct conflict with the religious leaders of Galilee. He usurps authority (9:3-4), eats with the wrong groups of people (9:10-13), behaves contrary to expectations (9:14-17), and openly displays his supernatural power (9:32-34). Our narrator looks inside the mind of Jesus and tells us his motivation. Jesus understands the dangerous nature of the world and has compassion for ordinary people who have no means to withstand it (9:36). But the power of those in authority is dependent upon their ability to harass the helpless sheep, and so Jesus' actions create opposition. It is then not surprising that when Jesus begins to instruct his followers in Matthew 10 to go out and minister to the world in the same way he has been ministering, he gives this warning: "Do not think that I have come to bring peace to the earth; I have not come to bring peace, but a sword. For I have come to set a man against his father, and a daughter against her mother, and a daughter-in-law against her mother-in-law;[29] and one's foes will be members of one's own household" (10:34-36, NRSV).

The Gospel of Matthew takes a significant turn here. As Jesus begins to encounter resistance and opposition, his statements about violence become frequent. He hints at violent judgment for those who do not accept the preaching of his followers (10: 15) and predicts the harsh persecution of the church in the future (10:16-23). The Missionary Discourse in Matthew 10 ends with a promise of reward to those who cooperate with the mission of Jesus and his disciples (10:40-42), but the risks are high, and as the passage quoted above indicates, the ultimate result is the rending of the societal fabric right down to the level of the family.[30]

Beginning in chapter 11, the opposition faced by Jesus and his followers becomes more severe.[31] Surprisingly, potential opposition comes from within. John the Baptist sends his disciples to Jesus, questioning Jesus' messianic credentials (11:3). Jesus' reply in 11:4-6 first makes clear that he has come to heal the world of all its wounds. At the same time, Jesus acknowledges that this kind of ministry threatens to create division. He heals the breach between himself and John by emphasizing the continuity between their tasks, but his compliments of John lead to the most revealing statement in the Gospel about the disruptive effects of the coming of the kingdom. In 11:12 Jesus says, "From the days of John the Baptist until now, the kingdom of heaven has been suffering violence, and violent ones plunder it." The translation of this verse is notoriously difficult, and much depends on uncertain decisions.[32] It is possible to construe the verse in a much different way, such as "From the days of John the Baptist until now, the kingdom of heaven has been coming forcefully,[33] and forceful ones take hold[34] of it."

The most thorough treatment of these difficulties has been that of Peter Scott Cameron. Cameron is more concerned with establishing the original form of the saying, using both the parallel in Luke 16:16 and a hypothetically reconstructed Semitic version. Though Cameron's methods are out of line with a narrative approach, his results may still be instructive. According to Cameron, Matthew has shaped and placed the saying in 11:12 to apply it specifically to Herod Antipas's treatment of John the Baptist.[35] Such an interpretation could plausibly be reached by a narrative analysis. Nevertheless, this is a classic case of translators and interpreters mysteriously assuming that the grammatical ambiguities they see in the text would have been completely lost on the writer. In light of the disruptive results of Jesus' missionary program in chapter 10 and the surrounding stories of the imprisonment and execution of John, the second rendering above seems particularly unlikely as an unambiguous meaning. The Missionary Discourse reveals that the kingdom of heaven comes violently ("I have not come to bring peace, but a sword," 10:34) and that it suffers violence ("When they persecute you in this town, run to the next one," 10:23). A collision of kingdoms is in process in Matthew's Gospel, and those addressed by Jesus must choose sides. If they choose to follow the way of the kingdom of heaven, then they will go forth into the world with a powerful message, but they may likely suffer John's fate, an early death.[36]

Matthew 11:12 proves to be a decisive turning point, for Jesus' message to his wider audience changes. In 11:20-24 he pronounces judgment and condemnation on whole cities because they have rejected his message. Conflicts with religious authorities that had been relatively mild and infrequent become stronger and almost constant as they clash with Jesus over Sabbath law (12:1-14), the source of his authority over demons (12:22-32), and proof of his identity (12:38-42). This series of conflicts ends when Jesus declares that his own familial relationships have been disrupted and reformed (12:54-58). A realignment is taking place and it begins with Jesus. Matthew 13 contains the Parable Discourse of Jesus in which he produces a series of portraits of the kingdom—sower, wheat and weeds, mustard seed, yeast, treasure, pearl, net. Garland has noted that the two scenes involving Jesus' family bracket this discourse.[37] Life in the kingdom requires the redrawing of lines of allegiance. The life-giving and protective resources of family must be abandoned, exposing the follower of Jesus to the dangers of the world.

Kingsbury, and others analyzing the Gospel of Matthew from a narrative perspective, are correct to see a major division at 16:21 as Jesus turns his attention toward Jerusalem. Matthew has placed the great confession of Peter in a powerful position at the end of the section leading up to this point. When Jesus questions his disciples in 16:13-16 about how they and the crowds understand Jesus' identity, Peter speaks up and declares his belief that Jesus is the Messiah. The result of this declaration is Jesus' description of the church's future. It will continue to clash with its opponents, in this case "the gates of Hades" (16:18), but it will be empowered by Jesus to withstand the challenge. As Jesus turns toward Jerusalem in 16:21, it is fitting that his first words are a prediction of his coming passion. Just as violent people seized John and killed him, they will also seize and kill Jesus when he arrives in Jerusalem for the final confrontation (16:21).

The journey to Jerusalem in Matthew 16–20 focuses on Jesus' interaction with his disciples. The dominant theme is the seeking of status and position. Jesus seems to contribute to the notion of a hierarchy among his disciples by taking only Peter, James, and John up to the Mount of Transfiguration. Fault lines develop among the followers of Jesus (18:1), and this is reflected in future conflicts within the church, which Jesus addresses (18:15-20). The disciples begin to jockey for position in the coming kingdom, an activity to which Jesus supplies a repeated and consistent response. Two parables, the unmerciful servant in 18:23-35 and the laborers in the vineyard, illustrate that the economic principles by which earthly kingdoms operate are not the way of the kingdom of heaven. But some of the ways of earthly kingdoms persist. In the former parable, the servant's unwillingness to follow the example set by the king results in his being tortured (18:34). In the latter parable, the generosity of the landowner causes grumbling among those with a greater sense of entitlement, and they are unable to enjoy the benefits of their labor.[38] No violent punishment is prescribed, but neither is the conflict fully settled.

The poignant story of the rich young man falls between these two parables. The meaning of this story is elusive. At the very least it declares that wealth will not insure position in the kingdom of heaven. In fact it may preclude it. At the end of this story, Jesus' response to the struggle among his followers for status and position is crystallized in the saying "the first will be last and the last first" (19:30). The saying is repeated in reverse in 20:16 and its echo appears in 20:27 after the request of James and John and the angry response of the other ten disciples. The goal of Jesus' followers should be to put themselves last, and the ultimate result of such an act matches the final fate of Jesus, to die a violent and untimely death (20:28).

HIS BLOOD BE ON US

As we enter Matthew's passion narrative, beginning in chapter 21, a vital critical issue comes to the surface. Modern narrative theory, when applied to ancient texts, struggles with the tension between original audience and modern audience. To what extent must a modern reader identify with Matthew's late-first-century community in order to enter Matthew's narrative world with the proper sensory equipment? Iser's implied reader and what many other theorists have labeled a "competent" reader are attempts to ease this tension. A host of questions persists, however. The text itself certainly provides cues that help define what an adequate reader should know and understand, but is this enough? Should the competent, modern reader be aware of the growing conflict between nascent Christianity and first-century Judaism that may have affected this evangelist's community?[39] Is there adequate information in the text to point the reader toward this understanding, or is external information necessary to bring about proper awareness? Has our understanding of this conflict reached a level of sufficient clarity that it merits a role in the reader's preunderstanding? Does such a presupposition have significant impact on how readers perceive Matthew's harsh anti-Jewish polemic?

As a literary method, narrative criticism is concerned with matters "in front of" the text. The historical conditions that gave rise to the text and other matters "behind" the text are often considered off-limits. Certainly, external information should be brought to the reading, but should it only be that which is clearly indicated by the text? For example, the abundance of geographical designations in the Gospels obviously prompts the modern reader to consult a map of first-century Palestine in order to understand the movements of Jesus. It is a harder question to determine whether the criticism of Judaism in the Gospel of Matthew prompts the reader to explore the state of Jewish-Christian relations at the time the Gospel was written. The abundance of misguided interpretation of Matthew's anti-Jewish statements throughout history and their tragic results lead me to the tentative assumption that a competent reader needs some understanding of the first-century context of these statements in order to read properly.[40]

Firm and specific conclusions about the state of church-synagogue relations at the time the Gospel of Matthew was written are not achievable. A likely general picture, however, can be developed with reasonable certainty. The Gospel itself contains ample references to a strained relationship. Note particularly the references to "their synagogues" in 4:23, 9:35, 10:17, 12:9, and 13:54. Other sources from this era indicate a decision to expel certain heretics from the synagogues.[41] Tension almost certainly existed between Christian Jews in Matthew's community and other Jews in the synagogues. At the very least, enough information is available to say this: Anti-Jewish statements in the Gospel of Matthew were written and originally read in the context of a minority group that perceived itself to be persecuted by a larger group. When the power dynamics are reversed, as they soon were and have remained during most of the succeeding 2,000 years, and a Christian majority applied these sayings uncritically to their understanding of the Jewish minority, the results were brutal and tragic. In light of this, it appears that modern readers of the Gospel of Matthew need to remain critically aware of how these texts potentially inform their perspective of current Jewish-Christian relations.[42]

The gathering storm of tension and conflict Jesus has brought to Galilee and to the lives of his followers strikes Jerusalem with a fury on the Sunday before Passover. When Jesus rides into the city, accompanied by song and a great procession, Matthew tells us that "the whole city was stirred." The entry into Jerusalem is no small, marginal event, but is seismic in its proportions. The arrival of Jesus is to Jerusalem what the great shout of the Old Testament holy war tradition was to the cities of ancient Canaan. The metaphorical earthquake provides the context for the most overt act of violence on Jesus' part in all of the Gospel. The destructive aspect of the clearing of the temple should not be overplayed, however.[43] True to Matthew's pattern, the disruption is pushed back beneath the surface. Jesus remains in the temple to heal the blind and the lame and to teach. His dispute with the temple authorities in 21:15-16 is relatively mild, considering the implications of the children worshiping him in the temple.

The violent nature of Jesus' actions in the temple requires that his apparent condemnation be understood carefully. The popular understanding of the prophetic quotation in 21:13 is that Jesus is specifically condemning the money-changing and dove-selling businesses because they extort money from the religious pilgrims coming into Jerusalem for Passover. Those who were sitting at the tables Jesus has just overturned are robbers. It may have been the case that these merchants were gouging their customers, but such an understanding of Jesus' rebuke is true neither to his statement itself nor to the prophetic contexts from which it is drawn. The first half of the statement, "My house shall be called a house of prayer," is part of Isaiah 56:7. This entire verse and its surrounding context specifically state that the sacrificial cult is a legitimate accompaniment to prayer. The second half, "but you have made it a den of robbers," is taken from Jeremiah 7:11. The acts specifically condemned in this context are not acts being committed in the temple itself. The lists in Jeremiah 7:6-9 include oppression of orphans and widows, stealing, murder, adultery, and idol worship. Most significant is the simple fact that robbers do not rob in their "den." They rob outside the den and then come to it in order to hide. The acts condemned by Jesus, therefore, cannot be those conducted in the temple itself, but those conducted on the outside. This view of the temple as a true "den" has been aptly expressed by Garland. The temple has, in Jesus' view, become "a sanctuary for religious knaves who believe that they can find automatic absolution from sin and fellowship with God through the sacrificial cultus."[44] One result of this understanding is that it does not single out religious authorities or the merchants for condemnation, but includes all of those present in the temple. There are no innocent bystanders in a "den of robbers."

The next act of Jesus is easily passed over by most readers, but may cause even greater difficulty for a few. In 21:18-19 Jesus curses and kills a fig tree for not bearing any fruit. Such an act of violence against a plant may seem a trivial matter, but the complete innocence of this living organism raises questions. Matthew does not include any overt reference to this being the wrong season for figs,[45] but it is reasonable to assume that a competent reader would know that fig trees in Palestine do not bear fruit around the time of Passover. Two observations may be of significance. First, the world of Matthew is one in which modern environmental sensitivities may not operate. That the fig tree is used as a prop to make a point, literally by the character Jesus and figuratively by the writer of Matthew, may have raised no difficulty at all for the Gospel's original readers. Second, the disruptive results of the coming of the kingdom in Matthew affect the innocent and the guilty. Jesus' explanation in 21:21 describes an extremely destructive act as a sign of faith. The coming of the kingdom is not to be an altogether pleasant experience. The destructive and deadly nature of the kingdom of God will be a repeated refrain in the teachings of Jesus during his final week in Jerusalem.

The next few days, depicted in 21:18–25:46, are filled with themes of conflict and reward and punishment. Garland has aptly described the feel of

Matthew 24–25 as a "dark mood of judgment."[46] This mood may begin even earlier for some readers. It is hard to mistake the image of Judaism rejecting Jesus and being replaced by the church. Jesus' earlier statement to his disciples, in 19:28, specifically claims that they will take over the seats of the twelve sons of Jacob. The parables of Jesus in this section are closer to detailed allegories than to the snapshots of the kingdom that are most common earlier in the Gospel. The first parable in this section, the two sons in 21:28-30, establishes a pattern of dividing people into groups. Jesus himself provides an interpretation of this parable by identifying his listeners, the chief priests, elders, and people in the temple with the dishonest second son and the tax collectors and prostitutes with the repentant first son.

The parable of the two sons is followed by the much more menacing parable of the wicked tenants. For Matthew's readers, who should surely be expected to be aware of the vineyard tradition of Isaiah 5, it is easy to associate the landowner with God. The parable tells a violent story of assault and murder. With a question, Jesus dupes his listeners into pronouncing their own destructive fate in 21:41. Their realization of this causes them to want Jesus arrested. In the parables that follow, the wedding banquet (22:1-14), the bridesmaids (25:1-13), the talents (25:14-30), and the sheep and goats (25:31-46), there is always an accepted group and a rejected group. The eternal punishment of the latter is always emphasized and serves to intensify the "dark mood."

Amid these parables stands the painful and complex chapter 23. This chapter contains Jesus' most virulent and sustained attack on the Judaism of his day. It consists primarily of the seven woes against the scribes and Pharisees. English translations of the Bible tend to divide the paragraphs so that the seven-woe sequence is apparent. The NRSV, for example, places all of the "woe to you" phrases, except for the second one in 23:25, at the beginning of a new paragraph. Matthew's penchant for repeating patterns is obvious. Jesus introduces the woe sequence with a description of the scribes and Pharisees that highlights their authoritarian leadership style and desire for the trappings of power. Alongside this description, Jesus projects a vision for the community of his own followers in 23:8-12. This vision eschews hierarchy and grasping for power and instead promotes humble service within an egalitarian social context. With these two models of community life laid out as a backdrop, Jesus launches into a withering assault on hypocrisy and reliance on the outward forms of religion. The language is harsh and the sequence builds toward the final woe, which stands out from the others because of its greater length. The seventh woe addresses the bloody confrontation of the past (23:34-35) and the looming, deadly clash that is to come.

Jesus concludes with a lamenting condemnation of Jerusalem at the end of the woe section.

Matthew 24 is a more specific description of the destruction of Jerusalem and the temple. This is "us-and-them" language at its most intense level. The condemnations and predictions of Matthew 23–24 divide the world into two clearly identified groups, the faithful and the unfaithful.[47] Jesus' faithful followers will not escape the immediate suffering caused by the coming storm. They will be tortured and killed (24:9), tempted (24:10), pursued (24:15-16), and confused (24:23-26). The hope that Jesus offers to those who remain in the faithful group comes only as a result of endurance (24:13) and steadfast labor (24:46). The parables surrounding these predictions illustrate the eschatological nature of their reward.

The world of Jesus' final week in Jerusalem is frightful and troubling. Jesus enters verbal war with his opponents and predicts the outbreak of a physical war after his death. He acknowledges a long line of victims in the past, from Abel to Zechariah (23:35). As a new phase of physical conflict looms, Jesus stands in line to be its first victim. The fate of his followers hangs in the balance. They are promised no safe and easy way, but are encouraged to remain steadfast in their faith by the promise of ultimate reward and, more problematically, the threat of eternal punishment.

In Matthew 26, events begin to accelerate. Jesus finishes his teaching and predicts not only his death, but the specific manner in which he will die (26:1-2). The temple officials plot his arrest and execution. An unnamed woman comes to Jesus in Bethany and anoints him for burial (26:6-13). Finally, Judas conspires with the chief priests so that Jesus might be arrested secretly and, thus, the stage is set for the crucifixion.

At the Last Supper, Jesus tells his disciples that they will desert him (26:31), but assures them of his resurrection and his faithful presence with them (26:32-33). The poetic fragment from Zechariah 13:7, introduced by a fulfillment citation, mitigates the guilt of the disciples. Not only has their desertion been foretold, but they are in some small way also victims of the efforts to kill Jesus. A process of increasing isolation begins here. In the anointing scene at Bethany, Jesus is with a larger group of followers. At the Last Supper he is with the twelve. In Gethsemane he leaves the twelve behind, taking only Peter, James, and John further along with him (26:37). Finally, he separates from them and is alone (26:39-42). The parallels between this sequence of separation and that leading up to Jacob's wrestling match in Genesis 32 are intriguing. Jesus has his own wrestling to do. Matthew makes no attempt to hide Jesus' human emotions. He is "grieved and agitated" (26:37). When he seeks companionship, twice he finds his disciples sleeping (26:40, 45).

The scene of Jesus' arrest is easy to picture in gentle terms. It opens with the kiss of Judas and ends with the willing submission of Jesus, but in the middle lies an armed confrontation ready to explode. A large crowd with swords and clubs accompanies Judas to arrest Jesus. Violent ones have come to take hold of him, fulfilling his statement in 11:12 just as the death of John the Baptist had. Is it a surprise to the reader that at least one of Jesus' disciples is armed with a sword? Jesus' saying about the sword in 10:34 is metaphorical in nature. There has been no direct indication in the Gospel of Matthew that the disciples carry weapons,[48] and so the sudden outburst of violence is startling. Just as surprising, however, is the suddenness with which it ends. If there is a large, armed crowd present, one would expect them to pounce on the unnamed disciple immediately when he strikes the high priest's slave. Jesus is able to halt the conflict, though, and he condemns the violent nature of his arrest in 26:55. He is prepared to go with them and understands that he must in order to fulfill the Scriptures. Again, a fulfillment citation in 26:56 serves to bring order. It orders the text by closing the arrest scene and the story within it as Jesus makes a reference to fulfillment in 26:54. In a sharp reversal of 10:34, to this situation Jesus brings not a sword but peace. Matthew makes clear that the arrest and conviction of Jesus is not at all what Judas expected. Whether he expected armed resistance and a revolt is impossible to say. Matthew 27:3-5 only tells us that he regretted what did happen to Jesus so much that he killed himself. Modern English translations are divided on whether to treat the Greek word used here as repentance or remorse, but either indicates that what happened did not meet his expectation. Jesus' submission continues as he refuses to defend himself against the charges in 27:11-14. Instead he obeys his own admonitions from the Sermon on the Mount (5:12, 39) and does not resist. The more submissive he becomes, however, the more intense the opposition against him grows. Matthew draws a striking contrast between Jesus and the angry mob that wants him dead. The crowd's actions become riotous before Jesus is finally sent to be crucified.

The crucifixion scene in Matthew is violent, of course. Jesus is stripped, beaten, and fitted with a crown of thorns. Jesus is utterly alone. Even the two crucified with him abuse him verbally.[49] Jesus is again tempted with the potential to overcome his killers with power. The passersby raise this possibility in 27:39-43. Jesus remains silent. In Matthew, as in Mark, Jesus speaks only one sentence from the cross, the cry of dereliction in 27:46. "My God, my God, Why have you forsaken me?" is the first line of Psalm 22. There are two schools of thought concerning this saying. Some, along with whoever named this saying the "cry of dereliction," understand this as a painful expression of Jesus' feelings of forsakenness at the moment. Others understand it as a reference to the whole of Psalm 22, which, in the manner of most lament psalms, proceeds through complaint to a statement of faith at the end. Either reading is possible.[50] We cannot know the extent to which Matthew's implied reader would be expected to know this psalm and how it ends.

The seismic effect of the triumphal entry is repeated at the moment of Jesus' death. Heaven and earth are ripped apart. On the curtain in the temple was painted a picture of the heavens. It is torn in two, and the rocks forming the earth are split in 27:50-51. In Matthew, the beginning of God's victory over death cannot wait for three days, but the resurrection begins immediately with the raising of the saints in 27:52. The rending of the earth is repeated again at the moment of Jesus' resurrection in 28:2. There is no need for the twelve legions of angels to which Jesus referred in 26:53. One angel is enough to overcome the guard and free Jesus from the tomb. Matthew 28:4 tells us cryptically that the guards "became like dead ones" at the appearance of the angel, but 28:11 assures us that they recovered. In Matthew the resurrection is a violent cataclysm, but it is not destructive. Order is restored to the scene as Jesus calms and reassures Mary and Mary at the tomb. Matthew comes to an end in orderly fashion as Jesus commissions his followers to a threefold task of making disciples, baptizing them, and teaching them, assuring them of his eternal presence.

REFLECTIONS

Our entry into the world of Matthew has revealed a pattern of orderliness disrupted by outbursts of conflict and violence.[51] This takes place both within the plot of the story and in the literary structure of the book.[52] Jesus enters into the world to fulfill or complete a long story. Matthew reminds the reader of that story using a carefully ordered genealogy. Those who know the Hebrew Bible well, however, know that the story is not so well ordered. The disruptions in the genealogy are reminders of that story's disruptive elements. Matthew promises God's presence at the beginning (1:23) and end (28:20) of the Gospel, but this presence does not insure peace. When Jesus is born, a king is threatened and children are murdered. When Jesus' ministry progresses, it begins to divide his family, as it will the families of his followers. Jesus encounters increasing conflict with political and religious leaders. As the climactic moment of his death approaches, his teaching becomes increasingly dark and frightening.

The same paradox confronts modern followers of Jesus. The gospel has the power to bring both life and death. Faith may be rewarded in some situations and may provide a calm, serene surface to life. For others it brings great danger. The challenge to those who wish to follow Jesus is how to live up to the ideals of the Gospel of Matthew in such a dangerous world. The Sermon on the Mount urges pacifism and love of enemy, but how does one start living in such a way when every day we live and move under a blanket of protection provided by a military threat of destruction and a law enforcement threat of punishment?

It is a striking coincidence how the last days of Jesus' life reflect a common, modern experience of death. The progressively isolating sequence of home to hospital to intensive care unit makes death for many a lonely experience. The added elements in Jesus' death are that he dies young and by physical violence at the hands of other human beings. The Gospel of Matthew seems uncertain how to handle this death. Hamerton-Kelly's analysis of the Gospel of Mark is appropriate to apply here. The "cry of dereliction" is Jesus' only word from the cross in each of the first two Gospels. How are we to understand the cry, "My God, my God, why have you forsaken me?" For Hamerton-Kelly, this is Jesus' refusal simply to be absorbed into the process of his death, his refusal to become a sacred hero.[53] This tension is easily removed in Luke with Jesus' saying, "Father, forgive them; for they do not know what they are doing" (Luke 23:34). This saying, however, is not in Matthew.[54] The presence of this verse in the reader's memory threatens to turn Matthew's Jesus into a compliant victim. Such a comfortable, stock character removes the powerful tension with which Matthew challenges its readers to struggle. Again, Hamerton-Kelly's description of Mark applies to some extent to Matthew. "The Gospel achieves a critical advance beyond sacred violence by certain elements in the plot that prevent it from becoming just another violent circle."[55] This effect is muted in Matthew, however, because of the frequent understanding of 27:25 as an invitation to vengeance. The difficulty of this verse gets at the heart of the challenge of reading Matthew. The way of the world is vengeance, but the way of Jesus is not. Jesus tells his followers to turn the other cheek (5:39). Jesus declares that his blood is shed for forgiveness (26:28). The cry of the crowd in 27:25, "Let his blood be on us and our children," can be understood as a blessing as easily as a curse. The reality of reading is that this is the reader's choice. The final word of Jesus on the sword is "put it away" (26:52). Yet Jesus' presence in the world is itself a sword (10:34). He did not come to bring peace, but he blesses the peacemakers (5:9). Live with that.

NOTES

[1] From "Lonesome Day" on the album *The Rising* (Sony, 2002).

[2] Benjamin Bacon, *Studies in Matthew* (New York: Holt, 1930), 143-261.

[3] Jack Dean Kingsbury, *Matthew: Structure, Christology, Kingdom* (Philadelphia: Fortress, 1975), 1-7.

[4] Ibid., 7-39.

[5] Kingsbury, *Matthew as Story* (Philadelphia: Fortress, 1986). In this study, Kingsbury was obviously influenced by the rapidly emerging body of narrative criticism of the Gospels, particularly the early work of David Rhoads and Donald Michie on Mark (*Mark as Story: An Introduction to the Narrative of a Gospel* [Philadelphia: Fortress, 1982]) and R. Alan Culpepper on John (*The Anatomy of the Fourth Gospel: A Study in Literary Design* [Philadelphia: Fortress, 1983]).

[6] Seymour Chatman, *Story and Discourse* (Ithaca: Cornell University Press, 1978), 53-56.

[7] Chatman himself demonstrated a sense of overconfidence in his method when he stated that the reader ". . . can see how easily a consensus is reached about which are the kernels and which are the satellites of a given story" (ibid., 56). This has not been the case with attempts to apply Chatman's model to the Gospel of Matthew.

[8] See Warren Carter, "Kernels and Narrative Blocks: The Structure of Matthew's Gospel," *CBQ* 54 (1992): 465-75; and F. J. Matera, "The Plot of Matthew's Gospel," *CBQ* 49 (1987): 233-53. Omission of the resurrection and crucifixion points to one of the pitfalls of precise schemes. Matera and Carter seem to assume that kernels are almost always at or near the beginning of a block. Carter's six-block structure would be more acceptable if the crucifixion replaced the entry into Jerusalem as the kernel of the fifth block. This block would then stand out in Matthew as the longest, the only one with the kernel at the end, and the most important.

[9] This phrase is taken from Chatman's definition of a kernel (see *Story and Discourse*, 53). Both Matera and Carter make direct use of this definition (see Carter, "Kernels and Narrative Blocks," 469, and Matera, "The Plot of Matthew's Gospel," 237-39).

[10] See Janice Capel Anderson, *Matthew's Narrative Web: Over, and Over, and Over Again* (Sheffield: Sheffield Academic Press, 1994), 43-44. See especially her list here of the seven general functions of repetition in narrative.

[11] Anderson, *Matthew's Narrative Web*; see the lists of repetitions up to eight words long (pp. 226-40) and a separate list of those nine words and longer (pp. 241-42).

[12] I have not included a discussion of Lohr's work here because it is not an explicitly narrative analysis. His attempt to define Matthew as a "giant chiasm" has had significant influence. As is typical of such grand schemes, many of its smaller components are astutely observed and described, even if the whole is not entirely convincing (C. H. Lohr, "Oral Techniques in the Gospel of Matthew," *CBQ* 23 [1961]: 403-35).

[13] Anderson, *Matthew's Narrative Web*, 134-41.

[14] See Carter, *Matthew: Soryteller, Interpreter, Evangelist* (Peabody MA: Hendrickson, 1996).

[15] See Wolfgang Iser, *The Act of Reading: A Theory of Aesthetic Response* (Baltimore: Johns Hopkins University Press, 1979); and Umberto Eco, *The Role of the Reader* (Bloomington: Indiana University Press, 1979).

[16] Carter, *Matthew*, 106-12. See especially his application of Eco's seven audience tasks to Matthew 8:1-2. Margaret Davies, in light of Iser's theory, has listed "the major conventions and

strategies by which the Gospel according to Matthew guides readers' responses" (see *Matthew* [Sheffield: JSOT Press, 1993], 17-28).

[17] Eco, *The Role of the Reader*, 7-8. See Eco's detailed description of the kinds of interactive tasks a reader performs (pp. 14-23).

[18] Iser, *The Act of Reading*, 28.

[19] Ibid., 125.

[20] See Anderson, *Matthew's Narrative Web*, 38-43.

[21] Ibid., 43-45.

[22] Anderson has pointed to the use of a repetitive pattern as a way of drawing attention to the women whose appearance is unexpected. The pattern in the way the women are mentioned, e.g., "by Rahab," is then broken when Mary appears in the phrase "Joseph the husband of Mary." This singles out Mary among the five women in the genealogy (*Matthew's Narrative Web*, 50).

[23] David E. Garland, *Reading Matthew: A Literary and Theological Commentary on the First Gospel* (New York: Crossroads, 1993), 16.

[24] These are quotations from the prophetic literature introduced by phrases such as "This happened in order to fulfill the word of the prophet...." The first one appears in 1:22-23. The Gospel of Matthew contains twelve of these, a number fraught with significance, of course. These sayings form the most noticeable thread that holds together the narrative of this Gospel.

[25] Along with the quotation from Jeremiah, the numerous parallels between Matthew 2 and the story of Moses in Exodus also serve this function. These parallels have been noted in many places. For a description of their narrative function, see Carter, *Matthew: Storyteller, Interpreter, Evangelist*, 204-205.

[26] See Davies, *Matthew*, 38. Again, the Jeremiah reference and the Moses allusions call attention to this pattern.

[27] Carter has given attention to the disruptive aspects of Jesus' life and teachings in Matthew and the tensions they create for the reader (*Matthew: Storyteller, Interpreter, Evangelist*, 261).

[28] Girard has applied his hermeneutical model to this text in a stimulating manner in *The Scapegoat*, trans. Yvonne Freccero (Baltimore: Johns Hopkins University Press, 1986), 69. The neighbors are troubled by the healing because the demoniac was the bearer of the whole town's collective madness. His insanity defined and preserved their sanity.

[29] This third pair is a rather strange inclusion for several reasons. It does not depict a close, biological relationship like the previous two and it lacks the expected parallel concerning son-in-law and father-in-law. In fact, it depicts a relationship that many expect to be contentious and seems to disrupt the logic of the statement. Could it be that Matthew's Jesus acknowledges that the greatest illustration of familial loyalty in Israelite tradition is Ruth's love for Naomi? Ruth's prior appearance in the genealogy of Matthew 1 makes this a tantalizing possibility.

[30] For Walter Wink, the family is an integral part of the "Domination System" Jesus intends to overthrow. Therefore, its disruption is necessary and it will fight back (*Engaging the Powers: Discernment and Resistance in a World of Domination* [Minneapolis: Fortress, 1992], 118-19).

[31] Garland, *Reading Matthew*, 45.

[32] For an overview of the difficulties and possibilities, see Donald A. Hagner, *Matthew 1–13*, WBC (Waco: Word, 1993), 306-307. For a far more extensive discussion, see Peter Scott Cameron,

Violence and the Kingdom: The Interpretation of Matthew 11:12 (Frankfurt am Main: Peter Lang, 1984).

[33] The difficulty of translating this verb is that in biblical Greek the forms known as middle and passive look exactly the same. The first translation of 11:12 above reflects a passive rendering and the second a middle (reflexive) understanding.

[34] Those arguing for a positive understanding of this final clause see it as a description of decisive discipleship. Margaret Davies has proposed a mixed translation, using the more middle form ("coming forcefully") of the first verb and the negative sense of reciprocal violence against the kingdom in the final clause (see *Matthew*, 89).

[35] Cameron, *Violence and the Kingdom*, 214-45.

[36] See Garland's argument that this is a warning to the disciples about future opposition (*Reading Matthew*, 128).

[37] Garland, *Reading Matthew*, 143.

[38] Justin K. Ukpong has called into question this fairly standard interpretation into serious question. See his "Reading with a Community of Ordinary Readers," in *Biblical Hermeneutics in Africa: Towards the 21st Century*, ed. Mary Getui, T. Maluleke, and Justin Ukpong (Nairobi: Acton Press, 2001), 188-212. Ukpong has contended that the landowner cannot be considered truly generous because he takes advantage of the most vulnerable in society and sets them against each other with his feigned generosity. If the last are to be first in the kingdom, according to the repeated statement that frames this parable, then it must be the poor in the story who speak the truth. If Ukpong's reading is correct, the parable still demonstrates that the kingdom disrupts accepted economic practices. The persisting element of the story would differ, though. Instead of the grumbling of the workers, it would be the manipulative, self-serving statements of the landowner.

[39] For a discussion of all the issues related to this problem, see Hagner, *Matthew 1–13*, lxviii-lxxv.

[40] Adding to the difficulty is the fairly obvious observation that this issue is much more subjective in nature than matters such as geography

[41] See the discussion in Hagner *Matthew 1–13*, lxviii. Hagner rightly dismisses any detailed conclusions drawn from potential relationships between the writing of the Gospel of Matthew and the decisions of the Council of Javneh. The dates of each are too uncertain to establish a chronology, and little is known about the council.

[42] Attempts to apply the hermeneutic of René Girard to the New Testament have been fruitful but have given rise to some difficulties. Chief among them is the seemingly inevitable identification of Pharasaic Judaism as the representation of Girard's "primitive sacred." Hamerton-Kelly has confronted this problem in the conclusion of his Girardian reading of the Pauline literature (see *Sacred Violence: Paul's Hermeneutic of the Cross* [Minneapolis: Fortress, 1992], 183-88). Hamerton-Kelly strained to show that the Judaism described in the New Testament only exemplifies the primitive sacred, as do many other religious realities. It does not embody the primitive sacred in its entirety. Hamerton-Kelly was largely successful in constructing this argument and is certainly correct that attempts to avoid this identification entirely diminish the conflict in a way that does not treat New Testament texts honestly. He goes on to accuse the church, in its second-century zeal to replace Israel, of exemplifying the primitive sacred itself (p. 187). A Girardian reading, therefore, need not be specifically anti-Semitic, though it has a definite potential to move in that direction.

[43] This is one of the places where our internalized "harmony" of the Gospels most threatens to distort our reading of Matthew's story. It is difficult to read Matthew 21:12-13 and not picture the

Jesus of John 2:13-22 with a whip in his hand. Matthew's portrayal is violent, to be sure, but not so much as John's.

[44] Garland, *Reading Matthew*, 212. I first became aware of this interpretive issue some years earlier when I was a student in David Garland's New Testament classes.

[45] Mark 11:13 does make this statement, and experienced readers of the Gospels can hardly help but recall it in this context.

[46] Garland, *Reading Matthew*, 240.

[47] Carter has argued that the death of Jesus in Matthew serves the purpose of "uniting Jews and Gentiles as the people of God" (*Matthew*, 222-23). This is difficult to see. Carter's focus at this point is the parables of Matthew 21–22. Some positive sense may be inferred from the simple fact that Jesus takes the time to teach in the temple. The dividing lines are not precisely Jewish/Gentile, but rather Church/Synagogue. Of course, there are Jews among the followers of Jesus, as there were in the church that was Matthew's original audience, but division dominates Matthew's passion narrative and those condemned are always Jews.

[48] For those familiar with the Gospel traditions, Luke 22:38 may come to mind. During Luke's passion narrative, the disciples indicate that there are two swords among them. This is hardly an arsenal, and the meaning of this exchange between Jesus and his disciples in the third Gospel is unclear. Most important here is the recognition that there is no parallel to this verse in Matthew.

[49] Luke's "good thief" surely enters the mind of experienced readers of the Gospel, but he is absent from Matthew's narration.

[50] For a fuller discussion of the alternatives and history of interpretation, see Hagner, *Matthew 14–28*, 844-45.

[51] That conflict is the key to the first Gospel is the conclusion of a growing number of commentators. For example, see Eugene Boring, "Matthew," in *The New Interpreter's Bible*, vol. 8 (Nashville: Abingdon, 1995), 115; Mark Allen Powell, "The Plots and Subplots of Matthew's Gospel," *JNS* 38 (1992): 187-204; and Kingsbury, *Matthew as Story*.

[52] The idea that the literary structure of a work and its meaning reflect each other is not new. James Muilenburg has best expressed it in his statements about the inseparability of form and content ("Form Criticism and Beyond," *JBL* 88 [1969)]: 1-18).

[53] Robert G. Hamerton-Kelly, *The Gospel and the Sacred: Poetics of Violence in Mark* (Minneapolis: Fortress, 1994), 123-24.

[54] It is also absent from some early manuscripts of Luke.

[55] Hamerton-Kelly, *The Gospel and the Sacred*, 123-24.

The Acts of the Apostles: Those Who Were Scattered

Old pirates yes they rob I
Sold I to the merchant ships
Minutes after they took I from the
Bottomless pit
But my hand was made strong
By the hand of the almighty
We forward in this generation triumphantly
All I ever had is songs of freedom
Won't you help to sing these songs of freedom
Cause all I ever had redemption songs, redemption songs

—Bob Marley[1]

THE NARRATIVE SHAPE OF ACTS

Any attempt to formulate a literary design for this book must contend with its relationship to the Gospel of Luke. The prologues of these two books, in Luke 1:1-4 and Acts 1:1-5, link them closely together, and this connection has been a factor in the interpretation of the book of Acts for most of its history. Distinct parallels have been drawn between the two books in terms of literary structure. At the same time, most readers recognize that Luke and Acts are different kinds of books. The tension between the likeness of these two books and the uniqueness of each will play a major role in describing the shape of Acts.[2]

A second major factor influencing a narrative appraisal of Acts is that this book provides, by far, the best source of information about the church during the first century. Historical interests in primitive Christianity have often dominated interpretation of the book of Acts.[3] For example, the book provides something of a chronology of the pastoral career of the Apostle Paul. Information about Paul is also found in bits and pieces in his epistles. The effort to draw connections and identify difficulties between these two sources of information about Paul has been the focus of much scholarly energy. Study of the book of Acts as a literary work has often been eclipsed by such concerns.

The transmission of the text of Acts provides some difficulty for any interpretive approach, narrative approaches included. There are two major textual traditions of Acts, which differ significantly enough to alter the narrative character of the book.[4] These two major traditions are commonly referred to as the Western text and the Alexandrian text. Because the Western text of Acts has many additions that make it a longer version, the Alexandrian text is considered by a majority of scholars to be the best witness to the book of Acts in its earliest form.[5] The reading of Acts presented here accepts that majority opinion and will follow the Western text of the book of Acts, as do the major English translations. At the same time, this is an appropriate point to acknowledge that a different version of a biblical book exists that might yield somewhat different interpretive results. It has been argued by some interpreters, for example, that the Western text is significantly more anti-Jewish than the Alexandrian text that is interpreted here.[6] A few specific illustrations of this effect will be presented at appropriate points below.

The presentation of characters undoubtedly plays a significant role in the literary development of Acts. The two major characters are Peter and Paul, and it is hard to miss the seismic shift from the former to the latter in the book. This issue intersects the discussion of the parallel character of Luke and Acts, because when parallel events appear in the two books, Peter is the character whose actions match those of Jesus in Acts 1–12, while Paul is the mirror image of Jesus in Acts 13–28.[7] Nevertheless, as Fitzmeyer has noted, the Peter and Paul sections overlap significantly.[8] This shift in the significance of characters is one of many major literary features in the book, but not the single decisive one.

Almost all interpreters of Acts have noticed the significance of the geographical progression presented in 1:8. Just before his ascension, Jesus says to his followers, "But you will receive power when the Holy Spirit has come upon you, and you will be my witnesses in Jerusalem, and all Judea, and Samaria, and unto the end of the earth." This progression is matched by the movement of the book as a whole and acknowledged at key turning points in the book at 8:5, 13:1, 15:35, 21:1, and 27:1.[9] Fitzmeyer has used these markers and the geographical scheme they follow to produce a seven-part outline for the book of Acts. With chapter 1 serving as a prologue, six narrative movements are established by the five markers listed above. Frank Stagg, taking a cue from the observation that Acts ends with an adverb, which he translated "unhinderedly," argued for an understanding of the book that emphasizes the ability of the gospel to break through barriers in a pattern of outward movement.[10]

AFTER HIS SUFFERING

One of the major challenges the book of Acts faces is the continuation of the gospel story beyond the crucifixion, death, and resurrection of Jesus. We have seen in the examination of some Old Testament books that the death of a major character often provides closure for the book. The Gospels in the New Testament follow this pattern to varying degrees. Of course, the resurrection provides a new twist to the story. We have also seen major characters like Moses, Joshua, and David make brief appearances in the next book to play a role in a new beginning. The death of Jesus provided his followers with their first major theological challenge. Acts 1:6 shows them still struggling with the question of a restoration of an earthly Israelite kingdom. While the resurrection temporarily delays Jesus' ultimate departure, the ascension comes quickly in Acts. The book seems to be in a hurry to establish the ascension as a beginning rather than an end.

If the story is to progress, the apostles must reach a new understanding of the death of Jesus as an event that is part of God's way of salvation. Likewise, the Twelve must be able to carry on this work, which means that they must also be able to face death.[11] Two important events take place at the end of Acts 1 that confirm and support this shift. First, the death of Judas provides a sense of God's retribution and a warning to those who might waver in their resolve.[12] Second, Peter's emergence as the leader of the Twelve fulfills Jesus' command in Luke 22:32 to "strengthen your brothers" in the times of threat that lie ahead.[13]

Acts 2:1-13 begins the fulfillment of the programmatic statement in 1:8 by telling the story of the coming of the Holy Spirit among the apostles, commonly known as Pentecost. In the wake of this event, the first stage of the church's ministry, centered in Jerusalem, is recounted in 2:14–8:3. The apostles quickly prove themselves able to continue Jesus' ministry by preaching, healing, and standing up to religious and civil authorities, risking imprisonment and death. Significant patterns of repetition within this part of Acts serve to highlight major issues. Most noticeable are the episodes of opposition in 4:1-22, 5:17-22, and 6:8–7:60. The first opposition faced by this young movement appears in 4:1-3 when the temple authorities arrest Peter and John as a result of their preaching and healing. At this point, the persecution of the church is mild. Peter and John are imprisoned overnight and released the next day with a warning to stop preaching (4:18). The prayer of the believers in 4:23-30 after the release of Peter and John explicitly connects the current experience of the apostles with the opposition faced by Jesus in Jerusalem. The prayer for boldness results in an experience reminiscent of the Pentecost event in v. 31.

The description of the church's sharing of possessions in 4:32-37 points backwards to a similar description in 2:43-47. At the same time, it introduces one of the most mysterious and troubling passages in Acts, the episode concerning Ananias and Sapphira. In 4:32-37 Barnabas sells a field and lays the proceeds "at the apostles' feet." This sets the stage for the story of Ananias and Sapphira. Clearly, we do not have enough information about the sociology of the early church to understand this bizarre event fully.[14] Connections to the Achan episode in Joshua 7 are apparent and are frequently discussed by commentators. This connection may reveal part of the significance of this text in Acts, but it still leaves many questions unanswered. Along with the upcoming story of the deprived Hellenist widows in 6:1-7, the Ananias and Sapphira story shows that there is also internal conflict within the church.[15] This appears to be a story about apostolic authority and the rigorous demands of membership in the Christian community. The most difficult question is whether devotion to this community and its cause ought to be motivated by fear of death. Unfortunately, we are unable to penetrate to the core of the story. Ananias and Sapphira may have been murdered by the apostles, who believed they were executing God's judgment. The direct cause of death goes entirely unmentioned. The point of the story is the indirect cause. "They put the Spirit of the Lord to the test" (5:9). Their deaths recall the death of Judas in Acts 1. In both cases, Satan is attributed with an attempt to destroy the unity of the church. Ananias and Sapphira are the opposite of Barnabas. The communal spirit that holds the church together is threatened by their actions. As in the case of Judas's betrayal and death, the obedience and authority of the apostles, particularly Peter, overcomes this threat. Reimer has argued that this text is not so much about punishment as it is about the deadly threat of sin. The Christian community is still subject to the terror of sin, and only absolute unity of spirit can combat it.[16]

A number of repetitions have already been observed in the early chapters of the book of Acts, and a larger pattern is beginning to emerge. The Jerusalem phase of the church's expansion falls into three similar cycles of action. These three sections, 1:12–4:23, 4:24–5:42, and 6:1–8:4, all lead to episodes of conflict between the church and the Jerusalem authorities. A number of interpreters have noticed that the conflicts and their results intensify in this progression.[17] Peter and John are only imprisoned overnight and warned in 4:13-22. In 5:33-42, the council wants to kill Peter and John, but, on the advice of Gemaliel, they beat them and warn them again. The climax comes in the final episode of conflict in

Acts 7 when Stephen is martyred. Other matching episodes, such as the healing stories (3:1-10 and 5:12-16), the dual reports about sharing of possessions (2:43-47 and 4:32-37), and the two dramatic prayer meetings (2:1-13 and 4:23-31), also serve to link these cycles of action together.

The role of the stoning of Stephen in the book of Acts is remarkable. This character has just been introduced in 6:5 as one of the leaders within the Hellenist faction of the Jerusalem church. The book of Acts shows little interest in the deaths of the apostles. It reports the death of only one of the Jerusalem leaders, James the brother of John, in 12:2. Even this report of an execution seems to be of little significance in its own right, but it helps set up the story of the death of Herod. Thus, Acts 7 stands alone as the only significant story of martyrdom in the whole book. The presence of this story of execution is partially explained by the pattern of intensification of persecution in Jerusalem described above, but where could such a directional pattern be leading? The answer to this question appears in 7:58–8:1 when Saul is introduced as a participant in the execution of Stephen. Stephen, therefore, becomes not only a martyr in first century Jerusalem, but a martyr within the book of Acts. He is killed in order to introduce the one who will become the most important character in the book. Thus, the destructive, painful side of growth and change is first revealed here and will become a prominent theme throughout the book of Acts. Within his speech, Stephen condemns his Jewish audience for murdering the prophets and Jesus (7:52). In the story surrounding his speech, Stephen is subsequently executed in the same way. For a brief moment, Stephen is the character in Acts who is a parallel to Jesus, as his sayings at the point of death in 7:59-60 reflect those of Jesus in Luke 23:34-36.[18] The book of Acts is approaching its critical nexus, where death and expansion come together, and the narrator must kill Stephen as the first step in this process. The Twelve are being moved into the background, but kept alive because they still have a role to play, even if it is mostly a silent one.

The persecution surrounding the execution of Stephen breaks the boundary that allows for the expansion of the church into Judea and Samaria in 8:1b-5. The growth pattern emerges in the story that introduces Stephen in 6:1-6. Key texts that emphasize "spread," "increase," or "advance" of the church appear in 6:1, 6:7, 9:31, and 12:24.[19] Along with the death of Stephen and the introduction of Paul, the section of Acts marked off by this expansion theme also includes the story of the death of Herod, the report of the execution of James, and the imprisonment of Peter. Death, expansion, and the shift of attention to Paul are themes that the book of Acts carefully intertwines in these pivotal chapters of the book (6–12). They ultimately clear the way for the commissioning of Paul and

Barnabas in 13:1-3.[20] A look at the parallel developments in Luke and Acts reveals that this is the point in Acts when Peter ceases to mirror Luke's Jesus and Paul takes over this role.[21]

The strangest element of Acts 6–12 is the report of the death of Herod. The person portrayed here is apparently the ruler known more precisely as Herod Agrippa I.[22] Herod is brought into the Acts narrative in 12:1-5, using the report of the execution of James and imprisonment of Peter. His death is reported in a bizarre and difficult scene in 12:20-23.[23] This text reports a conflict between Herod and the people of Tyre and Sidon. The people request a meeting with Herod and he agrees. At the meeting the people shout a saying implying the divinity of Herod. The narrator then reports that because Herod accepts glory that is due only to God, he is struck dead. Allen has labeled this a "death of tyrant type-scene" that fulfills a number of purposes.[24] Herod's failure to give glory to God is in contrast to the church's faithful recognition of God, and God's power over the tyrants of the world is portrayed.[25] More to the point, Herod's death provides an important transition. James, one of the Twelve to whom leadership of the church has passed from Jesus, is killed, making way for the transition of leadership to Paul.[26] The death of Herod parallels the death of Judas in Acts 1. The actions of each opponent, followed by his death, point the way to new leadership. Judas's death in Acts 1 shifted focus from Jesus to the Twelve, and Herod's death in Acts 12 shifts the story from the Twelve to Paul.[27] The Jerusalem apostles are retained in the background of the story, but their role has shifted, in Tannehill's words, from "initiator" to "verifier."[28] They will be used to verify the ministry of Paul in Acts 15.

In Acts 13 the gospel begins to approach its next boundary, one that will not be crossed without significant threats to the church's existence. As the ministry of Paul comes into view and he becomes the great apostle, conflict abounds within the developing story. Paul's power is immediately displayed in 13:4-12 as the one who was struck blind now has the ability to strike someone else, a magician named Bar-Jesus, blind. Paul's lengthy speech at the synagogue in Pisidian Antioch (13:17-41) points both backwards and forwards in the text of Acts. In many ways it is reminiscent of Peter's Pentecost speech in 2:14-36 and Stephen's speech in 7:2-53, but there are significant differences.[29] Like Stephen's speech, it is rejected by its Jewish audience. It is also the first of three long speeches given by Paul in Acts 13–20, which provide much of the shape of this portion of the book.[30] The reaction to Paul's speech here produces the first clear picture of the divide between Jews and Gentiles in the emerging church. The movement from a Jewish to a Gentile focus is repeated in a threefold pattern in Acts 13–14.[31]

Paul's declaration in 13:46 that the Jewish rejection of his message will cause him to turn to the Gentile audience begs the question of what will be the continuing role of the Jewish members of the early church. As mentioned earlier, the Jerusalem apostles are retained momentarily in the Acts narrative as verifiers of Paul's ministry. Paul's turn to the Gentiles here has already been verified by Peter's encounter with Cornelius in Acts 10.[32] The divide declared in Pisidian Antioch is confirmed when Paul and his company must flee Iconium to avoid physical persecution (14:5-6) and Paul suffers an actual attack in Lystra that nearly kills him (14:19-20). Acts attributes the attacks to "the Jews" in both instances. Throughout Acts 13–14, Paul suffers for his Gentile mission as a fulfillment of his commission in 9:15-16.[33]

After a few more stops in Asia Minor, Paul begins moving back toward Jerusalem. The return portion of his first journey mirrors the first half of the trip. Paul and Barnabas stop in Syrian Antioch where they were first commissioned, and the Gentile nature of their mission is reemphasized (14:27).[34] All of this serves as a prelude to the impending showdown in Jerusalem. The Jerusalem Conference in Acts 15 is the turning point of the story.[35] When the apostles in Jerusalem decide to allow Gentiles to enter the church without circumcision or adherence to Jewish dietary laws, they also determine that the rest of the book of Acts will be about Paul and his Gentile mission.[36] Peter will not appear in the book of Acts again, and James will be mentioned only once more, in 21:18.

FOR THE SAKE OF THE HOPE OF ISRAEL

The remainder of the book of Acts narrates three additional journeys of Paul, his second and third missionary journeys and his travel to Rome as a prisoner.[37] These two missionary trips follow essentially the same route and are recounted in 15:36–18:21 and 18:23–21:16. Whereas Paul's first missionary journey expanded the church into Asia Minor, these two journeys extend it to Greece and Macedonia. These travel narratives are filled with adventure, danger, persecution, and imprisonment. In them Paul is portrayed as the great apostle. Recalling the now seemingly silly story of the selection of Matthias by lot to replace Judas in 1:21-26, it now appears that one of the goals of Acts is to proclaim that Paul is the true twelfth apostle.

In 16:16-40, Paul and Silas, his new traveling companion, are beaten and imprisoned because Paul performs an exorcism. Issues of freedom and bondage fill this story. The young woman, who is a slave and is possessed by a spirit, calls Paul and Silas slaves. Paul calls the spirit out of her[38] and he and Silas are subsequently beaten and put into jail. An earthquake potentially frees them from prison, but their possible escape threatens the life of the jailer. The refusal of Paul and Silas to escape from their bondage results in the salvation of the jailer and his family. In the end, Paul and Silas receive an official release from prison along with an apology.

As Paul continues on his second missionary journey, Acts 17 relates two stories in which Paul's preaching has different results. The report of Paul's visits to Thessalonica and Boroea sound familiar. His preaching arouses the opposition of some in the local Jewish community. Some of the believers who have been hosting Paul and Silas are arrested during the uproar in Thessalonica. They are released and Paul and Silas escape to Boroea. This is in marked contrast to Paul's experience in Athens (17:16-33), where his preaching is received peacefully, if not enthusiastically. Paul's second journey reaches its westward extent with his arrival and lengthy stay in Corinth. The connections begin to intensify between the events in Paul's life and those in the life of Jesus. Paul has been coming into increasing conflict with Jews.[39] In Corinth, Paul is put on trial in front of the Roman proconsul, Gallio, but is released and begins his return trip to Jerusalem.

At this point Jerusalem has lost almost all significance. While some English translations mention the name of the city in Paul's itinerary in 18:22, the Greek text only hints at his visit there by saying that he "went up and greeted the church" in between his arrival at Caesarea and his visit to Syrian Antioch. On either side of this journey back to Israel are two visits to Ephesus (18:19-21 and 19:1-41) that propel the story quickly into the third missionary journey. This journey begins with the account of the events in Ephesus in 19:1-41. Because the third journey begins where the second left off, the trip to Jerusalem seems more a diversion than a return to the church's home base.

The narrative about Paul's stay in Ephesus is dramatic and astounding. The brief account of the ministry of Apollos in 18:24-28 sets the stage for Paul to arrive in Ephesus and to find a fledgling Christian community. Paul's encounter with this group of believers reveals that the ministries of John the Baptist and Jesus have not been fully integrated.[40] These disciples have received only the baptism of John. The story of Paul's introducing them to the baptism of Jesus allows for the portrayal of the coming of the Holy Spirit upon these people, much like the Pentecost event in 2:1-13. The text even notes that "about twelve" of them are gathered at this event. Lest Paul be characterized as a divisive figure, as he might be understood in the events that follow, this story shows a Paul who is able to unite factions within the early Christian movement.[41] Meanwhile, Paul's personal power is magnified to an even greater extent than before. Following a general account of Paul's miracles, two stories display the disruption Paul's preaching brings to both the Jewish and Gentile elements of the city of Ephesus.[42] The stories of the sons of Sceva (19:13-20) and the worshipers of Artemis (19:23-41) are linked by their shared concern for the disruptive effect Paul's presence has upon those who use false religious practices for economic gain. The story of the seven sons of Sceva demonstrates that it is Paul who has true power over life and death, like Jesus. Not only do many of the practitioners of magic cease their activities, but they destroy the books that guide these practices. The narrator provides us with the monetary value of the books in 19:19. The interruption of the market for silver goods related to the worship of Artemis creates a riot in 19:28-34. When the riotous crowd seizes companions of Paul, the fearless Paul wants to jump into the crowd to save them and has to be restrained by other followers of Jesus (19:30). As Paul begins to move back toward Jerusalem and the end of his third journey, it becomes apparent that the effects of his message are becoming significant enough to gain the attention of civil authorities (19:40). The power of the gospel and the power of the state are headed for a confrontation, and the life of Paul will be the point of the collision.

Following these events in Ephesus, Paul begins to make his way back toward Jerusalem. The narrator inserts the strange story of Eutychus at 20:7-12, which reemphasizes Paul's power, this time over death itself, as Paul raises the young man for whose death he is partly responsible. Eventually, Paul will make his way back to Jerusalem, where his presence will cause a riot that parallels the one in Ephesus (21:27-35).[43] Bracketed between these two events, along with the demonstration of Paul's power over death in the Eutychus incident, is Paul's reflection on his own death. Paul's statements to the Ephesian elders who come to meet him in Miletus again connect his life to the life of Jesus. Paul's statement, in 20:25, that he will not see them again echoes the passion predictions of Jesus in the Gospels.[44] Unlike the disciples of Jesus, Paul's friends understand what he is saying to them, and the scene ends with an emotional departure in 20:36-38. This scene is replayed in briefer form in the moving farewell between Paul and the believers in Cyprus in 21:5-6. As Paul nears Jerusalem, the tone of the story is heavy with emotion. In the remainder of Acts 21, Paul's arrival in Jerusalem, his visit to the temple, and the turmoil that follows serve to link Paul's life to the passion of Jesus.[45]

Acts 23 begins the account of Paul's trials. Like Jesus in Luke, Paul will be tried a total of four times, but Paul's trial will take place on a much larger stage, the entire Roman Empire. Following the trial before the chief priests and the council in Jerusalem (23:1-11), the discovery of a plot to kill Paul leads to his removal to Caesarea. Paul's Roman citizenship affords him the right of a trial before Roman authorities (23:27). He subsequently faces his second trial, this time before the governor in Caesarea. Following this trial, Paul remains a prisoner for a long time, until Festus replaces Felix as governor. Paul's dealings with Festus, in 25:1-12, succeed in moving his case up the line of authority to King Agrippa. The actions of Festus concerning Paul protect Paul from another plot to take his life (25:3). It is unclear whether this Festus protects Paul knowingly or by accident, but it is difficult to escape the underlying notion in the book of Acts that these events are divinely engineered both to protect Paul and to move him to Rome. All of the mechanisms of the empire appear to be in the service of the goal of bringing the gospel to the heart of the empire itself.

Acts 26 presents Paul's trial before King Agrippa. The entire progress of the book of Acts is pulled forward into Paul's speech before Agrippa in 26:2-23, beginning with the persecution of the church in Jerusalem (26:10-11), continuing through Paul's conversion (26:12-18), and culminating with Paul's mission to the Gentiles (26:19-23). The end of Paul's speech reaffirms before Agrippa the suffering, death, and resurrection of Jesus, the Christ (v. 23). The result of this trial is that Paul is declared innocent (26:32) but is sent off to Rome because of his appeal to the emperor (27:1).

Acts 27:1–28:10 contains an astounding story of Paul's voyage from Caesarea, the subsequent shipwreck, and the resulting time Paul spends on the island of Malta. The shipwreck story serves to display Paul's continuing power and God's continuing provision for Paul.[46] Though he is a prisoner of the empire, and even the power of nature is arrayed against him in the vivid account of the storm (27:13-44), Paul's life is spared and his presence and command of the situation is the source of salvation for all of those aboard the ship. Paul predicts the shipwreck (27:10), but his warnings go unheeded. After his prediction is fulfilled, Paul predicts their rescue (27:1-2), a series of events that also comes to pass.[47] Once on Malta, Paul is bitten by a snake (28:3-4). Given all of Paul's misfortunes, observers might conclude, as do the residents of Malta in 28:4, that there is some kind of divine sentence or curse against Paul.[48] The shipwreck and snakebite story serve, however, to overturn this assumption, since Paul survives. If Paul is able to overcome these apparent signs of divine disfavor, then his imprisonment should not be taken as a sign of disfavor either.

For all the trouble the book of Acts has gone to in order to bring Paul to Rome, the account of his activity there is stunningly brief. The abbreviated ending has been the occasion of much interest, particularly in reference to the purpose of the book of Acts. Most surprising is the absence of a report of Paul's death. Instead the book ends with a number of tensions still at work. Despite

Paul's identity as apostle to the Gentiles, he speaks to the Jews in Rome. The response of the Jews is mixed (28:24-25), yet Paul condemns them harshly as a group, using the words of Isaiah 6:9-10, and turns attention to the Gentiles (28:28). The last words of Acts states Paul proclaims the gospel "without hindrance," yet he remains a prisoner.[49]

REFLECTIONS

The unresolved tensions of Acts, both political and theological, are still operative for the church of the twenty-first century. The relationship between Christianity and Judaism is still an open wound. The root of this conflict is present in the book of Acts as well as in the Gospels.[50] Contemporary Judaism and contemporary Christianity are both multifaceted and diverse. Carroll ably demonstrates the complexity of the relationship in his telling of the story of a group of Carmelite nuns who attempted to establish a place of prayer at the site of the Auschwitz concentration camp and the controversy that followed.[51] While some elements of the church and some elements of Judaism have made progress in efforts at dialogue, others remain in open conflict. The fate of the modern nation of Israel and the relationship between church and state in other nations are continuing sources of friction. Outside of the narrative of Acts, the one who has been introduced as the Apostle Paul attempts to resolve this tension in Romans 1–11, but his argument is so incomprehensible that the church has done little with this portion of Scripture other than to pluck out small pieces to use as proof-texts in debates over other issues.

Followers of Jesus still wonder what to make of suffering and what to do with power. The church in Acts, and Paul in particular, have in Jesus a clear expression of suffering for a divine purpose. The Gospel of Luke did not have to end with the death of Jesus because it had the story of the resurrection to tell, but Acts will not be able to resurrect Paul, so it cannot kill him. Arthur C. McGill has profoundly expressed this difficulty in his understanding of suffering and power. The cross itself is the ultimate expression of God's power, which resides in self-giving love. Our temptation is to see the cross as temporary defeat and the resurrection as final victory.[52] The understanding of the church's task in the book of Acts hangs in the same perilous balance. Will the church seek to change the world by exerting power over it, or will it choose the way of suffering and self-giving love? Paul, at once unhindered and in chains, embodies this choice.

NOTES

[1] From "Redemption Song," which appears on several of Bob Marley's albums.

[2] For a fuller discussion of the effects of reading Luke and Acts together, see Robert C. Tannehill, *The Narrative Unity of Luke-Acts: A Literary Interpretation*, vol. 2 (Minneapolis: Fortress, 1994), 7-8. Mikeal C. Parsons and Richard I. Pervo have raised important questions about the narrative unity of Luke and Acts and have effectively argued that the idea needs further refinement (*Rethinking the Unity of Luke and Acts* [Minneapolis: Fortress, 1993], 45-83).

[3] See Tannehill's discussion of this issue (*The Narrative Unity of Luke-Acts*, vol. 2, 3-4).

[4] For a thorough discussion of the textual problems of Acts, see P. Head, "Acts and the Problem of its Texts," in *The Book of Acts in Its Ancient Literary Setting*, ed. Bruce W. Winter and Andrew D. Clarke (Grand Rapids: Eerdmans, 1993), 415-44.

[5] This kind of textual issue has not been faced yet in this study. Of course, there are numerous variant readings in all of the books that have been examined. Generally, these variant readings are the haphazard result of centuries of handwritten transmission of biblical books. The closest we have come to a text that exists in two systematically different forms is the book of Samuel. The Hebrew and Greek texts of Samuel that have been transmitted to us differ significantly, and there may be discernable patterns (see the discussion of 1 Sam 16–18 in chapter 4). Nevertheless, the overall narrative character of the book does not seem significantly different in the two versions.

[6] For a discussion of this issue, and other more minor ones, see Robert W. Wall, "The Acts of the Apostles: Introduction, Commentary, and Reflections," in *The New Interpreter's Bible*, vol. 10 (Nashville: Abingdon, 2002), 17-18.

[7] For a helpful list of the parallel elements in Luke and Acts, see Mark Allan Powell, *Fortress Introduction to the Gospels* (Minneapolis: Fortress, 1998), 88.

[8] Joseph A. Fitzmeyer, *The Acts of the Apostles: A New Translation with Introduction and Commentary*, Anchor Bible (New York: Doubleday, 1997), 119-20.

[9] See the discussion of this issue in Fitzmeyer, *The Acts of the Apostles*, 119, and Wall, "The Acts of the Apostles," 13.

[10] See Frank Stagg, *The Book of Acts: The Early Struggle for an Unhindered Gospel* (Nashville: Broadman, 1955), 1-18. Stagg also pointed to the six other occurrences of this root word in Acts (p. 2). He acknowledged but wished to limit the influence of Oscar Cullman's argument that the presence of forms of the word "unhindered" indicated the use of an ancient baptismal formula. See Cullman, *Baptism in the New Testament*, trans. J. K. S. Reid (London: SCM, 1953).

[11] On these developments in Acts 1, see Tannehill, *The Narrative Unity of Luke-Acts*, vol. 2, 24-25.

[12] Of course, the story of the death of Judas in Acts 1:16-20 causes difficulty because of its conflict with the account in Matthew 27:3-10. Did Judas kill himself or did God kill him? Apparently, both traditions were present in the early church. For more detail on this issue, see Ernst Haenchen, *The Acts of the Apostles* (Philadelphia: Westminster, 1971), 159-60.

[13] Tannehill, *The Narrative Unity of Luke-Acts*, vol. 2, 20-21.

[14] For an extensive socio-historical discussion of this text, particularly with regard to the role of Sapphira, see Ivoni Richter Reimer, *Women in the Acts of the Apostles: A Feminist Liberation Perspective* (Minneapolis: Fortress, 1995), 1-30.

[15] Tannehill, *The Narrative Unity of Luke-Acts*, vol. 2, 47.

[16] Reimer, *Women in the Acts of the Apostles*, 16-24. Reimer also contended that, in the case of Sapphira, submitting herself to the authority of her husband instead of the community and God led to her death (p. 24).

[17] See, for example, Tannehill, *The Narrative Unity of Luke-Acts*, vol. 2, 63-65, and Charles H. Talbert, *Reading Acts: A Literary and Theological Commentary on the Acts of the Apostles* (New York: Crossroad, 1997), 72-74.

[18] Note that the two parallel sayings are peculiar to Luke among the Gospels. In addition, there are textual problems surrounding the sayings in Luke. This leads to the likelihood, from a historical perspective, that Luke's Jesus is shaped to match Stephen. In terms of the development of the Luke-Acts narrative, however, Stephen now reflects Jesus.

[19] For a more complete discussion of this feature, see F. Scott Spencer, *Acts* (Sheffield: Sheffield Academic Press, 1997), 62.

[20] Tannehill, *The Narrative Unity of Luke-Acts*, vol. 2, 159.

[21] See, for example, Powell, *Fortress Introduction to the Gospels*, 88.

[22] Labeling this character as simply "Herod" serves to associate him with the villainous character in Luke who imprisoned and killed John the Baptist (Luke 3:19-20 and 9:9), threatened Jesus (13:31), and took part in Jesus' trial (23:6-12).

[23] This difficult passage and its background have been treated in a book-length analysis by O. Wesley Allen Jr. in *The Death of Herod: The Narrative and Theological Function of Retribution in Luke-Acts* (Atlanta: Scholar's Press, 1997).

[24] Allen, *The Death of Herod*, 74. The death of Herod Agrippa I is also reported by Josephus in *Antiquities*, but Josephus's depiction is significantly different.

[25] Allen, *The Death of Herod*, 91-92.

[26] Ibid., 130-36.

[27] Ibid., 201.

[28] Tannehill, *The Narrative Unity of Luke-Acts*, vol. 2, 102-103.

[29] On the structure of this speech and comparisons to the speeches of Peter and Stephen, see Fitzmyer, *The Acts of the Apostles*, 507-508.

[30] On the narrative function of these three speeches, see Tannehill, *The Narrative Unity of Luke-Acts*, vol. 2, 164-75.

[31] This shift is illustrated in 13:4-12, 13:13-52, and 14:1-23. For a thorough demonstration of this pattern, see Talbert, *Reading Acts*, 125-26.

[32] On this connection, see William Willimon, *Acts* (Atlanta: John Knox, 1988), 125.

[33] Talbert, *Reading Acts*, 125-26.

[34] On the two meetings in Syrian Antioch (13:1-3 and 14:25-27) as an inclusion surrounding this section of Acts, see Talbert, *Reading Acts*, 125-26.

[35] Fitzmyer, *The Acts of the Apostles*, 538-39.

[36] Each of the movements toward a Gentile audience in Acts 11–15 is confirmed by Jerusalem. On this pattern, see Talbert, *Reading Acts*, 136.

[37] An alternative to the traditional view of three Pauline missionary journeys has been offered by Talbert who essentially fuses what are typically labeled the second and third missionary journeys into a single trip (16:6–20:3a). He then proposes a parallel structure shared by this trip and the first

one in 13:1–16:5. This is, in part, recognition of the little significance the text gives to the return to Jerusalem in 18:22, which will be discussed further below (*Reading Acts*, 146-47). This proposal has significant appeal, but the traditional view of three missionary journeys will be retained in the discussion here. That both of these readings are possible may signal the success the narrator of Acts has achieved in removing Jerusalem from the center of the narrative.

[38] Reimer appropriately warns against assuming that Paul liberates this woman. In fact, this could have made her life more difficult by putting her in the status of an ordinary slave. See *Women in the Acts of the Apostles*, 183-84. Moreover, it appears that Paul's motive for exorcising the demon was not the welfare of the woman, but simply to stop her from annoying him. Why does he wait several days before acting?

[39] Talbert has observed, also at this point, that Acts increases its attention to the "prophecy-fulfillment pattern," which provides another sense of connection between Paul in Acts and Jesus in Luke. Acts 18:9-18 is an obvious example of this pattern. See *Reading Acts*, 168.

[40] The Gospel of Luke is also at pains to integrate these two movements, spending much greater energy than any of the other Gospels to define the relationship between Jesus and John the Baptist in Luke 1:5-80.

[41] On the background of this passage and the various ways of understanding the relationship among Paul, Apollos, the church in Ephesus, and this small group of believers, see Haenchen, *The Acts of the Apostles*, 552-57. Historical-critical assessments of the many difficulties in this text will, of course, make use of information from the epistles, particularly Ephesians and 1 Corinthians. The use of this information is problematic in a straightforward narrative appraisal of Acts.

[42] On the role of power in these stories, see Talbert, *Reading Acts*, 172-81.

[43] For a comparison of these two events, see Tannehill, *The Narrative Unity of Luke-Acts*, vol. 2, 242-44.

[44] Tannehill, *The Narrative Unity of Luke-Acts*, vol. 2, 264-65.

[45] Talbert has also observed the ways in which this visit of Paul to Jerusalem matches his visit in Acts 15 (*Reading Acts*, 191-92).

[46] This whole section concerning Paul's journey to Rome, in Acts 27–28, serves to reverse standard, theological assumptions about a human being who is suffering many trials. On this theme, see Fitzmyer, *The Acts of the Apostles*, 766-84.

[47] On this prediction and fulfillment pattern in Acts 27, see Talbert, *Reading Acts*, 218-19.

[48] Talbert has demonstrated that these stories in Acts follow common type-scene patterns in Greco-Roman literature and that such stories are used to demonstrate divine approval or disapproval (*Reading Acts*, 221-25).

[49] On all of these unresolved tensions and the mixture of openness and closure at the end of Acts, see Tannehill, *The Literary Unity of Luke-Acts*, vol. 2, 353-57.

[50] The bibliography on this issue is voluminous. Recently James Carroll has summed up the history of the issue and its current state in his monumental work *Constantine's Sword: The Church and the Jews* (New York: Mariner, 2001). On the New Testament root of this conflict and its connection to the book of Acts, see pp. 129-34.

[51] Carroll, *Constantine's Sword*, 308.

[52] Arthur C. McGill, *Suffering: A Test of Theological Method* (Philadelphia: Westminster, 1982), 95-98.

Living and Dying

It's hard to know when to give up the fight
Two things you want will just never be right
It's never rained like it has before tonight . . .

Strange how hard it rains now
Rows and rows of big dark clouds
When I'm still alive underneath this shroud
Rain, Rain, Rain.

—Patty Griffin[1]

On Ash Wednesday in 1998 I sat in the chapel of the Mekane Yesus Theological Seminary in Addis Ababa, where I was a member of the faculty and dean of the department of theology. The school's Lutheran heritage placed great emphasis on the contemplation during Lent on Jesus' suffering and death. I remember closing my eyes and imagining Jesus on the cross and being stunned by what I saw. For the first time in my life, I was consciously aware that I was looking at a dying man who was younger than me. If the tradition of Jesus being thirty-three years old at the time of his death is correct, then I was about five years late coming to this realization; nevertheless, it taught me something profound about how we experience biblical stories. As a child, an adolescent, and a young adult, I saw Jesus primarily as a great role model, even to the point of being willing to "give his life for his friends." As an adult in middle age, I see Jesus primarily as a courageous young man who was unjustly executed for what he believed. I suspect that my perspective is due for another seismic shift when my son reaches the approximate age of Jesus at the time of his death. When I enter the biblical narrative, I do so as a particular reader with a particular identity and set of experiences.

I realized that a narrative world is shaped to some extent by the reader who enters it. Justo L. Gonzalez speaks beautifully of his realization of this principle in relation to the issue of poverty in the Bible: "Thus, the question becomes more complicated. It is no longer simply, what does the Bible say about the poor? It is also and foremost, what does the Bible say when read from the perspective of the poor? Or, in other words, what do the poor find in the Bible that the nonpoor easily miss?"[2]

This journey through the worlds of six biblical books has a number of purposes. Among them is the attempt to find a way to do biblical theology that takes the horizons of both text and reader seriously. Because the narrative worlds created by biblical books are significantly different from the modern world we inhabit, we have entered them carefully and deliberately. I argued in the introduction, following Ricoeur and Gadamer, that meaningful reading involves a sense of correspondence between the world of the reader and the world of the text. This is no simple process because modern readers are far removed from the worlds of the Bible. Two extremes must be avoided. First, the attempt to determine objectively the intent of the author, whether or not this is truly possible,[3] threatens to overwhelm and deny the world of the reader. Second, simply asking "What does this text mean to me or to you?" obscures the narrative world that the text builds. Thus, in each of the preceding six chapters, I have attempted to draw a roadmap at the beginning by examining the literary design of the book. This has involved looking at the ways that the field of biblical studies has progressed in establishing a sense of the structure of each book. This is not a fully objective process, but it is a best effort to take the apparent design of the whole book seriously at the beginning as guide for reading.

It has been my observation that readers of the Bible have become more acutely aware of how issues of life and death are portrayed. Conversation about such issues on many levels has become more common in recent years. In a decidedly post-September 11 work, *Is Religion Killing Us?: Violence in the Bible and the Quran*, Jack Nelson-Pallmeyer referred to violence in sacred texts as "the elephant in the room."[4] He correctly implies by this phrase that this is a vital topic that we have too often pretended was not there. Perhaps the question in his title is too simplistic, however. Life is killing us. Our sacred texts acknowledge this, none more poignantly than Genesis. The vital question is how we will respond to the portrayals of life and death in our sacred texts. We can allow the predicaments of the text, favoritism and rejection, slavery, or genocide to become our predicaments by a simplistic reading that simply emulates biblical heroes. Alternatively, however, we might allow the same texts to expose our lives and reveal us as human beings who struggle against many of the same forces of life and death that entangle the biblical characters.

Biblical texts are produced by communities amid their own struggles for survival. The imprints of this struggle are placed upon the text and carried forward into the dangerous contexts of every generation of readers.[5] The characters in the book of Genesis struggle to find a place in the world and to resolve conflict with other human beings, including their own family members. The text attempts to negotiate God's position in all of this struggle and conflict. Throughout human history, much of this difficulty has been resolved or avoided by the spreading out of human beings on the face of the earth, just as the brothers in Genesis move away from one another. There are no more New Worlds for us to sail to, however, and globalization is returning us to the pre-Babel state of not being scattered. How will we live with each other? The book of Judges raises the pitch of the discussion as a large group of people, Israel, struggles to find its identity and place in the world. The conflicts here are among emerging nations. The silence of Judges concerning the times of peace determines that violence and death will shape the narrative. Because Judges is a book that argues for a new sense of order, disorder is the story it needs to tell. It falls victim to the same reality as our modern media. Nonviolent stories require far more imagination and effort to tell. The result is a portrayal of life that is untrue. Goodness does not receive its fair share of attention, and our anxiousness about the world multiplies. If Genesis establishes that God is on our side, Judges discovers that God will not stay on our side, and a more reliable system of human order and power must be put into place.

The book of Samuel likely contains a mixture of pro-monarchy and anti-monarchy voices. The result is a surprisingly honest reflection on the dynamics of power. Ultimately, even the greatest of human personalities crumbles beneath the weight of power and it becomes the master of us all. At the end of Samuel, David is as powerless as Hannah at its beginning. Power is not the answer and we, like the characters in these stories, are left with the task of living faithfully within a world where the unpredictable movements of power dominate. Ezra-Nehemiah stands on the opposite side of the experience of exile from the book of Samuel. The difficulty of telling a story that is not about war is apparent here, and the narrative is admittedly more difficult to read. The story is not without conflict and death, and abusive power is still at work. In a situation of renewal of community, questions of identity become ultimate. Can identity be established around a productive center without the construction of boundaries that exclude? Can I know who I am and where I belong without saying who does not belong?

It is tempting to think that when we cross the boundary from the Old Testament into the New Testament, the questions we have raised will find some clear resolution. Instead, we discover that the same tensions between order and conflict, identity and confusion, and life and death persist. The Gospel of Matthew struggles with these tensions as both the form and content of its narrative move back and forth from calm order to disruptive chaos. Modern, false prophets peddle the gospel as a sure path to personal success, but discipleship in Matthew brings mixed and unpredictable results. Living peacefully causes violence and gentleness brings harsh response. Jesus did not fit easily into the world, so he was violently removed. Yet, even this story of death is contained within God's abiding presence. Acts continues the story of Jesus, as told by Luke, by telling a matching story of the church. All of the ambiguities are retained as members of the early church kill and are killed, reject and are rejected, control and are controlled. The ministry of the Apostle Paul becomes the primary vehicle of the biblical story in the second half of the book of Acts, and the story ends with the life of Paul and the life of the church hanging in the balance. The church is in a struggle for its life, both in establishing its internal sense of identity and in finding its place in a brutal world.

It is tempting to boil the biblical story down to extracted principles that are pure and consistent. The Bible tells messy stories of life and death and we can accept these stories as a beginning point for our theology, but it is difficult to accept them as the end. Biblical theology runs aground, however, if it leads away from the Bible's own narrative form. On the contrary, the invitation must be to move back and forth between our stories and those of the Bible, bringing them into contact so that they might shape themselves around each other and we might live and die faithfully in the dangerous world they form together.

NOTES

[1] From the song "Rain" on the Patty Griffin album *1,000 Kisses* (Ato Records, 2002).

[2] Justo L. Gonzalez, *Santa Biblia: The Bible through Hispanic Eyes* (Nashville: Abingdon, 1996), 57-58.

[3] Though I believe this goal is not attainable, any claim that it is sets up the reading of one interpreter as the objective norm by which others are evaluated.

[4] Jack Nelson-Pallmeyer, *Is Religion Killing Us?: Violence in the Bible and the Quran* (Harrisburg PA: Trinity Press International, 2003), xiv.

[5] A detailed example of this phenomenon is eloquently demonstrated in the work of James Carroll on the New Testament and its reception, particularly in reference to the church's treatment of the Jewish people (see Carroll's *Constantine's Sword: The Church and the Jews* [New York: Mariner, 2001], 67-122). As Carroll illustrates, the conflicts in the text are a complicated mixture of the conflicts within the events reported and the conflicts within the authors' communities. The lenses thorough which readers later perceive these texts add an additional dimension to this already complex situation.

Bibliography

Ackerman, Susan. *Warrior, Dancer, Seductress, Queen: Women in Judges and Biblical Israel.* New York: Doubleday & Co., Inc., 1998.

Allen, O. Wesley Jr. *The Death of Herod: The Narrative and Theological Function of Retribution in Luke-Acts.* Atlanta: Scholar's Press, 1997.

Alter, Robert. *The Art of Biblical Narrative.* New York: Basic Books, 1981.

———. *Genesis: Translation and Commentary.* New York: W. W. Norton & Co., 1996.

———. *The David Story: A Translation with Commentary of 1 and 2 Samuel.* New York: W. W. Norton & Co., 1999.

Anderson, Janice Capel. *Matthew's Narrative Web: Over, and Over, and Over Again.* Sheffield: Sheffield Academic Press, 1994.

Auerbach, Erich. *Mimesis: The Representation of Reality in Western Literature.* Princeton: Princeton University Press, 1953.

Bacon, Benjamin, *Studies in Matthew.* New York: Holt Publishing, 1930.

Bal, Mieke. *Death and Dissymmetry: The Politics of Coherence in the Book of Judges.* Chicago: University of Chicago Press, 1988.

———. *Murder and Difference: Gender, Genre, and Scholarship on Sisera's Death.* Bloomington: Indiana University Press, 1988.

———. *Lethal Love: Feminist Literary Readings of Biblical Love Stories.* Bloomington: Indiana University Press, 1987.

Bar-Efrat, Shimon. *Narrative Art in the Bible.* Trans. Dorothea Shefer-Vanson. Sheffield: Almond Press, 1989.

Barrick, W. Boyd. "Saul's Demise, David's Lament, and Custer's Last Stand." *JSOT* 73 (1997): 25-41.

Berlin, Adele. *Poetics and Interpretation of Biblical Narrative.* Sheffield: Almond Press, 1983.

Berry, Wendell. *A Timbered Choir: The Sabbath Poems 1979–1997.* Washington, DC: Counterpoint Press, 1998.

Blenkinsopp, Joseph. *The Pentateuch: An Introduction.* New York: Doubleday & Co., Inc., 1989.

Boesak, Alan. *Black and Reformed: Apartheid, Liberation and the Calvinist Tradition.* Johannesburg: Skotaville Press, 1984.

Bonino, José Míguez. "Genesis 11:1-9: A Latin American Perspective." In *Return to Babel: Global Perspectives on the Bible*, ed. John Levison and Priscilla Pope-Levison, 13-36. Louisville: Westminster John Knox Press, 1999.

Boring, Eugene. *Matthew*. The New Interpreter's Bible, vol. 8, ed. Leander Keck. Nashville: Abingdon Press, 1995.

Bowman, Richard G. "Narrative Criticism in Judges: Human Purpose in Conflict with Divine Presence." In *Judges and Method: New Approaches in Biblical Studies*, ed. Gale A. Yee, 17-44. Minneapolis: Fortress Press, 1995.

Brenner, Athalya, editor. *A Feminist Companion to Judges*. Sheffield: Sheffield Academic Press, 1993.

Brettler, Marc. "The Book of Judges: Literature as Politics." *JBL* 108 (1989): 395-418.

Brettler, Mark. "The Composition of 1 Samuel 1–2." *JBL* 116 (Winter 1997): 601-12.

Brueggemann, Walter. *Theology of the Old Testament: Testimony, Advocacy, Dispute*. Minneapolis: Fortress, 1997.

———. *Genesis*. Interpretation. Atlanta: John Knox Press, 1982.

———. "1 Samuel 1—A Sense of a Beginning." In *Old Testament Theology: Essays on Structure Theme, and Text*, ed. Patrick D. Miller, 219-34. Minneapolis: Fortress Press, 1992.

———. "2 Samuel 1–24—An Appendix of Deconstruction." In *Old Testament Theology: Essays on Structure, Theme, and Text*, ed. Patrick D. Miller, 235-51. Minneapolis: Fortress, 1992.

———. *Power, Providence, and Personality: Biblical Insight into Life and Ministry*. Louisville: Westminster, 1990.

Cahill, Thomas. *The Gifts of the Jews: How a Tribe of Desert Nomads Changed the Way Everyone Thinks and Feels*. New York: Doubleday & Company, Inc., 1998.

Cameron, Peter Scott. *Violence and the Kingdom: The Interpretation of Matthew 11:12*. Frankfurt am Main: Peter Lang Publishing, 1984.

Carroll, James. *Constantine's Sword: The Church and the Jews*. Boston: Houghton Mifflin Co., 2001.

Carter, Warren. "Kernels and Narrative Blocks: The Structure of Matthew's Gospel." *CBQ* 54 (1992): 465-75.

Carter, Warren. *Matthew: Storyteller, Interpreter, Evangelist*. Peabody MA: Hendrickson Publishing, 1996.

Cartledge, Tony W. *1 & 2 Samuel*. Smyth & Helwys Bible Commentary. Macon GA: Smyth & Helwys Publishing, Inc., 2001.

Cassuto, Umberto. *A Commentary on the Book of Genesis*. 2 volumes. Trans. I. Abrahams. Jerusalem: Magnes Press, 1964.

Chatman, Seymour. *Story and Discourse*. Ithaca: Cornell University Press, 1978.

Comstock, Gary. "Truth or Meaning: Ricoeur versus Frei on Biblical Narrative." *Journal of Religion* 66 (1986): 117-40.

———. "Two Types of Narrative Theology." *Journal of the American Academy of Religion* 55 (1987): 687-717.

Crossan, John Dominic. *The Historical Jesus: The Life of a Mediterranean Jewish Peasant*. San Francisco: HarperSanFrancisco Publishing, 1991.

Culpepper, R. Alan. *The Anatomy of the Fourth Gospel: A Study in Literary Design.* Philadelphia: Fortress Press, 1983.

Davies, Gordon F. *Ezra and Nehemiah.* Berit Olam. Collegeville MN: Liturgical Press, 1999.

Davies, Margaret. *Matthew.* Sheffield: JSOT Press, 1993.

Diamant, Anita. *The Red Tent.* New York: Picador USA, 1998.

Dillard, Annie. *A Pilgrim at Tinker Creek.* New York: Quality Paperback Books, 1974.

Eco, Umberto. *The Role of the Reader: Explorations in the Semiotics of Texts.* Bloomington: Indiana University Press, 1978.

Edward Edinger, *The Bible and the Psyche: Individuation Symbolism in the Old Testament.* Toronto: Inner City Books, 1986.

Ellingsen, Mark. *The Integrity of Biblical Narrative: Story in Theology and Proclamation.* Minneapolis: Fortress Press, 1990.

Exum, J. Cheryl. "The Centre Cannot Hold: Thematic and Textual Instabilities in Judges." *CBQ* 52 (1990): 410-29.

————. *Fragmented Women: Feminist (Sub)versions of Biblical Narrative.* Valley Forge PA: Trinity Press International, 1993.

————. "Aspects of Symmetry and Balance in the Samson Saga." *JSOT* 19 (February 1981): 3-9.

————. *Tragedy and Biblical Narrative: Arrows of the Almighty.* Cambridge: Cambridge University Press, 1992.

Fishbane, Michael. *Biblical Text and Texture: A Literary Reading of Selected Texts.* New York: Shocken Press, 1978.

Fitzmeyer, Joseph A. *The Acts of the Apostles: A New Translation with Introduction and Commentary.* Anchor Bible. New York: Doubleday & Co., Inc., 1997.

Fokkelman, Jan P. *Narrative Art in Genesis: Specimens of Stylistic and Structural Analysis.* Assen: Van Gorcum Press, 1975.

————. "Genesis." In *The Literary Guide to the Bible,* ed. Robert Alter and Frank Kermode, 36-52. Cambridge: Harvard University Press, 1987.

————. "Exodus." In *The Literary Guide to the Bible,* ed. Robert Alter and Frank Kermode, 53-65. Cambridge: Harvard University Press, 1987.

————. *Narrative Art and Poetry in the Books of Samuel: A Full Interpretation Based on Stylistic and Structural Analyses.* 4 volumes. Assen: Van Gorcum, 1981–1993.

Frei, Hans. *The Eclipse of Biblical Narrative: A Study in Eighteenth and Nineteenth Century Hermeneutics.* New Haven: Yale University Press, 1974.

————. *The Identity of Jesus Christ: The Hermeneutical Bases of Dogmatic Theology.* Philadelphia: Fortress Press, 1975.

Friedman, Richard Elliott. *The Disappearance of God: A Divine Mystery.* Boston: Little, Brown, and Company, 1995.

Frye, Northrop. *The Great Code: The Bible and Literature.* San Diego: Harcourt Brace & Co., 1981.

Gadamer, Hans Geroge. *Truth and Method.* London: Sheed and Ward Publishers, 1975.

Garland, David E. *Reading Matthew: A Literary and Theological Commentary on the First Gospel.* New York: Crossroads Publishing, 1993.

Girard, René. *Violence and the Sacred.* Trans. Patrick Gregory. Baltimore: Johns Hopkins University Press, 1977.

———. *The Scapegoat.* Trans. Yvonne Freccero. Baltimore: Johns Hopkins University Press, 1986.

———. *Things Hidden Since the Foundation of the World.* Trans. Steven Bann and Michael Metteer. Stanford: Stanford University Press, 1987.

Githuku, Sammy. "Taboos on Counting." In *Interpreting the Old Testament in Africa,* ed. Mary Getui et al., 113-18. New York: Peter Lang Publishing, 2001.

Gonzalez, Justo L. *Santa Biblia: The Bible through Hispanic Eyes.* Nashville: Abingdon Press, 1996.

Grabbe, Lester. *Ezra-Nehemiah.* New York: Routledge Press, 1998.

Gunn, David M. *The Story of King David: Genre and Interpretation.* Sheffield: JSOT Press, 1978.

———. *The Fate of King Saul: An Interpretation of a Biblical Story.* Sheffield: Sheffield University Press, 1980.

Gunn, David M., and Danna Nolan Fewell. *Narrative in the Hebrew Bible.* Oxford: Oxford University Press, 1993.

Haenchen, Ernst. *The Acts of the Apostles.* Philadelphia: Westminster Press, 1971.

Hagner, Donald A. *Matthew 1–13.* WBC. Waco: Word Books, 1993.

Hamerton-Kelley, Robert. *Sacred Violence: Paul's Hermeneutic of the Cross.* Minneapolis: Fortress Press, 1992.

———. *The Gospel and the Sacred: Poetics of Violence in Mark.* Minneapolis: Fortress Press, 1994.

Hamlin, E. John. *At Risk in the Promised Land: A Commentary on the Book of Judges.* Grand Rapids: William B. Eerdmans Publishing Co., 1990.

Head, P. "Acts and the Problem of its Texts." In *The Book of Acts in Its Ancient Literary Setting,* ed. Bruce W. Winter and Andrew D. Clarke. Grand Rapids: William B. Eerdmans Publishing Co., 1993.

Hertzberg, Hanz Wilhelm. *1 and 2 Samuel.* Trans. J. S. Bowden. Philadelphia: Westminster Press, 1964.

Humphreys, W. Lee. *The Character of God in the Book of Genesis: A Narrative Appraisal.* Louisville: Westminster John Knox Press, 2001.

———. *The Tragic Vision and the Hebrew Tradition.* Philadelphia: Fortress Press, 1985.

Iser, Wolfgang. *The Act of Reading: A Theory of Aesthetic Response.* Baltimore: Johns Hopkins University Press, 1978.

Jones, Gareth Lloyd. *The Bones of Joseph: From the Ancient Texts to the Modern Church.* Grand Rapids: William B. Eerdmans Publishing Co., 1997.

Josipovici, Gabriel. *The Book of God: A Response to the Bible.* New Haven: Yale University Press, 1988.

Kimball, Charles. *When Religion Becomes Evil.* San Francisco: HarperSanFrancisco Publishing, 2001.

Kingsbury, Jack Dean. *Matthew: Structure, Christology, Kingdom.* Philadelphia: Fortress Press, 1975.

Kirsch, Jonathan. *The Harlot by the Side of the Road: Forbidden Tales of the Bible.* New York: Ballantine Books, 1997.

Kugel, James. *The Bible as It Was.* Cambridge MA: Belknap Press, 1997.

Lacoque, André and Paul Ricoeur. *Thinking Biblically: Exegetical and Hermeneutical Studies.* Trans. David Pellauer. Chicago: University of Chicago Press, 1998.

Lee, David. *Luke's Stories of Jesus: Theological Reading of the Gospel Narrative and the Legacy of Hans Frei.* Sheffield: Sheffield Academic Press, 1999.

Levison John and Priscilla Pope-Levison, editors. *Return to Babel: Global Perspectives on the Bible.* Louisville: Westminster John Knox Press, 1999.

Licht, Jacob. *Storytelling in the Bible.* Jerusalem: Magnes Press, 1978.

Lohr, C. H. "Oral Techniques in the Gospel of Matthew." *CBQ* 23 (1961): 403-35.

Lindbeck, George. *The Nature of Doctrine: Religion and Theology in a Postliberal Age.* Philadelphia: Westminster Press, 1984.

Lindars, Barnabas. *Judges 1–5: A New Translation and Commentary.* Edinburgh: T & T Clark Ltd., 1995.

Matera, F. J. "The Plot of Matthew's Gospel." *CBQ* 49 (1987): 233-53.

McCarter, Kyle. *1 Samuel: A New Translation with Introduction and Commentary.* Garden City, NJ: Doubleday & Co., Inc., 1980.

McEntire, Mark. "Surviving Genesis: Dangerous Worlds both Narrative and Real." In *Studies in Jewish Civilization 10*, ed. Leonard Greenspoon, 215-26. New York: Fordham University Press, 1999.

———. *The Blood of Abel: The Violent Plot of the Hebrew Bible.* Macon GA: Mercer University Press, 1999.

———. "Cain and Abel in Africa: An Ethiopian Case Study in Competing Hermeneutics." In *The Bible in Africa*, ed. Gerald O. West and Musa W. Dube, 248-59. Leiden: Brill Publishers, 2000.

———. *The Function of Sacrifice in Chronicles, Ezra, and Nehemiah.* New York: Mellen Biblical Press, 1993.

———. "Letters in Stories and Stories in Letters: An Intertextual Exploration of Ezra 4–5 and Galatians 1–2." *Perspectives in Religious Studies* 27 (Fall 2000): 249-61.

Meyers, Jacob M. *Ezra-Nehemiah: Introduction, Translation, and Notes.* Anchor Bible. Garden City NY: Doubleday & Co., Inc., 1965.

Miles, Jack. *God: A Biography.* New York: Vintage Press, 1995.

Mitchell, Stephen. *Genesis: A New Translation of the Classic Biblical Stories.* New York: HarperCollins Publishing, 1996.

Moore, George F. *A Critical and Exegetical Commentary on Judges.* Edinburgh: T & T Clark Ltd., 1895.

Mosala, Itumaleng. *Biblical Hermeneutics and Black Theology in South Africa.* Grand Rapids: William B. Eerdmans Publishing Co., 1984.

Mudge, Lewis. "Paul Ricoeur on Biblical Interpretation." In Ricoeur, *Essays on Biblical Interpretation*, ed. Lewis Mudge, 1-10. Philadelphia: Fortress Press, 1980.

Muilenburg, James. "Form Criticism and Beyond." *JBL* 88 (1969): 1-18.

Nash, Roderick. *Wilderness and the American Mind*, 3rd edition. New Haven: Yale University Press, 1982.

Nelson-Pallmeyer, Jack. *Is Religion Killing Us: Violence in the Bible and the Quran.* Harrisburg PA: Trinity Press International, 2003.

Nicol, George G. "The Alleged Rape of Bathsheba: Some Observations on Ambiguity in Biblical Narrative." *JSOT* 73 (1997): 43-54.

Noth, Martin. *The Deuteronomistic History.* Sheffield: Sheffield Academic Press, 1981.

Oduyoye, Modupe. *The Sons of God and the Daughters of Men: An Afro-Asiatic Interpretation of Genesis 1–11.* Maryknoll NY: Orbis Press, 1984.

Olson, Dennis T. "The Book of Judges: Introduction, Commentary, and Reflection." In *The New Interpreter's Bible*, vol. 2, ed. Leander Keck, 721-888. (Nashville: Abingdon Press, 1998.

Olyan, Saul M. "Honor, Same, and Covenant Relations in Ancient Israel." *JBL* 115 (Summer 1996): 201-18.

Pagels, Elaine. *Adam, Eve, and the Serpent.* New York: Vintage Press, 1989.

Parson, Mikeal C., and Richard I. Pervo. *Rethinking the Unity of Luke and Acts.* Minneapolis: Fortress Press, 1993.

Polzin, Robert. *Moses and the Deuteronomist: A Literary Study of the Deuteronomistic History: 1 Samuel.* San Francisco: Harper & Row Publishers, 1980.

———. *Samuel and the Deuteronomist: A Literary Study of the Deuteronomistic History: 1 Samuel.* San Francisco: Harper & Row Publishers, 1989.

———. *David and the Deuteronomist: A Literary Study of the Deuteronomistic History: 2 Samuel.* Bloominton: Indiana University Press, 1993.

Prickett, Stephen. *Words and the Word: Language Poetics and Biblical Interpretation.* Cambridge: Cambridge University Press, 1986.

Powell, Mark Allan. *Fortress Introduction to the Gospels.* Minneapolis: Fortress Press, 1998.

Reimer, Ivoni Richter. *Women in the Acts of the Apostles: A Feminist Liberation Perspective.* Minneapolis: Fortress Press, 1995.

Rhoads, David, and Donald Michie. *Mark as Story: An Introduction to the Narrative of a Gospel.* Philadelphia: Fortress Press, 1982.

Ricoeur, Paul. *Time and Narrative.* Volume 1. Chicago: University of Chicago Press, 1984.

———. *Essays on Biblical Interpretation.* Ed. Lewis Mudge. Philadelphia: Fortress Press, 1980.

Rost, Leonhard. *The Succession to the Throne of David.* Trans. Michael D. Rutter and David M. Gunn. Sheffield: Almond Press, 1982.

Roth, Robert Paul. *The Theater of God: Story in Christian Doctrine.* Minneapolis: Fortress Press, 1985.

Rowley, H. H. "The Chronological Order of Ezra and Nehemiah." In *Ignace Goldziher Memorial Volume*, vol. 1, ed. D. S. Lowinger and S. Somogyi, 127-40. Budapest: Globus Press, 1948.

Rudolph, Wilhelm. *Esra und Nehemiah.* Tübingen: J. C. B. Mohr Publishing, 1949.

Sanford, John. *King Saul, the Tragic Hero.* New York: Paulist Press, 1985.

Schneider, Tammi J. *Judges.* Berit Olam. Collegeville MN: Liturgical Press, 2000.

Schwartz, Regina M. *The Curse of Cain: The Violent Legacy of Monotheism.* Chicago: University of Chicago Press, 1997.

Scott, Bernard Brandon. *Jesus, Symbol-Maker for the Kingdom.* Minneapolis: Fortress Press, 1981.

Scullion, John J. "The Narrative of Genesis." In *The Anchor Bible Dictionary,* vol. 2, ed. David Noel Freedman. New York: Doubleday & Company, Inc., 1992.

Shaver, Judson R. *The Torah and the Chronicler's History Work: An Inquiry into the Chronicler's Reference to Laws, Festivals and Cultic Institutions in Relationship to Pentateuchal Legislation.* Atlanta: Scholars Press, 1989.

Smith, Daniel L. *The Religion of the Landless: The Social context of the Babylonian Exile.* Bloomington IN: Meyer Stone Publishing, 1989.

Soggin, J. Alberto. *Judges: A Commentary.* Trans. J. S. Bowden. Philadelphia: Westminster Press, 1981.

Spencer, F. Scott. *Acts.* Sheffield: Sheffield Academic Press, 1997.

Stagg, Frank. *The Book of Acts: The Early Struggle for an Unhindered Gospel.* Nashville: Broadman Press, 1955.

Steinmetz, Devora. *From Father to Son: Kinship, Conflict and Continuity in Genesis.* Louisville: Westminster John Knox Press, 1991.

Sternberg, Meir. *The Poetics of Biblical Narrative: Ideological Literature and the Drama of Reading.* Bloomington: Indiana University Press, 1985.

Stiver, Dan R. *Theology after Ricoeur: New Directions in Hermeneutical Theology.* Louisville: Westminster John Knox Press, 2001.

Sweeney, Marvin A. "Davidic Polemics in the Book of Judges." *VT* 47 (1997): 517-29.

Talbert, Charles H. *Reading Acts: A Literary and Theological Commentary on the Acts of the Apostles.* New York: Crossroad Publishing, 1997.

Tannehill, Robert C. *The Narrative Unity of Luke-Acts: A Literary Interpretation.* Volumes 1 and 2. Minneapolis: Fortress Press, 1994.

Trible, Phyllis. *Texts of Terror: Literary Feminist Readings of Biblical Texts.* Philadelphia: Fortress Press, 1984.

Thiselton, Anthony C. *New Horizons in Hermeneutics: The Theory and Practice of Transforming Bible Reading.* Grand Rapids: Zondervan Publishing, 1992.

Tov, Emanuel. *Textual Criticism of the Hebrew Bible.* Minneapolis: Fortress Press, 1992.

Throntveit, Mark. *Ezra-Nehemiah.* Louisville: Westminster John Knox Press, 1992.

Ukpong, Justin K. "Reading with a Community of Ordinary Readers." In *Biblical Hermeneutics in Africa: Towards the 21st Century,* ed. Mary Getui, T. Maluleke, and Justin Ukpong, 188-212. Nairobi: Acton Press, 2001.

Wall, Robert W. "The Acts of the Apostles: Introduction, Commentary, and Reflections." In *The New Interpreter's Bible,* vol. 10, ed. Leander E. Keck, 1-365. Nashville: Abingon Press, 2002.

Watson, Francis. *Text and Truth: Redefining Biblical Theology.* Grand Rapids: William B. Eerdmans Publishing Co., 1997.

Westermann, Claus. *Joseph.* Minneapolis: Fortress Press, 1996.

Van Wijk-Bos, Johanna W. H. *Ezra, Nehemiah, and Esther.* Louisville: Westminster John Knox Press, 1998.

Wilder, Amos N. "The World Story: Biblical Version." In *Jesus' Parables and the War of Myths: Essays on Imagination in the Scriptures.* Philadelphia: Fortress Press, 1982.

Williams, James G. *The Bible, Violence, and the Sacred: Liberation from the Myth of Sanctioned Violence.* San Francisco: HarperSanFracisco, 1991.

Williamson, H. G. M. *Ezra-Nehemiah.* Word Biblical Commentary. Waco: Word Books, 1985.

Willimon, William. *Acts.* Atlanta: John Knox Press, 1988.

Wink, Walter. *Engaging the Powers: Discernment and Resistance in a World of Domination.* Minneapolis: Fortress Press, 1992.